PARLIAMENTS AND LEGISLATURES SERIES

SAMUEL C. PATTERSON
GENERAL ADVISORY EDITOR

Party Discipline and Parliamentary Government

EDITED BY
SHAUN BOWLER,
DAVID M. FARRELL,
AND RICHARD S. KATZ

OHIO STATE UNIVERSITY PRESS
COLUMBUS

Library of Congress Cataloging-in-Publication Data

Party discipline and parliamentary government / edited by Shaun Bowler,
    David M. Farrell, and Richard S. Katz.
        p.   cm. — (Parliaments and legislatures series)
    Based on papers presented at a workshop which was part of the European
Consortium for Political Research's joint sessions in France in 1995.
    Includes bibliographical references and index.
    ISBN 0-8142-0796-0 (cl : alk. paper). — ISBN 0-8142-5000-9 (pa : alk.
paper)
    1. Party discipline—Europe, Western.   2. Political parties—Europe,
Western.   3. Legislative bodies—Europe, Western.
I. Bowler, Shaun, 1958–   . II. Farrell, David M., 1960–   .   III. Katz,
Richard S.   IV. European Consortium for Political Research.   V. Series.
JN94.A979P376   1998
328.3'75'094—dc21   98-11722
                                                                              CIP

Text design by Nighthawk Design.
Type set in Times New Roman by Graphic Composition, Inc.
Printed by Bookcrafters, Inc..

The paper used in this publication meets the minimum requirements of the
American National Standard for Information Sciences—Permanence of Paper
for Printed Library Materials. ANSI Z39.48-1992.

9 8 7 6 5 4 3 2 1

Contents

Foreword

Party Discipline and Parliamentary Government brings together empirical studies of the internal cohesiveness of political party groups in European parliaments, along with the leadership behavior that conduces to disciplined parties in parliament. The purview of these studies includes parliamentary party behavior in Great Britain, Ireland, Switzerland, Norway, Spain, Hungary, and the European Parliament, with less extensive inclusion of parliamentary behavior in a number of other countries. The original papers upon which these chapters are based were first exposed to the public view in a workshop, "Party Discipline and the Organization of Parliaments," that Shaun Bowler and David Farrell organized for the European Consortium for Political Research meetings in Bordeaux, France, in 1995.

Students of American legislative politics are highly sensitive to the fact that the U.S. Congress and the state legislatures often do not exhibit party discipline in their voting behavior: members of the legislative party do not vote against members of the other party a very high proportion of the time. Party government is not a preponderant feature of American legislative decision making. Although party voting is by no means insignificant or trivial in American legislatures, it plays a far more important role in the parliamentary parties in European assemblies.

Central as party discipline and cohesion are to the performance of many European parliaments, the phenomena have not been investigated extensively. The studies in this anthology take a very large leap forward in knowledge about parliamentary party discipline. Because the parliamentary cohesiveness of the governing majority may be a coalition of several party groups, the joint problems of cohesiveness and discipline in multiparty parliaments are intriguing and fertile. More broadly, these careful and cogent studies contribute to better understanding of the nature of legislature or parliamentary politics altogether.

In the American context, legislative parties may contribute primarily by addressing the policy or status preferences of their members, by supporting a legislative program either on ideological grounds or for the purpose of facilitating reelection of their members and leaders, or both. In European parliamentary systems, the legislative assembly has as its preeminent function the formation of a majority coalition—composed of one large party or several smaller ones—sufficient to establish and support a government. Accordingly, party discipline plays a significantly different role in the parliamentary systems than in separated systems such as that of the United States, where the executive is chosen quite independently of the legislature.

The studies in this book are illuminating. These authors move away from a crude consideration of parliamentary parties as unitary actors to investigate what goes on inside them in terms of the formation of intraparty consensus and leadership support. The true policy preferences and attitudes of the MPs may, for instance, be belied by an analysis operating only at the party level, as illustrated by the views of the British MPs toward the Maastricht Treaty. Even the less well-understood continental European parliaments exhibit very high, although varying, levels of parliamentary party cohesiveness. Indeed, some parliamentary parties harbor more loyal, better disciplined members than others. Moreover, national parliamentary parties are, in turn, nested in a transnational assembly, the European Parliament. These fascinating variations are investigated in innovative ways in the following chapters.

Samuel C. Patterson

Preface

This book emerged from a series of papers presented at a workshop, "Party Discipline and the Organization of Parliaments," held during the Joint Sessions of the European Consortium for Political Research, at the Institut d'Etudes Politiques de Bordeaux, France, April 27–May 2, 1995. During the course of five days of stimulating discussion, it became clear to all of us around the table that there was a crying need for a comparative study on this important subject. It was agreed that the workshop organizers (Bowler and Farrell), together with the most forceful of the participants (Katz), should try to pull a selection of the papers together as an edited volume. As always happens with such exercises, we could not include all of the papers presented in the workshop, either because they were already committed elsewhere or because their subject matter did not quite fit the overriding theme of the book. But this does not take from the fact that each of these colleagues played a vital role in seeing this project come to fruition and we want to record a special thanks to them: Herbert Döring, John Huber, Stephen Ingle, Robin Kolodny, Petr Kopecky, Lia Nijzink, Kaare Strøm, Marc van den Muyzenberg, Ania van der Meer-Krok-Paszkowska, and Matti Wiberg.

Given the transatlantic dispersion of the authors and editors, the relative speedy completion of this volume is testimony to the wonders of e-mail, but more especially to the conscientiousness of our authors. Final completion was facilitated by David Farrell's stay at Harvard, in the first part of 1997, as a fellow at the Shorenstein Center on the Press, Politics, and Public Policy, Kennedy School of Government. We are grateful to Samuel Patterson for his advice and support throughout, to our reader for very helpful feedback and advice that helped to improve the manuscripts, and most especially to Charlotte Dihoff, Beth Ina, and the rest of the staff at Ohio State University Press.

PART I

Theories and Definitions

1

Party Cohesion, Party Discipline, and Parliaments

SHAUN BOWLER, DAVID M. FARRELL, AND RICHARD S. KATZ

In 1993, British Prime Minister John Major had to threaten errant Conservative backbenchers with a suicidal snap election to ensure their support in passing a parliamentary bill ratifying Britain's signature of the 1992 Treaty on European Union (the Maastricht Treaty). On a regular basis in postwar, prereform Italy, prime ministers fell at the hand of factions within their own party, which meant that the average life span of Italian governments could be measured in months rather than years (see chap. 11 of this volume). These are just two examples of a problem that all party leaders share: party discipline in parliament. In the first case we are dealing with what is supposedly *the* example of a "cohesive" parliamentary system; in the second, with what was one of the best examples of a parliamentary system that was far from cohesive (e.g., as shown by the range of factions in the Italian chamber).

Cohesion and discipline matter in the daily running of parliaments. The maintenance of a cohesive voting bloc inside a legislative body is a crucially important feature of parliamentary life. Without the existence of a readily identifiable bloc of governing politicians, the accountability of the executive to both legislature and voters falls flat. It can be seen, then, as a necessary condition for the existence of responsible party government (Katz 1987; Castles and Wildenmann 1986). For some, the maintenance of a majority voting bloc is simply the necessary condition for winning the parliamentary game. Majorities rule, and whoever can form (and keep together) a majority wins the legislative game, shaping policies and programs in order to keep on winning in the future. For others, and especially for those who write on coalition politics, the existence of strong and stable parties is an almost hidden assumption from which to begin theorizing about the existence of the broader, governmental, coalition game. For a variety of scholars, then, the existence of unified blocs of legislators is a major part of the political landscape, constituting a central normative requirement, a beginning assumption, or a part of the parliamentary game. However, despite being so centrally important to the theory and practice of parliamentary government, discussion of this topic is relatively underdeveloped.

This book aims at going some way toward filling this gap. We begin, in this chapter, by outlining what we understand these rather amorphous terms of *cohesion* and *discipline* to mean. The argument is developed through the drawing of three sets of distinctions. We start, in the first section, with some basic definitional distinctions between *party coherence* and *party discipline*. This is followed, in the second section, by a discussion on levels of analysis, where we explore differing explanations of the sources of party coherence and discipline both inside the legislature and outside (or electorally). In the next section, a third distinction sharpens our focus on who, or what, is being "disciplined."

Distinguishing Party Cohesion and Party Discipline

In a now neglected but nonetheless valuable exploration of this topic, Ozbudun (1970) distinguishes between *party cohesion* and *party discipline*. Often the two terms are used interchangeably in the literature, but Ozbudun makes a strong case that they are analytically distinct and should be kept that way. He sees them as referring to two quite distinct components, each of which contributes to a unified party bloc in parliament, but with different determinants and differing effects. Ozbudun (1970, 305) defines cohesion as "the extent to which . . . group members can be observed to work together for the group's goals." He breaks party discipline down into two parts: first, that "followers regularly accept and act upon the commands of the leader or leaders," and second, that the leader has "ways and means of inducing recalcitrant members to accept and act upon . . . commands" (305). According to these definitions, therefore, whenever we observe members of legislatures voting as a bloc or otherwise acting in unison, this can be because the members agree with each other or because they are being made to act in accord with each other despite their personal preferences (or, perhaps, a combination of the two).

Clearly, the two concepts are related. Presumably discipline is needed when cohesion is low and is not needed in its more coercive forms when cohesion is high. But getting those who disagree with each other to submit to the rigor of common discipline is no easy feat. As Ozbudun observes (1970, 331), "The only parties which have not adopted disciplinary measures are also the least cohesive ones." There is at least one obvious explanation for this: if members of a group disagree so very much, they are unlikely even to be able to agree that they should be forced to act in concert.

We might think of the relationship between cohesion and discipline in the following way. Below some minimal level of coherence, it is impossible, at least within the confines of democratic politics, to impose discipline. Above some relatively high level of coherence, the imposition of discipline is pointless, since the members agree anyway. Between these two extremes—where cohesion is high enough so that members agree to some sort of broad organizational goals and structure, yet falls far short of unanimity—party discipline has scope to act upon a legislative grouping to produce unified action.

Electoral and Legislative Discipline

In the same way that these forces may apply at different times, they may apply at different points in the party political process. Here we elaborate a distinction between electoral and legislative politics and the different demands involved in fighting elections and winning legislative battles. Each of these differing demands has been offered as the root explanation for the rise of unified parties in legislatures, especially in the nineteenth century. The first category of explanation focuses on electoral politics and the rise of extraparliamentary organizations. The second category argues that it is within legislatures themselves that we find the rise of unified parties. This relates to Duverger's (1951) classic distinction between parties originating within parliaments and those emerging from the grassroots outside of parliament.

The Impact of Electoral Machines

Many of the early party scholars noted the impact of extraparliamentary organizations in producing distinct voting blocs within parliaments (e.g., Duverger 1951; Ostrogorski 1902). Best (1995) argues that the emergence of political parties in the constituent assemblies of Paris and Frankfurt in 1848 is directly attributable to the polarizing effect of mass politics. And the degree of polarization of the electorate, and hence of the party system, is seen as a major determinant of the willingness of members to cross to the other side (e.g., Epstein 1956; Kornberg 1967; Best 1995): for instance, in a highly polarized party system, the distance (whether psychological or political) between the parties may be so wide as to deter members from wanting to defect.

Of course, one of the major impacts of extraparliamentary organization is upon the selection of candidates for office. To the extent that nomination politics are controlled by the party machine (brought about by mass enfranchisement), the party can ensure the cohesion of a legislative body by weeding out potential troublemakers. This is helped by the fact that the act of joining a party is explicitly contractual. In many cases, on joining a party or standing as a candidate, individuals must sign a pledge in which they declare that this is the only party of which they are a member and in which they promise to support the general aims and constitution of the party. The following example is not untypical: "I hereby agree to be bound by the objective, federal and state platforms of the Australian Labor Party. I also agree to be bound by decisions of the state executive taken in accordance with these rules" (Australian Labor Party, South Australia Branch 1986–87, 12).

The New Zealand Labour Party makes its candidates take similar pledges and can expel for six years "any member of the party who stands as a candidate in opposition to, or publicly campaigns against, an official Labour candidate" (*New Zealand Labor Party* 1984, 27). These features are not confined to modern or even antipodean experience. Ostrogorski wrote in the context of the late–nineteenth-century Birmingham caucus, which marked one of the earliest developments of a self-consciously disciplined cadre within the British system, although by several accounts this innovation was brought more strongly to the fore by the Parnellite block of Irish Home Rulers, whose members also had to sign an oath of loyalty to the party (Farrell 1973). Duverger, too, notes the beginnings of constituency influence in this period when he discusses the example of a Mr. Forster in the Bradford of 1878 who fought against the incorporation of such a clause into the constitution of his local party: "Throughout the country there arose a lively controversy over the problem of the relations between Members of Parliament and caucuses. Finally there was a compromise, quite favourable to the party. If Forster had not died during the following legislature he would not have been renominated by the party caucuses at the elections" (Duverger 1951, 188–89).

Thus, members of a political bloc take part in a voluntary and contractual relationship that essentially confers a series of obligations upon the individual to support the party. Fulfillment of many of these obligations is quite difficult to measure. For instance, the obligations can be couched in such vague terms that fulfillment is almost impossible to monitor. A typical example here is the requirement in the New Zealand Labour Party that candidates swear to "wholeheartedly support" fellow candidates (*New Zealand Labor Party* 1998, clause 242). Parties need to be careful in vetting before they select. It is a very important component in recruiting members to the legislature that there be some preexisting loyalty to the party itself. Kornberg's study of Canadian legislative parties pays particular attention to the preexistence of loyalty and to the "internalization" of party loyalty (Kornberg 1967, 136).

It is here, perhaps, that the real significance of extraparliamentary organizations comes into its own. One of the major impacts of extraparliamentary organization is upon the selection of candidates for office, and control over candidate nomination plays a large part in controlling the composition of the legislative caucus (Schattschneider 1942, 64). To the extent that nomination politics are controlled by the center, the party can ensure the cohesion of a legislative body by vetting its parliamentary candidates (Gallagher and Marsh 1988). To a certain extent, this may interact with the kind of electoral system in place. The party-list proportional representation systems, for example, are likely to be associated with the central (or perhaps regional) allocation (and withdrawal) of nominations. By contrast, district-based electoral systems (such as the single-member simple-plurality system used in the United Kingdom) tend to be associated with more localized control over nominations (see Katz and Mair 1992, tables D.5).

The picture has been complicated in recent years by changes to party rules that apparently amount to an even greater role for party members but that also reflect closer scrutiny of the process by the top leadership, which is both anxious to avoid potential embarrassments and seeking to maximize electoral returns through vote management strategies. This paradoxical process is perhaps best shown by the reforms within the "New Labour" Party in Britain that introduced membership mail voting for candidate selection, while at the same time permitting greater vetting rights to the party's national executive to weed out potential problem cases (see Webb 1994).[1] The issue of local party control over candidate nomination was a cause of some difficulty to the British Conservative Party national leadership in the 1997 general election, when efforts were made to prevent one of its MPs from being reselected as parliamentary candidate due to intense media and opposition party scrutiny into accusations of financial impropriety. Despite the best (and quite public) efforts of Conservative Party "high command," the local party went ahead and selected the candidate, as was their prerogative under the party's rules.

Overall, then, whether the process of candidate nomination is controlled locally or nationally should have a clear impact upon where the legislative member directs his or her loyalty. Local party organizations and local caucuses can be quite disruptive, allowing, and possibly compelling, local members with a strong local following to disobey the legislative line. To the extent that this is the case, the much-vaunted system of British parliamentary cohesion (certainly in the Conservative Party of today) is likely to be far less secure than perhaps expected. Local nomination means not only that legislators have a local base from which to oppose strong leaders but also that they face local demands that may lead to dissent. As Whiteley and Seyd demonstrate in chapter 3, in the current climate of deep division within the British Conservative Party over the European issue, it is quite a rational strategy for a Conservative backbench MP to defy the national leadership, for the very reason that the MP will enjoy the support of local party activists. Such an occurrence is much less likely when nominations are centrally controlled. Wherever one's place on the party list is determined by party leaders, the minds of candidates are likely to be much more concentrated on loyalty to the party line (Bowler, Farrell, and McAllister 1996). This leads to the rather straightforward hypothesis that centralized nomination procedures should lead to greater party cohesion. Though it is not an easy hypothesis to test, several chapters in this volume certainly lend support to the importance of the electoral system (i.e., the distinction between proportional representation list systems and single-member simple-plurality systems) as a relevant factor in explaining differing levels of parliamentary coherence.

Parliamentary Incentives

A second branch of explanations locates the sources of coherence at the level of the legislature itself. Cox and McCubbins (1993) present what is perhaps the fullest argument in favor of this view. Parties, they argue, operate as a kind of legislative cartel aimed at making rules favorable to their own members. While their argument is applied to the case of the twentieth-century U.S. Congress, it is quite clear, from historical accounts of the eighteenth-century British parliament, that a similar argument held there too as rival Whigs and Tories jockeyed for control of the executive (Holmes 1987).

Party leaders, one presumes, would like nothing better than a majority in the legislature made up of like-minded individuals willing to vote early and often in accord with the leader's suggestions. The more typical state of affairs, however, is something far less idyllic from the party leader's point of view. Once a legislature has been elected, the problem remains of getting legislators to act in concert (see chap. 2 of this volume). After all, once elected, members of a given legislative body are formal equals, typically not allowed to take advice or instruction from those outside the chamber; they may need to be encouraged even to attend roll calls and meetings, let alone to vote or participate in other respects. And several studies show that, at least when answering survey questions, parliamentarians bridle very quickly at the idea that matters of personal conscience can be subjected to the discipline of the party line (see especially Kornberg 1967, 132). This necessarily makes unity in the face of difficult political decisions that much harder to attain. A prime example of this point is offered by the ongoing debacle within the British Conservative Party over European integration (see chaps. 3 and 4 of this volume).

Worse still is the constant threat of defection. Even if one argues that there are advantages to be gained from banding together, as for instance has been suggested by coalition theorists, the problem still remains that members of the "in" group may be lured away by the blandishments and offers of the "out" group in order to gain a better (individual or private) payoff. Thus, parenthetically, even as coalition theorists discuss coalitional behavior within European legislatures (Laver and Schofield 1990), they presuppose the existence of parties whose own stability as coalitions they may not be able to explain (see, however, chap. 2 of this volume for one explanation; see also chaps. 11 and 12 of this volume and Aldrich 1995).

When discussing the cohesion of legislators, considerable attention is paid to the array of carrots and sticks that leaders use to create or enforce discipline. We can discuss these in two broad groups, as generic incentives and as procedural devices.

Typically, legislative leaders have at their disposal a range of inducements to place in front of individual members. Patronage and committee appointments (and withdrawal of same) are the most commonly used, especially in parliamentary systems, where, provided the party is in government, plum jobs within the executive itself are available, as are jobs for supporters or public works for members' districts (see Blondel and Cotta 1996). Also available to leaders (in government and opposition) are whips' offices, organizations that allow leaders to identify and deal with potential rebels. It was the business of the Chief Whip, wrote one, "to know all about every man in his party who counted, and to have a wide and correct view of what was going on in the opposite party. . . . It was his duty to scent dissatisfaction, the formation of disloyal cliques, and, in short, any danger to the party arising from dislike of particular measures, personal jealousies and ambitions, irritations caused by personal inefficiencies of ministers, and all possible causes of mischief arising from complexities of human nature" (Gladstone 1927, 520).

The creation of the whips' office represents one of the great parliamentary innovations, predating the rise of modern or mass parties. This is an organization specifically devoted to the maintenance of unified action by a political bloc. Holmes (1987, 300) traces it back to the "whipping of sorts" among Whigs and Tories at the beginning of the eighteenth century, when the major problem was simply getting supporters to show up in London. A regional whipping structure was established in which individuals were responsible for fellow members from the same region. This helped to mobilize supporters of the parties and to provide access to the kinds of social incentives and gatherings—such as the prestigious Kit-Cat Club—that might sway the minds of reluctant MPs. Gladstone (1927, 522) dates the existence of permanent appointments concerned with patronage to as early as 1711. More contemporary accounts provide a similar description of the range of activities and inducements of the whips, even down to the persistence of a regional structure (Silk 1987, 47; see chap. 7 of this volume for discussion of the Spanish *portavoz*).

Procedural measures, depending upon parliamentary maneuvers, can be equally influential tools in bringing about bloc unity. Some measures can be quite rudimentary, such as the use of open roll call votes where member loyalty or disloyalty can be monitored (as discussed for the Swiss case in chap. 5 of this volume). A good reason why such a measure might be wanted by the party leadership is provided by the practice in Italy over much of the postwar period, where secret voting in the parliament facilitated extensive "sniping" as members voted against their own party line in blissful anonymity. Introducing votes of confidence can be seen as quite a blunt instrument with which to club members of the governing party into line, but it is a measure that Prime Minister John Major found useful on not a few occasions in recent British parliamentary practice.

Other procedural maneuvers may be more subtle as party leaders manage legislative votes in such a way as to ensure that divisive issues are simply not brought to the floor or alternatively are not posed as party-political issues, thereby avoiding the appearance, and even the possibility, of disloyalty (e.g., Gladstone 1927; Loewenberg 1967; Silk 1987). An example of this practice is offered by the Irish parliament, in which, on controversial matters relating to public morality, MPs are permitted to vote according to their individual "conscience" and no whip is imposed; similar examples are provided by the Norwegian case (as discussed in chap. 6 of this volume) and also by the British House of Commons during its regular votes on whether to reintroduce hanging. The French Fifth Republic's constitution provides yet another escape route for the government: in certain areas the government is allowed to bypass the floor entirely and rule by decree, thereby blunting the scope for disloyalty in the governing party.

Legislative and electoral behavior are, of course, interrelated. If the central party leadership controls nomination or use of the party label at election time, then the range of carrots and sticks available to it widens perceptibly. Cox's (1987) study of the nineteenth-century British parliament sets out an argument in which developments inside the chamber and among the wider electorate are interconnected. In a sense, for Cox the responsible party model of government does not simply require party loyalty in the legislature; it creates it. He describes a process where the cabinet becomes ever more important as an actor in its own right. In the light of this, the voters pay much more attention to the government of the day and much less attention to constituency service matters. In putting less pressure on members to serve local interests and directing more attention to party politics matters, electoral competition removed an important impetus to dissent and increased the pressure to conform. Part of the beauty of this system is that disloyal parliamentarians can be punished not only by the party leaders but also by the voters.

To the extent that electoral incentives, and in particular reelection incentives, shape legislators in fundamental ways, these are clearly the most important incentives to have in favor of unity. For instance, the ability of dissident British parliamentarians to insulate themselves from disciplinary measures has been noted. Epstein (1956, 372) cites a couple of cases in which the Labour Party of the 1950s was unable to discipline members after the rebels had received assurances of support from local party organs (something that would be unheard of in the Labour Party of Tony Blair). If elections stress the local and particular, then one would reasonably expect reelection-motivated candidates to be less willing to submit to the confines of party discipline for prolonged periods. On the other hand, if elections turn on governmental performance, and if party organization reinforces this, then we are likely to see something quite different. This discussion suggests a number of straightforward cross-system comparisons that are explored throughout this volume: for example, that we should expect unity to be higher in parliamentary systems than presidential ones; party leaders to be able to discipline legislators more easily in party-based systems than in candidate-based systems (see Katz 1986 for discussion on preferential electoral systems); cohesion to be more difficult to maintain in systems characterized by high levels of localism or clientelism; and the "nationalization" of electoral politics to have aided central party cohesion (i.e., a possible temporal dimension).

In addition to the costs of electoral punishment incurred by specific individuals within some settings, defections may also raise suspicion among other actors. Coalition theorists, for example, typically make the assumption that any given member of a coalition may be bribed away to join a rival. But perhaps there are restrictions on the degree to which coalition members wish to be seen as bribable. Prospective coalition partners themselves would presumably rather ally with reliable partners. A single defection from a coalition may not imply massive unreliability;

Table 1.1

Party Cohesion as a Function of Party Competition

	Competition		
	One-Party State (%)	*Weak Minority (%)*	*Two Parties (%)*
Cohesion			
Strong	7	31	63
Moderate	7	31	32
Weak	86	38	5
N	14	13	19

Source: Golombiewski (1958, 501).

Note: Observations are U.S. states.

persistent defections, however, can easily be seen as an indication of likely future behavior. Given a choice, political entrepreneurs, who are in the process of building coalitions, would rather not team up with unreliable partners. Hence, in coalition systems, actors wishing to become part of a winning coalition may suppress tendencies to jump ship or to be seen as too openly quarrelsome for fear of being seen as "difficult" partners.

Party competition more generally understood can also be seen as one of the factors shaping party cohesion and discipline. Competitive pressures—the fear of losing (a majority or a vote) and the hope of winning—can promote a powerful concentration of attention. Not all acts of dissent need be closely watched and quelled. Elections help provide some guide to how monitoring should take place and how much effort should be expended on trying to maintain party coherence: monitoring and coercion, after all, are rather costly activities. One way in which costs to the leadership can be reduced is simply not to enforce discipline when there is no point. This can be illustrated by some evidence provided by a U.S. study from 40 years ago.

In his study Golombiewski (1958, 501) makes the point that "party cohesion is a direct function of the degree of competition between political parties." His empirical evidence certainly seems to bear this out. As table 1.1 shows, there is a clear relationship between coherence and competitive position, and this is particularly evident in the case of one-party states (see also Mezey 1995, 204–5). If a party has little or no chance of winning or losing power, then there would seem to be no real point in maintaining unity or even trying to impose costly disciplinary measures. There is, however, a hidden asymmetry between the position of a losing and a winning party. If a party cannot gain a majority, then imposing discipline may well be pointless (since, by definition, the party cannot win). On the other hand, a party with a massive majority can still lose power through massive defections. Some kind of unity should therefore be maintained in majority parties but may be allowed to slip in the smaller parties.

It is not only the position of the leadership with regard to cohesion that is affected by the party's competitive position; there are also effects on the individual parliamentarians, as shown by the often-noted phenomenon in the United Kingdom that party cohesion is easier to maintain when the government has a small majority than when it has a big one. A specific example of this is provided by the Irish Fianna Fáil party after its stunning electoral victory in 1977, when it won more than 50% of the popular vote and a substantial majority of seats in Parliament. As the electoral returns were flowing in and pundits were pontificating on what they saw as the unassailable position of the party leader, Jack Lynch, he was less sanguine, expressing doubts about his ability to maintain discipline over a parliamentary party in such a secure position (Farrell and Manning 1978). His doubts proved well founded. Within two years of his stunning electoral victory, he was thrown out of office as the result of a backbench coup (Farrell 1987).

So far, we have argued for the existence of an important definitional distinction between cohesion and discipline. The second distinction, between levels of analysis, to some extent overlies the first. Getting and keeping control over who gets into the legislative caucus can help (or, in some cases, can hinder) cohesion. Once in the parliament, however, the cast of players is fixed and cannot be changed. This raises one final area of concern: just who is being disciplined?

Party Discipline: Top Down or Bottom Up?

The discussion so far has been couched largely in terms of the ability of legislative leaders to mobilize and produce a unified voting bloc when the occasion demands. The "problem" of party discipline phrased in this way is the standard one: How can leaders keep backbenchers in line? But there is another way of looking at the problem: How can backbenchers discipline leaders and get them to promote policies and positions that are to the backbenchers' liking? The rank and file may be wary of a "leadership" (broadly defined) that seeks to desert the "true" grassroots cause by following an electoral agenda entailing the watering down of ideological content. Mezey (1993, 346) comments, "Party discipline may be partially the product of anticipated reaction—that is, leaders deciding not to propose policies that they know their followers will oppose."

In this regard, factions and factionalism can be seen as especially important. If acting as a disciplined bloc is valuable within a parliament, it should also be valuable within a party (McAllister 1991). Factionalism has long been a subject of considerable interest to scholars working on predominant party systems. For this reason, much of the work on factions focuses on such cases as Italy, Japan, and the U.S. southern states (see Katz 1980; Key 1949; Sartori 1976; Thayer 1969; von Beyme 1985). More or less by definition, factions exist to voice claims within the party as a whole. These claims may be aimed at personalities or policies, and according to Panebianco (1988) they carry with them dangers of indiscipline and incoherence within parties. While this line of argument clearly has some merit, there are reasons for thinking that factions can help rank-and-file members discipline their leadership, either by providing faction leaders to take part in policy discussions (reporting back to their members) or by making it clear to party leaders that a block of votes will desert if some policy line is crossed. In this sense, factions help party leaders understand where their support or opposition lies within the party and the levels of this support or opposition—factors that were crucially important to British Prime Minister Major in trying to hold the line on Europe within his divided party (see chaps. 3 and 4 of this volume). Factions can also provide useful testing grounds for up-and-coming party leaders (Loveday and Martin 1966).

Rather than being necessarily harmful, then, factions can have some use in helping to show party leaders which policies and actions are tolerable and which are not. Similarly, the very presence of factions can help the rank and file themselves understand what is permissible by making them aware of the size of different voting blocks within the party. Rather than simply quitting the party and forming or joining a rival, a group of dissenters might instead decide to stay with the party and try to change its direction from inside. The nature of party competition may also have a role to play here. It could be argued that as the ideological divide between parties increases, so too does factionalism within each party; otherwise, as parties blur into each other, dissidents may find it easier to jump ship. In Hirschmann's terms (1970), factions can be seen as an example of "voice" in preference to "exit."

By the same token, whips' offices need not simply be organizations to impose discipline by the leaders upon the rank and file but can also be viewed as organizations through which the rank and file keep the leaders informed. Again, early English evidence seems to bear this out. If getting supporters to actually vote was a problem for the eighteenth-century Whigs and Tories, so was getting policies endorsed by these supporters (Holmes 1987, 289–93). It was found necessary to take account of backbench opinion, to canvass support, and to seek to persuade. Coordination meetings were established to bring more supporters on board. The whips' office thus existed as much to provide leaders with information relating to where the backbench could be led as to provide backbenchers with directions over where the leader wanted to go.

In short, party cohesion and discipline are very much two-way streets, and certainly much more so than the emphasis on whipping—with its connotations of disciplining the unruly rank and file—might suggest. While it may be true that there is an asymmetry between leaders and followers, given that the former have access to patronage and the ability to play divide and rule, whereas the latter must overcome problems of collective action and rivalry, leaders can still be disciplined by the rank and file.

To return to Hirschmann (1970) for a moment, there is, of course, always the option of "exit": disillusioned MPs can jump ship, either moving to a new party or becoming independents. This phenomenon, entitled variously as "faction hopping," "fraction hopping," or "political tourism" (or being "flicked off" in the case of Bulgarian MPs ejected from their parliamentary parties; see Karasimeonov 1996, 55), has been a prominent feature of parliamentary life in the new democracies of East and Central Europe (see the various articles in *Journal of Legislative Studies* 1996; contrast this with the virtual absence of faction hopping in Norway, discussed in chap. 6 of this volume). In chapter 8 of this volume, Ágh shows how in the Hungarian case, as the process of what he calls "parliamentarization" has unfolded, the number of MPs switching parties has plummeted to negligible levels. This is consistent with earlier cases of parliamentary institutionalization (on postwar West German experience, see Schüttemeyer 1994).

Party Cohesion and Discipline

Even this brief review suggests that the topic of party cohesion and discipline is a much richer subject for study than might at first be assumed. Complicating this picture even more is an interpretation of party cohesion/discipline as a dynamic process rather than as the necessarily static property of a party. Some of the features identified in this chapter suggest that some elements contributing to party cohesion are more or less permanent features of the political landscape. Nomination procedures, for example, can exist unchanged for lengthy periods, as can the electoral systems to which they are related and the many rules of parliamentary procedure. These kinds of factors, then, can contribute to a snapshot picture of party cohesion at any one time, possibly even over the relatively long haul.

But our description would suggest that the balance between cohesion and discipline or, perhaps more accurately, between the two features' degree of presence or absence, provides a more unstable and shifting set of political problems. In this light, an understanding of party cohesion and discipline might require a fuller appreciation of these dynamics. For example, certain political problems are likely to depend, at least in part, upon the competitive position of a party in both legislative and ideological terms. Close-fought races between fiercely ideological rivals are, one presumes, likely to help foster cohesive parties. On the other hand, as either of these two measures of competitiveness slackens, much more may be demanded of disciplinary measures. As majorities mount, for example, it seems less important to ensure that each and every party member toes the line exactly: some examples of dissent can be tolerated much more readily. And here, in these different sets of circumstances, may well lie an account of the different types of party leadership.

Leaving aside the idiosyncracies of personality, it is possible to see distinct themes of party leadership. At times, party leaders may seem more like generals guiding their disciplined troops into the lobbies. Examples such as Margaret Thatcher or Newt Gingrich suggest a highly cohesive and willing body of legislators, willing to do or die. In these ideologically charged circumstances, where perhaps also nomination procedures have produced a willing body of supporters, leadership may be less a matter of leading than of leashing. At other times, however, parties are not nearly so compliant. For instance, in the context of highly diverse intraparty ideological divisions within the British Labour Party during the 1980s, or perhaps the Conservative Party of today, the *generalissimo* style of leadership is unlikely to work. Rather, a model of leadership in which the peace is kept, possibly simply an agreement to keep to the status quo, becomes the hallmark of leadership by consensus. The leader keeps the party together, but basically by herding people together while letting the party go where it wants (e.g., Sam Rayburn as Speaker of the U.S. House; John Major as Conservative Party leader in Britain).

Of course, legislative settings are hardly all or nothing. "Generals" and "shepherds" may be pure types, but pure types are rarely seen, and then often fleetingly. We are more likely to find party leaders shuttling between these types. In very fragmented settings, with multiple parties and multiple factions, or possibly simply a party in a minority position, leadership may become primarily a matter of tactics above all; it may then become the task of stitching together a temporary coalition for the purpose of achieving a specific goal.

Outline of What Follows

In a recent overview of the state of the discipline, Michael Mezey (1993, 356) makes the telling observation that "most of the legislative literature is firmly rooted in time and place, and for much of the subfield the place is Washington, D.C., and the time frames are usually current." This volume goes some way toward meeting both objections by its coverage of a wide set of different cases outside of the United States and also by its treatment of parliamentary systems at different stages of historical development. While some of the chapters focus on relatively familiar settings, such as the United Kingdom or Italy, many of the other chapters examine less well-known examples, such as Spain, Switzerland, Hungary, Ireland, and Norway. Some cases involve well-established parliamentary systems; other cases—notably Hungary, Spain, and the European Parliament—have much more recent origins.

In addition to the wide range of settings, this volume also provides a number of different perspectives on the topics of party cohesion and discipline. As this introduction has suggested, there are a variety of different dimensions to the topic of parliamentary cohesion, involving relationships between the party grassroots and the legislative caucus, the use of roll call votes, and other procedural devices. These themes, among others, are taken up in the chapters that follow.

We begin, however, with a more abstract and detailed focus on the question of why should we expect to see party cohesion. If legislators are formal equals, and if the temptation to jump ship is ever present, why should we see parliamentary parties exist and persist in unified form for such long periods of time? The next chapter, by Laver and Shepsle, suggests one set of answers to this, based on the idea of discipline acting as a "kind of gravitational force" pulling legislators together into parties. Once some rudimentary form of party organization exists, the benefits available to such a group provide powerful inducements to members and enemies alike. There are clearly many benefits to acting in concert. By operating as a single voting bloc, a party can seek to control policy, committees, procedures, and even government. Once the bloc has gained access to such things, it is also in a position to reward loyal friends and punish traitors.

Laver and Shepsle's "portfolio allocation" approach makes a significant contribution to the study of coalitions, particularly in that it removes the standard assumption of parties as unitary actors, permitting a focus on the motivations of individual politicians. Laver and Shepsle's chapter has the added significance of helping to group much of the discussion in the remainder of this volume. Their analogy of parliamentary parties "emerging from the primeval slime" can be read in two ways.

First, as headlined in Ágh's chapter on Hungary (chap. 8), and as discussed in the Spanish case by Sánchez de Dios (chap. 7) and in the two chapters on the European Parliament (chaps. 9 and 10), the Laver-Shepsle analogy can be seen as relating to the establishment and institutionalization of cohesive parliamentary parties in emergent political systems. Second, it can be viewed in a more day-by-day sense, as relating to the establishment and survival of governments in multiparty parliamentary systems. As Mershon (chap. 11) and Mitchell (chap. 12) demonstrate, there is good reason for coalition theory to finally stop treating political parties as monolithic, unitary actors, for they evidently are not. In multiparty systems, which exist across much of Europe, governments emerge out of deals struck between party leaders who have one eye firmly fixed on their backbenchers. Ultimately, the survival of the government will depend on the maintenance of coalition discipline. In short, without party cohesion in parliament, a coalition government in unlikely to have much of a future.

NOTE

1. For comparative treatment of recent changes in party rules on candidate selection, see Mair (1994) and Gallagher and Marsh (1988).

REFERENCES

Aldrich, John H. 1995. *Why Parties?* Chicago: University of Chicago Press.

Australian Labor Party, South Australia Branch. 1986–87. *Constitution and Rules.* Adelaide: Australian Labor Party, South Australia Branch.

Best, H. 1995. *Disorder Yields to Order.* In *Parliaments, Estates and Representation,* vol. 15. Aldershot, UK: Ashgate.

Blondel, Jean, and Maurizio Cotta, eds. 1996. *Party and Government: An Inquiry into the Relationship between Governments and Supporting Parties in Liberal Democracies.* New York: Macmillan.

Bowler, Shaun, David M. Farrell, and Ian McAllister. 1996. "Constituency Campaigning in Parliamentary Systems with Preferential Voting: Is There a Paradox?" *Electoral Studies* 15: 461–76.

Castles, F., and R. Wildenmann, eds. 1986. *The Future of Party Government.* New York: de Gruyter.

Cox, Gary. 1987. *The Efficient Secret.* Cambridge: Cambridge University Press.

Cox, Gary, and M. McCubbins. 1993. *Legislative Leviathan: Party Government in the House.* Berkeley: University of California Press.

Duverger, M. 1951. *Political Parties.* New York: John Wiley.

Epstein, Leon. 1956. "Cohesion of British Parliamentary Parties." *American Political Science Review* 2: 360–77.

Farrell, Brian. 1973. "The Paradox of Irish Politics." In Brian Farrell, ed., *The Irish Parliamentary Tradition.* New York: Macmillan.

———. 1987. "The Context of the Three Elections." In Howard R. Penniman and Brian Farrell, eds., *Ireland at the Polls, 1981, 1982 and 1987: A Study of Four General Elections.* Durham, NC: Duke University Press.

Farrell, Brian, and Maurice Manning. 1978. "The Election." In Howard R. Penniman, ed., *Ireland at the Polls: The Dáil Elections of 1977.* Washington, DC: American Enterprise Institute.

Gallagher, Michael, and Michael Marsh, eds. 1988. *Candidate Selection in Comparative Perspective: The Secret Garden of Politics.* Newbury Park, CA: Sage.

Gladstone, Viscount. 1927. "The Chief Whip in the British Parliament." *American Political Science Review* 21: 519–28.

Golombiewski, R. 1958. "A Taxonomic Approach to State Political Party Strength." *Western Political Quarterly* 11: 390–420.

Hirschmann, A. 1970. *Exit, Voice and Loyalty.* Cambridge, MA: Harvard University Press.

Holmes, G. 1987. *British Political Parties in the Age of Anne.* London: Hambledon Press.

Karasimeonov, Georgi. 1996. "The Legislature in Post-Communist Bulgaria." *Journal of Legislative Studies* 2: 40–59.

Katz, Richard S. 1980. *A Theory of Parties and Electoral Systems.* Baltimore: Johns Hopkins University Press.

———. 1986. "Intraparty Preference Voting." In Bernard Grofman and Arend Lijphart, eds., *Electoral Laws and Their Political Consequences.* New York: Agathon Press.

———, ed. 1987. *Party Governments: European and American Experiences.* New York: de Gruyter.

Katz, Richard S., and Peter Mair, eds. 1992. *Party Organizations: A Data Handbook.* Newbury Park, CA: Sage.

Key, V. O. 1949. *Southern Politics in States and Nation.* New York: Knopf.

Kornberg, A. 1967. *Canadian Legislative Behavior.* New York: Holt, Rinehart & Winston.

Laver, Michael, and Norman Schofield. 1990. *Multiparty Government: The Politics of Coalition in Europe.* London: Oxford University Press.

Loewenberg, G. 1967. *Parliaments in the German Political System.* Ithaca, NY: Cornell University Press.

Loveday, P., and A. Martin. 1966. *Parliaments, Factions and Parties: The First Thirty Years of Responsible Government in New South Wales, 1856–1889.* Melbourne, Australia: Melbourne University Press.

Mair, Peter. 1994. "Party Organizations: From Civil Society to the State." In Richard S. Katz and Peter Mair, eds., *How Parties Organize.* Thousand Oaks, CA: Sage.

McAllister, Ian. 1991. "Party Adaptation and Factionalism within the Australian Party System." *American Journal of Political Science* 35: 206–27.

Mezey, Michael L. 1993. "Legislatures: Individual Purpose and Institutional Performance." In Ada W. Finifter, ed., *Political Science: The State of the Discipline II.* Washington, DC: American Political Science Association.

———. 1995. "Parliament in the New Europe." In Jack Hayward and Edward C. Page, eds., *Governing the New Europe.* Cambridge: Polity Press.

New Zealand Labor Party Constitution and Rules. 1984. Wellington: Standard Press Ltd.

New Zealand Labor Party Constitution and Rules. 1998. Wellington: Standard Press Ltd.

Olson, David M., and Philip Norton, eds. 1996. "The New Parliaments of Central and Eastern Europe." Special issue. *Journal of Legislative Studies* 2.

Ostrogorski, M. 1902. *Democracy and the Organization of Political Parties.* New York: Macmillan.

Ozbudun, E. 1970. *Party Cohesion in Western Democracies: A Causal Analysis.* Beverly Hills, CA: Sage.

Panebianco, A. 1988. *Political Parties: Organization and Power.* Cambridge: Cambridge University Press.

Sartori, Giovanni. 1976. *Parties and Party Systems.* Cambridge: Cambridge University Press.

Schattschneider, E. E. 1942. *Party Government.* Westport, CT: Greenwood Press.

Schüttemeyer, Suzanne S. 1994. "Hierarchy and Efficiency in the Bundestag: The German Answer for Institutionalizing Parliament." In Gary W. Copeland and Samuel C. Patterson, eds., *Parliaments in the Modern World: Changing Institutions.* Ann Arbor: University of Michigan Press.

Silk, P. 1987. *How Parliament Works.* London: Longman.

Thayer, Nathaniel. 1969. *How the Conservatives Rule Japan.* Princeton, NJ: Princeton University Press.

von Beyme, Klaus. 1985. *Political Parties in Western Democracies.* New York: St. Martin's Press.

Webb, Paul. 1994. "Party Organizational Change in Britain: The Iron Law of Centralization?" In Richard S. Katz and Peter Mair, eds., *How Parties Organize.* Thousand Oaks, CA: Sage.

2

How Political Parties Emerged from the Primeval Slime: Party Cohesion, Party Discipline, and the Formation of Governments

MICHAEL LAVER AND
KENNETH A. SHEPSLE

By far the easiest way to construct models of interparty competition is to assume that parties behave as if they are unitary actors, which is of course not at all to assume that they actually are unitary actors. It clearly can sometimes make sense to treat life inside a political party as a black box. Most obviously, if members of a party are willing to submit themselves to party discipline, then the party may well look like a unitary actor in terms of its dealings with the outside world.

In relation to government formation, for example, individual political parties are almost always either in the government or outside it. It is very rare indeed for one fragment of a party to be in government while another is in opposition (Laver and Schofield 1990). We can thus describe the membership of coalition governments in terms of which parties are in the coalition and which are not—treating each party in this sense as if it were a unitary actor.

Although many interesting political phenomena can be described by treating parties as if they were unitary actors, we clearly do need to consider what goes on inside parties if we want to include an account of party decision making in a model of some political process. The danger of the unitary actor assumption in this context is that it may encourage us to take a quite unwarranted anthropomorphic view of how parties decide. For example, we may be seduced into thinking that a party will behave "in its own best interest"—and this is indeed an assumption shared by most models of interparty competition. This is effectively to assume that a party in some sense has its own utility function and a decision-making process designed to maximize this. Yet a political party comprises a group of individuals, and each individual not only has his or her own utility function but is clearly capable of autonomous action. Given this, the well-known logic of collective action implies that it is far-fetched to assume that individual members of this group will always act to maximize their collective utility. For this reason, we must obviously have a model of intraparty decision making before we can forecast how a political party is likely to behave in some specific circumstance. In this important sense, we need a model of intraparty politics before we can develop a realistic model of interparty competition.

An interesting early foray into this field was made by Gregory Luebbert (1986), who set out to develop an account of government formation that assumed, among other things, that a party leader is motivated above all else by the desire to remain party leader, even if this means on occasion sacrificing what to others might seem to be the best interests of the party. Empirically, it has been argued that certain Irish party leaders, for example, have taken their party into coalitions in circumstances when their party could quite possibly have governed alone, but only under another leader (Laver and Arkins 1990; Laver and Shepsle 1996). There is no job market for party leaders analogous to the market for company CEOs; parties do not transfer party leaders in the way that soccer teams transfer star players. It is thus clear that most party leaders have nowhere to go in politics but downhill and are likely to fight very hard to stay on top, even if their parties suffer some collateral damage in the process. Immediately we see that the interests of a party leader may well diverge from those of other sections of the party; only if we have an account of intraparty politics can we explore this type of phenomenon systematically.

It seems very likely on the face of things, of course, that it is not only party leaders who will have a distinctive political agenda. Those who would like to be party leader may have different views; so may the party's cabinet ministers, those who would like to be cabinet ministers, rank-and-file legislators who are concerned above all else with their reelection prospects, candidates who would like to be rank-and-file legislators as soon as possible, activists who joined the party to have some impact on policy, rank-and-file members who view the party as a sort of social club, and so on. To the extent that each of these types of intraparty actors has a say in what parties decide to do, its diverging views must be taken into account.

We set out in this chapter to explore ways in which an analysis of intraparty decision making might illuminate one important feature of intraparty politics—the making and breaking of governments in parliamentary democracies. We have elsewhere developed a model of the making and breaking of governments (Laver and Shepsle 1996). An important feature of our model is the assumption that the effective preparation, making, and implementation of policy decisions in parliamentary democracies depend in important ways upon the policy preferences of the cabinet minister in charge of the government department with jurisdiction over the policy area at issue. In the present context, this assumption is crucial because it means that the basic units of analysis are cabinet ministers and potential cabinet ministers, not political parties. Normally, one simplifies the analysis by assuming that all actual and potential cabinet ministers belonging to the same party have the same policy preferences, but this comes very close to making the unitary actor assumption. We discuss how this assumption can be relaxed in our earlier treatment of cabinet government (Laver and Shepsle 1996); in the present chapter, we elaborate in greater detail the consequences of intraparty preference heterogeneity for government formation and legislative party competition.

We develop this argument as follows. In the section "What Are Political Parties Made Of?" we discuss the basic building blocks of a model of intraparty politics: the external environment that sets the context for party decisions, the diversity of tastes within parties, the sections of the party with an input into decisions, the decision-making regime within the party, and the meaning and extent of party discipline. In the section "Intraparty Politics and Government Formation," we sketch our model and discuss why, in the context of government formation and for two quite different intraparty decision-making regimes, factions with diverse tastes might nonetheless submit to the discipline of a single party. Finally, we draw some conclusions from all of this about the strategic forces that might draw and hold parties together as units and that might indeed provide some of the basic logic that underlies the formation of political parties in the first place.

What Are Political Parties Made Of?

The External Environment

Political parties have many roles in parliamentary democracies. Not only do they supply members of governments and other political elites, but they also offer stimuli for voters at election time, construct interpretations of important events, provide important social networks, and so on. It is inconceivable that we could model the functioning of some abstract notion of a "political party" without having a clear sense of the particular role or roles in which we are interested.

As we have already indicated, our main concern in this chapter is the making and breaking of governments, which we take to be one of the pivotal processes in parliamentary democracy. To a very large extent, therefore, the environment in which we are interested comprises the legislature, the executive, and the relationship between these. While other environments (especially the electoral environment) are obviously important for a full understanding of the functioning of political parties, the setting that we focus on here is the formation of governments in parliamentary democracies.

One result of this is that, to the extent that we do consider electoral feedback to party decision making, we take it as an exogenous input to the making and breaking of governments rather than as an interaction effect that forms an intrinsic part of our model. In short, we assume that politicians thinking about government formation regard the electorate rather as they regard Nature, as a machine meting out rewards and punishments in some probabilistic manner. The key interactions in our model take place between party politicians in parliament.

Tastes

The most fundamental reason why political parties are not unitary actors is that different politicians have different tastes. If all politicians in the same party had identical tastes, there would be no intraparty conflict of interest and thus no policy basis for intraparty politics. The fact that it does not seem very reasonable to assume that all politicians in the same party have identical tastes is what put intraparty politics on the agenda.

Of course, when we come to model politics within parties, we do not do this in the abstract but have some particular context and purpose in mind. Thus, we must consider the diversity of those tastes in a party that are systematically relevant to the purpose at hand. Just because one politician likes steak very rare while another likes it burnt to a cinder, we need not assume that this has a bearing on intraparty politics. We must confine our attention, in short, to a diversity of relevant tastes.

This, like so many other things in political science, is easy to say but impossible to do, since what will ultimately turn out to be relevant to our main interests is not necessarily self-evident at the outset. It is hard to specify, a priori, which are and which are not relevant tastes. To make some progress, however, we probably will not raise too many eyebrows if, when we consider government formation, we confine ourselves to tastes about public policy *on issues that will certainly, or might conceivably, come up for decision by governments within the time horizons of the actors concerned.* Diversity of tastes on such issues is what makes politics within parties relevant. An important implication of this is that *changes* in the relative importance of issues can change politics within parties. Arguably, for example, the increasing salience of European policy ultimately undermined Margaret Thatcher's position as leader of the British Conservative Party. Ultimately, this led to a sudden and dramatic replacement of a party leader who had once seemed invulnerable, and it would have done so even if the party had comprised precisely the same members as before with precisely the same policy positions on Europe (Garry 1995).

Factions

Politicians within parties often align themselves with groupings that we can think of as factions. Factions can be based upon almost anything. Since we are concerned here with the tastes of politicians with respect to current or anticipated issues in public policy, however, we concentrate on factions comprising politicians with similar tastes in public policy. What precisely we mean by *similar,* of course, will determine how many factions we are likely to recognize for a given distribution of opinion within the party. At one extreme, if we draw very fine distinctions, every member of every party can be shown to have different views about everything of relevance. With this approach, there will be as many factions as there are politicians. At the other extreme, a hungry tiger might regard all politicians as the same, fail to observe any differences of taste between them, and effectively put them all into one faction.

The way in which one sees the factional structure of a political party, therefore, depends very much on one's point of view. For the most part, this is a problem of operationalization that should not concern us too much at this stage. What we do need to settle now is that parties can be thought of as comprising factions of politicians with similar tastes in public policy. These factions range in scale, according to exigencies of the analysis, from a single politician to the party as a whole. We will need to determine the factional structure of a party as an operational matter before we can analyze a particular case, but for the time being we will take this as given.

Decision-Making Regimes

Once we recognize different factions with different tastes within a party, it becomes important to know how these factions interact to determine courses of action for the party. Specifically, we need to know about the formal rules by which the party makes its decisions—its decision-making regime. Obviously, parties can operate on the basis of any one of a huge number of possible decision-making regimes, each of which could be modeled. For the sake of simplicity, however, we consider two possible decision-making regimes in what follows.

The first of these requires us to make the smallest step possible from the unitary actor assumption: it involves parties in which decisions are taken by an autocratic party leadership. All party decisions are assumed to be taken either by a single autocratic leader or by a leadership faction, all members of which share the same tastes. On the face of things, this may not seem to depart at all from the unitary actor assumption, but it does so in one important respect. The diversity of tastes in the party means that there are nonleadership factions to which it is possible to assign control over key aspects of public policy. This can have an important bearing upon government formation, as we show below. The first decision-making regime that we consider, therefore, involves autocratic decisions by the leader or leadership faction, given diversity of tastes among party politicians.

The second decision-making regime that we consider requires us to make a very large step from the unitary actor assumption and see a party as a microcosm of the wider political system. We might think of this regime as a "delegate conference" regime, in which all key decisions are taken by a representative body, which might even be the legislative party as a whole. Each faction within the party has a weight, and the party has a decision rule that specifies how such weight should be aggregated. There are many possible decision rules, of course, but we concentrate here on majority voting. Decisions within the party under this regime, in short, are taken by majority vote at a representative delegate conference.

While many other decision rules not only are theoretically possible but actually exist within real-world political parties, we begin our explorations by focusing on these two. Since they represent quite distinct extremes, they enable us to see as clearly as possible the extent to which the intraparty politics of government formation is affected by the party's decision-making regime.

Discipline

We take party discipline to involve a member's abiding by a decision taken by the party's decision-making regime, whether or not he or she supported the particular decision taken. Perfect party discipline arises when all members abide by all party decisions, including all of those that they opposed during the decision-making process and that run counter to their private preferences. Complete indiscipline arises when every member acts regardless of any decision taken by the party, in accordance with private preferences—in effect, as if the party did not exist at all. In an undisciplined environment, members may of course act in accordance with party decisions, but they do this because of the correlation between party decisions and private preferences, not as a result of deferring in their actions to party decisions.

One of the central issues that our model illuminates is why a politician would in fact submit to party discipline rather than behave as an independent actor. Essentially, as we shall see, this happens because party discipline creates more powerful bargaining units that are able to drag eventual government policy outputs on a wide range of issues closer to the ideal points of those subjecting themselves to the discipline.[1] The next section develops this argument.

Intraparty Politics and Government Formation

Outline of the Portfolio Allocation Model of Government Formation

The portfolio allocation model of government formation has been extensively described and empirically elaborated elsewhere (Laver and Shepsle 1996). We do no more here than briefly summarize its key features for the purposes of setting up our argument about party discipline.

The portfolio allocation approach is based fundamentally on the distinctive roles of legislature and executive in Western parliamentary democracies. While the executive is formally responsible to the legislature and must resign if it loses a vote of confidence or no confidence, almost all policy making and implementation takes place within the executive. If a government makes any policy a matter of confidence, then the legislature can change government policy only by changing the government. While most European executives operate formally on the principle of collective cabinet responsibility, most of the actual process of making *and implementing* policy inevitably takes place within government departments. Only government departments, each the political responsibility of a cabinet minister, have the resources and technical competence to develop implementable policy proposals within their jurisdictions.

Cabinet ministers thus have two roles. They are members of a body (the cabinet) that takes *collective responsibility* for government policy; they are also *individually responsible* for the departments that do much of the work of developing and implementing real-world policy proposals. It is in this important sense that cabinet *decision making* is not collective. By virtue of their role as department heads, cabinet ministers have disproportionate influence on the substance of cabinet decisions within their jurisdiction. This has the important implication that substantive policy outputs in a given area will change with the changing tastes of the minister put in charge of the department with jurisdiction. If we assume that the tastes of actual and potential cabinet ministers are common knowledge (revealed, in effect, during the apprenticeship that politicians must serve before being added to the roster of *ministrables*), then the making and breaking of governments is informed *and influenced* by forecasts of the policy outputs resulting from the appointment of each *ministrable* to each government department.

This postulated relationship simplifies the job of analyzing government formation, since it implies that there is in fact a finite number of possible cabinets, representing the number of ways of allocating a given number of *ministrables* to a given number of cabinet portfolios. A very much simplified characterization of this portfolio allocation problem, assuming two key policy dimensions (finance and foreign policy) and three sets of *ministrables* (to be thought of as parties or factions), is shown in figure 2.1. For the time being, we assume that each set contains

Figure 2.1 A Finite Set of Portfolio Allocations

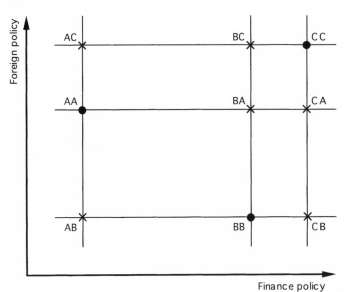

ministrables with identical preferences on the two key policy dimensions. That is, each set of *ministrables* can be taken for now to constitute a unitary party.

Assuming that each policy dimension is under the jurisdiction of a different cabinet portfolio, figure 2.1 shows that there are in effect just nine portfolio allocations with substantively different implications for public policy. Both portfolios can be given to the same set of *ministrables.* If both are given to party A, then government policy is forecast to be at AA. If both are given to party B, government policy is forecast to be at BB. Alternatively, one portfolio can be given to a politician from one party, while another portfolio is given to a politician from another party—in effect, this is a coalition cabinet. If the finance portfolio is given to a politician from party A and the foreign affairs portfolio is given to a politician from party B, then forecast government policy is at AB, and so on. Each of the nine points on the "lattice" in figure 2.1 is a distinct government, with the first letter in the label identifying the party assigned the finance ministry and the second letter identifying the party controlling the foreign ministry.

The portfolio allocation approach takes this finite set of governments as its raw material and uses two simple and uncontroversial assumptions about the making and breaking of governments to derive a model of

Figure 2.2   The "Winset" of a BA Cabinet

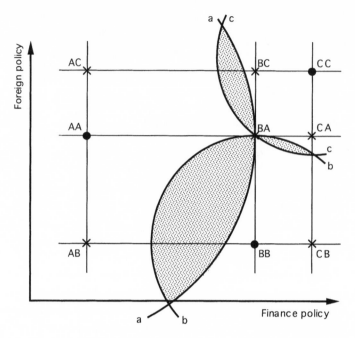

government formation. The first assumption is that an equilibrium cabinet must be able to win legislative majorities on votes of confidence or no confidence. Note that this definitely does *not* imply that the cabinet itself must comprise parties with a legislative majority between them. The second assumption is that no party can be forced into government against its will. Note that this means that every party has an effective *veto* over the formation of any cabinet in which it participates.

We will not repeat the full implications of the model and their derivation here (see Laver and Shepsle 1996 for this). Two key results are crucial for the argument that follows, however. Figure 2.2 shows how three parties A, B, and C, any two of which are required to form a legislative majority, feel about BA, the cabinet giving the finance portfolio to party B and the foreign affairs portfolio to party A. Party A prefers any cabinet inside the indifference curve *aa,* each of which is closer to its ideal policy than BA; Party B prefers any cabinet inside curve *bb;* and party C prefers any cabinet inside curve *cc.*

Any two parties command a legislative majority between them, and the shaded area in figure 2.2 shows those parts of the policy space preferred to the policies of a BA cabinet by some pair of parties and thus preferred to the policies of BA by some legislative majority. This is the "winset" of BA. Note that, although the (shaded) winset of BA is quite large, it contains the forecast policies of not a single one of the eight alternative cabinets. This implies that cabinet BA is in equilibrium, since, if BA were the status quo cabinet, then some legislative majority would have both the incentive and the ability to block any move leading to an alternative cabinet.

The BA cabinet has the distinctive property that it is at the dimension-by-dimension median (DDM) position in the policy space, in the sense that it comprises the party containing the median legislator on each key policy dimension. A DDM cabinet whose winset contains no alternative cabinet is obviously an important equilibrium feature of the government formation process. If it is the status quo, it should remain the status quo. Laver and Shepsle (1996) show that for any cabinet not at the DDM, at least one alternative cabinet can be found that is preferred to it by some legislative majority.

A striking feature of Laver and Shepsle's theory, however, is that the DDM cabinet with an empty winset is not the only candidate for equilibrium. To see why, consider that parties can veto the formation of cabinets in which they participate, the implications of which are shown in figure 2.3.

This shows how the same three parties feel about another cabinet—the "minority" administration in which both key portfolios are controlled by party B. Once more, party A prefers any cabinet inside curve *aa;* party C prefers any cabinet inside curve *cc.* Obviously, party B prefers no alternative cabinet to the one in which it gets both key portfolios. The shaded area is the set of policies preferred by both party A and party C to those of a cabinet comprising only party B. Note that two cabinets, BA and BC, lie inside this shaded area. In other words, BA and BC are preferred to BB by both party A and party C, *who between them control a legislative majority.* If BB were the status quo cabinet for some reason, why would parties A and C not combine to defeat it and install either BA or BC instead?

The short answer is that parties A and C, despite their legislative majority, do not have the power to install either BA or BC, since party B, a member of both alternative cabinets, can veto each of these. This creates the intriguing situation in which the only alternatives to BB that command majority support can be vetoed by party B, which has both the incentive and the ability to prevent these from replacing BB. Laver and Shepsle (1996) call a party in this position a "strong" party.

Figure 2.3 BB Is a "Strong" Party

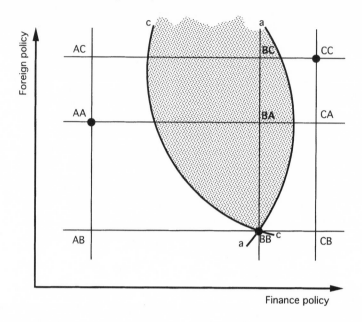

A strong party is one that can veto any alternative cabinet that is preferred by a legislative majority to the cabinet in which the strong party gets all key portfolios. If the strong party's ideal cabinet is the status quo, and if its threats to veto such alternatives are credible, then the strong party's ideal cabinet is in equilibrium. Laver and Shepsle (1996) show that there can be at most one strong party in any party system but that there may be no strong party for particular configurations of parties.

Laver and Shepsle thus derive two equilibrium concepts—the DDM cabinet with no alternative cabinet in its winset and the strong party cabinet. There will always be a DDM cabinet, although this does not always have an empty winset and thus does not always represent an equilibrium. There is often a strong party. And there may be both a strong party and a DDM cabinet with an empty winset. In such cases, strategic standoffs can occur, though we may assume that sophisticated political actors have good information about which parties are likely to win such standoffs. While there is much more to the portfolio allocation approach than we have outlined here, we now have sufficient tools to use the approach in an exploration of the impact of the government formation process on party discipline.

Party Discipline and Bargaining Power

The portfolio allocation model can easily be adapted to take account of intraparty politics because it is fundamental to the approach that government ministers have a combination of agenda power and implementation authority sufficient to pull policy outputs within their ministry's jurisdiction toward their preferred policy position in predictable ways. Assuming that parties are unitary actors amounts to assuming that all ministerial candidates from the same party are forecast to implement the same policies in a particular jurisdiction. This must be either because all ministers from the same party have the same policy preferences, which seems rather unlikely, or because parties are able to control absolutely the actions of their own ministers within their departments, which is also implausible. Once we make the plausible assumption of a diversity of tastes within parties, then a deeper consideration of intraparty politics is obviously needed.

In assuming a diversity of tastes within parties, we are stipulating that each party has a roster of senior politicians, each with a particular policy reputation, from which it selects ministerial nominees to the cabinet. These politicians are important resources for the party, since they allow the party to underwrite certain policy positions in government by making the appropriate ministerial appointment.

A vital consequence of any intraparty diversity in policy positions is thus that it allows the party to make different ministerial nominations to a given portfolio and thereby to generate different forecasts of the policy implications of including the party in government. To get an empirical sense of this, consider the following extract from an analysis in the *Financial Times* (June 3, 1996) of the policy consequences of different possible ministerial nominations to the Israeli cabinet that formed after the 1996 elections:

> How Mr. Netanyahu carries out his task . . . will be the first real indicator of the policy direction of Israel in the key issues of Middle East peace, the national economy, and the religious-secular status quo. . . . Mr. Netanyahu's first task is to decide how to distribute the big three posts—finance, defence and foreign affairs. . . . The prime-minister elect has promised the defence ministry to Mr. Yitzhak Mordechai. . . . However, senior generals . . . have let it be known that they will resign if Mr. Mordechai became defence minister. . . . [A] Treasury run by Mr. Sharon would be problematic. He is on the extreme right wing of the party and is a champion of the country's need

to keep hold of Arab lands and build a greater Israel by massive new investment in Jewish settlements in the West Bank. Such a policy would not only threaten the Middle East peace process but would kill urgent efforts to cut the budget so as to reduce inflation. . . . If Mr. Netanyahu were to decide to place at the finance ministry a more moderate Likud figure, such as Mr. Dan Meridan, the favourite candidate of the business community, that would mean some other post for Mr. Sharon.

The analysis goes on in this vein, and similar articles have been written during the formation of cabinets in most parliamentary democracies. By responding to the different policy forecasts generated by different possible ministerial nominations, a party may seek to improve its strategic prospects in government formation. We explore the implications of this matter for party discipline by relaxing the unitary actor assumption in two stages.

First, we relax it very gently by considering parties that include a diversity of tastes but that are very centralized in the sense that they are run on authoritarian lines by their leadership factions. This has the consequence that all strategic decisions are taken in terms of indifference curves centered upon the ideal point of the leadership faction but that party leaders can take advantage of the diversity of tastes among their stable of *ministrables*.

Second, while retaining the assumption of diversity of tastes, we consider parties in which power is more decentralized. We take the specific (and very decentralized) example of a party that takes all strategic decisions on government formation by way of majority voting at a delegate conference proportionately representing all tastes within the legislative party. In either case, we take party discipline to involve abiding by the party's validly taken strategic decisions, even when those concerned would choose a different course of action if they were not party members.

Diversity of Tastes in Autocratic Parties

Figure 2.4 shows a system with six independent political actors—A_1, A_2, B_1, B_2, C_1, and C_2—each with one-sixth of the total weight. Actors may be individual politicians or factions comprising politicians with identical tastes. One actor may fuse with another by giving its legislative weight to, and submitting to the strategic decisions of, the other actor. Both actors remain in politics, and their ideal points remain

Figure 2.4   A System with Three Parties, Each with Two Factions

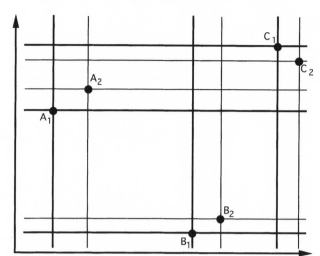

unchanged. Indeed, fusions are reversible, so that one faction may split from another with which it previously fused if the strategic environment changes.

Once a fusion has taken place, there is now one two-faction party where before there were two one-faction actors. The autocratic decision-making regime means that the party leadership is controlled by one faction and that all of the party's legislative weight can be deployed by this faction. The nonleadership "out" faction has tastes but no legislative weight. This is why we need consider only the indifference curves of the leadership faction to determine the strategic decisions that underpin the making and breaking of governments. In the present context, the key question that we must answer concerns whether it will ever be rational for one actor to cede its legislative weight and strategic autonomy to another in this way. If it is rational to do this in certain circumstances, then we have uncovered a strategic logic behind such fusions, and indeed behind a more general process that may cause political actors to bind themselves together into larger political units.

Figure 2.5 shows that it can indeed be rational to do this in certain circumstances. If each actor is independent, then there is no strong party. Consider now the situation that arises if there is a fusion between one of the three pairs of adjacent actors, with the leadership of the new party being given to one or the other actor. (There are, of course, many other potential fusions, but for the sake of clarity we do not consider

Figure 2.5 B₁ and B₂ Find It Rational to Fuse

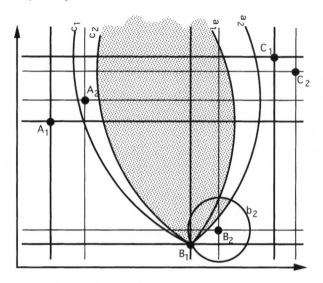

them here, since the restricted set of examples just mentioned allows us to make our main point.) We can investigate the effects of each possible merger.[2] When we do so, we find that mergers of either the A or the C pairs of actors, if all other actors stay independent, do not make much of a strategic difference but that a merger between the two B actors has a dramatic strategic effect. Whichever B faction is given the leadership, party B becomes a strong party as a result of the merger.

Figure 2.5 illustrates this. The winset of B_1 before any merger is shown as the shaded area. This is the intersection of any four of the indifference curves of the A_1, A_2, B_2, C_1, and C_2 factions through B_1 (the respective curves are labeled in lower case). B_1 is not a strong party because its winset contains several points in which it does not participate and that it therefore cannot veto. These are B_2A_1, B_2A_2, B_2C_2, and B_2C_1.[3]

Every one of these points, however, involves the participation of B_2. If B_2 joins B_1 and submits to B_1's discipline, then B_1 can also veto cabinets involving the participation of B_2. In effect, B_1 can prohibit B_2 from going into cabinet, and as a result, the new fused party B is a strong party. If it can win strategic standoffs against the other actors, it may be able to impose policy positions involving only actors from party B. The result would be that cabinet policy would be pulled toward both B_1 *and* B_2 as a result of the merger, an outcome preferred by both factions.

Figure 2.6 Parties C_1 and C_2 Fuse, Undermining the Position of B_1

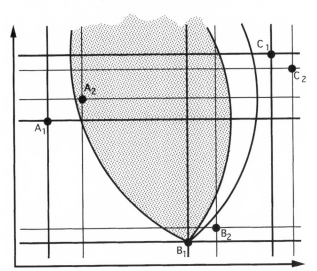

What has happened is that B_2 has produced an outcome it prefers by ceding its weight and strategic autonomy to B_1. It thus appears rational for B_2 to fuse with B_1 and to submit to the discipline of a party dominated by B_1. This is the central theoretical point of this chapter.

This is not the end of the story, however, for now things get complicated! Consider the potential responses of the other actors to the merger of B_1 and B_2 and the consequent creation of a strong party B. There is nothing much that the two A actors can do, but if the two C actors merge and if party C's leadership is controlled by C_1, then party B ceases to be able to impose B_1B_1. This is because, when C_2 cedes its weight and strategic autonomy to C_1, C_2's indifference curve is effectively deleted, and C_2's weight is added to C_1 when winsets are calculated. The effect is to increase the size of the B_1B_1 winset, as shown in figure 2.6.[4] There is now a set of cabinets in the winset of B_1B_1 that do not involve party B and that B therefore cannot veto.

As it happens in this case, party B is in fact a strong party because it has a strategic response to this move by the C actors. The leadership faction, B_1, can cede the foreign affairs portfolio to the "out" faction, B_2. As figure 2.7 shows, if this happens, then B remains a strong party. All alternatives in the winset of B_1B_2 involve the participation of one or other of the B factions, which the leadership of party B can veto. Thus, the fusion of the B factions does indeed appear to be a rational

Figure 2.7   Party B Is Strong if B_1 Cedes a Portfolio to B_2

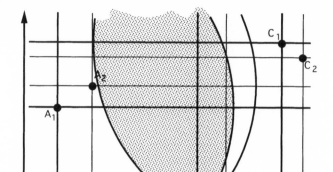

move, increasing the probability of government outputs favored by both factions. Note, moreover, that the fusion of the C factions also appears to be rational, pulling the eventual equilibrium toward both of them.

The theoretical example in figure 2.7 highlights a clear strategic logic for an intriguing empirical feature of the process of nominating party notables to cabinet portfolios in the real world—the fact that party leaders sometimes nominate their internal party opponents to high public office. A typical seat-of-the-pants explanation for this phenomenon is that party leaders like to have their opponents "inside the tent pissing out, rather than outside the tent pissing in" and that in this way they not only keep an eye on political opponents within the party but use the doctrine of collective cabinet responsibility to silence their opposition. The portfolio allocation approach shows us that interparty politics may also have an important impact on intraparty ministerial careers. A given government may be in equilibrium only if particular ministerial nominations are made to certain key positions. A particular *ministrable* may have too soft a reputation on balancing the budget to be made finance minister in a particular equilibrium cabinet, for example, or too hawkish a reputation to be put in charge of defence or foreign affairs. Alternative ministerial nominations from within the party, which may come from the ranks of the party's "out" factions, may be needed to sustain it in office by making its policy positions acceptable to other parties. In this way, interparty politics affect the intraparty allocation of cabinet positions.

Diversity of Tastes in Democratic Parties

Politics within "autocratic" parties, as we have modeled it, essentially consists of a leadership faction setting both policy and legislative strategy, constrained only by the possibility that factions will leave the party if some alternative becomes more attractive. We model politics within "democratic" parties, in contrast, as a microcosm of politics in the legislative system as a whole:

- Decisions within the party are taken by majority vote at a party meeting that is representative of the legislative party as a whole.
- Party discipline implies that all members of all party factions will abide by party decisions once taken.
- *Ministrable* politicians from factions within a party can be required by the party to hold cabinet portfolios. Factions are thus different from parties in the wider system in this sense. What they do within their department, however, is beyond party control (see above).

Given this model of decision making, democratic intraparty politics becomes distinct from autocratic intraparty politics only when there are three or more factions, each with less than majority weight in the party—otherwise, the majority faction behaves as if it were the leadership faction in an autocratic party.

Figure 2.8 shows a modified version of the previous example. To keep things simple, parties A and C are seen as unified parties, located at A_1 and C_1 respectively. Party B, however, has three factions, B_1, B_2, and B_3, none with majority weight within the party. Any two of the factions are decisive within the party's decision-making regime.

If any or all of the three factions leave the party, then there is no strong party in the system, and B_1A_1 is the only candidate for a cabinet equilibrium in our model, a DDM with an empty winset, shown by the shaded area. This seems a likely outcome of the government formation process.

If the three B factions accept the discipline of a single party with a democratic decision-making regime, then the situation is quite different. There are nine ways in which the two key portfolios can be given to the

Figure 2.8   The Strength of a United Party B

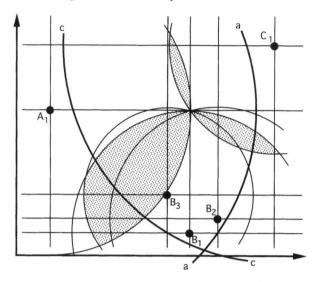

three B factions. As the heavy indifference curves show, any one of these nine allocations would make B a strong party. (The curve labeled *aa* shows how party A feels about the one of these nine allocations that is furthest from its ideal point; the curve labeled *cc* shows how party C feels about the allocation furthest from its ideal point.) These two curves show the outer bounds of the winsets of the nine party B allocations, and some party B faction participates in every point within these bounds, making a fused party B strong, whichever of the points it selects. In this important sense, which of the nine points it selects is entirely a matter for party B.

Figure 2.9 therefore concentrates upon the internal politics of party B. It shows that within party B, *the B_1 faction is a strong faction in the sense that it participates in any intraparty portfolio allocation in the intraparty winset of its ideal point.* If the B_1 faction can win standoffs with the other factions, then it may well be able to impose its ideal point as party policy, and we know from the original Laver-Shepsle propositions that even if the strong faction cannot win standoffs, party policy will be either B_1B_1 or B_1B_2. Since all of the B factions prefer both of these points to B_1A_1—the likely cabinet equilibrium if any of them split from party B—it is rational for them to submit to the discipline of party B. Whether party B's policy position is B_1B_1 or B_1B_2 will depend upon the ability of the strong B_1 faction to win intraparty standoffs with the other B factions.

Figure 2.9 The Strength of the B_1 Faction inside Party B

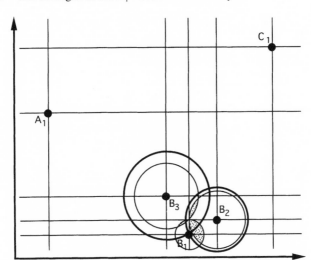

The theoretical possibility of strong party factions, highlighted in the example shown in figure 2.9, is one possible explanation for what can often appear to be the dominant position of some particular faction within a given party. Within the party, the dominant faction occupies an equivalent strategic position to that of a strong party in the wider legislative party system; note that the dominant faction's position may well be a product of the configuration of parties in the political system as a whole. This type of analysis has potentially far-reaching consequences, since the identity of the strong faction should have a major impact on the policy positions taken by single party governments, while the fact that this identity is affected by the configuration of the wider party system shows ways in which changes in the legislative party system outside a one-party government may affect policy developments inside it.

The key to the previous example was that all of the B factions preferred the predicted equilibrium cabinet arising from submitting to the discipline of party B to the predicted outcome if they defected. As might be expected, this is not always the case. Figures 2.10 and 2.11 show a slight modification of the example in figures 2.8 and 2.9; the B_3 faction is somewhat closer to the center of the policy space and thus somewhat further from the other B factions.

We immediately note several important differences between the two situations. If we consider only policy points within party B, B_1 remains a strong faction. However, the situation is complicated by the fact that

Figure 2.10   The B_3 Faction Prefers Coalitions with Other Parties to B_1's Ideal Point

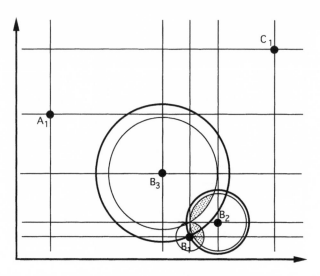

Figure 2.11   Party B Remains a Strong Party if It Stays United

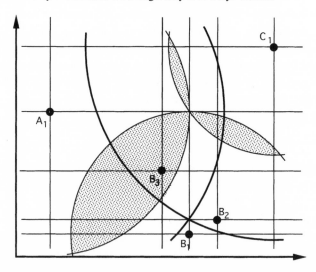

B_3 now actually prefers both B_3A_1 and B_1A_1 to B_1B_1, the ideal point of the B_1 faction. While B_1 can veto B_1A_1, it cannot veto B_3A_1. It looks likely that B_1 will not be able to impose B_1B_1, although B_1B_2 is preferred by B_3 to either B_3A_1 or B_1A_1. Figure 2.11 shows that if B_1B_2 is adopted as party B's policy position, then party B remains strong. Indeed, since

Figure 2.12 The B_3 Faction Would Be a Strong Party if It Defected from Party B

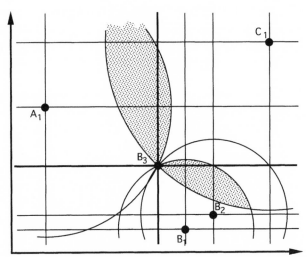

B_3B_3 is now in the (shaded) winset of the DDM cabinet, B_1A_1, party B's strong party status is enhanced in the sense that at least one rival candidate for an equilibrium cabinet has been removed from the picture.[5]

A much more significant difference between the two cases, however, is revealed by figure 2.12, which shows that *the B_3 faction would be a strong party in the wider party system if it defected from party B*. It participates in every cabinet in the (shaded) winset of its ideal point.

If B_3 expects to be able to win standoffs with the other parties, then it may well be rational for it to defect from party B—although in anticipation of this, the other B factions might agree to set party policy at B_3B_3. If B_3 does not expect to be able to win standoffs, then the equilibrium cabinet will nonetheless be in the shaded winset of B_3B_3. Note that neither B_1B_1 nor B_1B_2 is in this winset, although B_1B_3 is. If B_3 is not expected to win standoffs, then the other B factions could preempt B_3's defection by setting party B policy at B_1B_3. Nonetheless, the real prospect of the defection of B_3 does have a significant impact both on the policy position of party B and the eventual equilibrium cabinet.

In more general terms, figures 2.11 and 2.12 show that the portfolio allocation approach offers the possibility of being able to model the impact of the government formation process on the incentives for factions to defect from existing parties. If a particular faction would find itself in a powerful strategic position in the government formation process as a party in its own right if it were to defect, then such defection not only would seem rational but might force other party factions to make major policy concessions to avert this. Once more, changes in the configuration of the wider legislative party system may, by changing the balance of power within parties in this way, have a major impact on intraparty politics (for further discussion, see chaps. 11 and 12 of this volume).

Conclusion

Unlike most other theoretical accounts of party competition, the portfolio allocation approach focuses upon individual politicians rather than on monolithic parties. This allows us to address the issue of intraparty politics in general and of party discipline in particular. What we see when we look at party competition in this way is quite fascinating.

First, we see that a party may gain strategic leverage from having politicians with both diverse tastes and the discretion to do something about these if they get into government. By changing ministerial nominees, the party can change the policies that it is forecasted to implement if it gets into office, to its strategic advantage.

In the present context, the most important thing we see, however, is that there are incentives for independent parties or factions not only to fuse but also to submit to the discipline of other factions with different tastes, ceding strategic autonomy in the expectation of generating more favored government policy outputs than would otherwise arise. The strategic benefits of party discipline thus act as a kind of gravitational force, providing a logic that holds together what on the face of things may appear to be diverse parts of a single party. Indeed, if we imagine a primeval political soup through which political actors were scattered at random, then the processes described above should lead to a series of combinations of actors into ever-larger entities that come to look more and more like the political parties we have come by now to know and love. At the same time, our approach, as we saw in the final example that we discussed, can identify circumstances in which it may be rational for a faction to defect from a party and set up in business on its own.

Obviously, what have been presented here are no more than sketches of what might be at work. Much needs to be done on developing a formal model of the processes sketched above. What the examples show clearly, however, is that our model of government formation can be used to generate an account of the role of party discipline as the strategic force that binds factions together into larger and more effective legislative players in the government formation game.

NOTES

1. Of course, there are many explanations, in both the formal theory and the more substantive literatures, for the emergence and maintenance of parties. Formal theoretical arguments, for example, often emphasize the repeat-play nature of electoral/governance cycles and the "brand name" benefits that a party label provides to prospective and incumbent legislators (see Cox and McCubbins 1993). What distinguishes our explanation is that it depends entirely on politics *inside* Parliament, so that policy-oriented parliamentarians would want to coalesce into factions and parties even if there were no electoral benefits from so doing.

2. We do this using a custom-written computer program, WINSET, which identifies strong parties, empty-winset DDMs, and other strategic features of a given party configuration. The WINSET program, which runs under DOS, is freely available for personal research and teaching use via Internet. The program itself, program manuals, and sample data files can be downloaded by connecting to FTP.TCD.IE, logging on as user "anonymous" and supplying a complete e-mail address as a password. The latest release versions of all files are located in the directory /PUB/POLITICS, which contains a README file describing what is available.

3. The situation for B_2 before a merger is similar.

4. Because B_2 has fused with B_1, its indifference curve is also deleted in figure 2.6.

5. That is, the DDM cabinet no longer has an empty winset.

REFERENCES

Cox, Gary W., and Mathew D. McCubbins. 1993. *Legislative Leviathan: Party Government in the House.* Berkeley: University of California Press.

Garry, John. 1995. "The British Conservative Party: Divisions over European Policy." *West European Politics* 18(4): 170–89.

Laver, Michael, and Audrey Arkins. 1990. "Coalition and Fianna Fáil." In Michael Gallagher and Richard Sinnott, eds., *How Ireland Voted 1989.* Galway: Centre for the Study of Irish Elections.

Laver, Michael, and Norman Schofield. 1990. *Multiparty Government: The Politics of Coalition in Europe.* London: Oxford University Press.

Laver, Michael, and Kenneth A. Shepsle. 1996. *Making and Breaking Governments.* Cambridge: Cambridge University Press.

Luebbert, Gregory. 1986. *Comparative Democracy: Policy-Making and Government Coalitions in Europe and Israel.* New York: Columbia University Press.

PART II

The "Westminster Model"

In the U.S. literature on Congress, it used to be common practice to draw comparisons between the relatively low levels of party cohesion in Congress and the highly cohesive "Westminster model," in which parliamentary discipline and cabinet collegiality combined to ensure a relatively smooth passage of legislation through the British House of Commons. Furthermore, the belief of the U.K. political science tradition, from Samuel Finer onwards, was that any of the rare incidents of internal party division and factionalism were a feature more of the Labour Party than of the Conservatives. It is not only the U.S. literature that treats the United Kingdom as an ideal type. For instance, in his book *Democracies* (Yale University Press, 1984), Arend Lijphart uses the Westminster model as the basis for his "majoritarian" system, one of the characteristics of which is a "cohesive majority party" ensuring cabinet dominance.

Recent literature has started to blunt some of the sharper edges of these U.S.-U.K. contrasts. Scholars in the United States have begun to assert the importance of party, while work in the United Kingdom has gone some way toward undermining the view of British parliamentary parties as monoliths (see the citations in chaps. 3 and 4 of this volume). Here we present two chapters that go even further toward undermining the received view of the Westminster model as one that should form the ideal type in contrast to that of the United States. British parties have revealed evidence of "seismic" differences, and, if anything, this has been a far greater problem of late for the Conservative Party than for Labour. The two chapters in this part set out the nature and extent of these divisions. They also discuss their causes, a combination of both the issue of European integration (the principal factor) and, as Whiteley and Seyd (chap. 3 of this volume) point out, institutional developments in British politics (such as the rise of candidate-centered local politics and the decline of local government) that have served to ennoble the constituency politician.

According to Whiteley and Seyd's analysis of the attitudes of party members—and contrary to the long-held canons of British political science—the local Conservative selectorates appear quite prepared to sanction dissension by their parliamentary representatives: "An MP who gratifies local sensibilities, and who does a reasonable amount of constituency service, can persistently rebel in the House of Commons, without being unduly concerned that this will lead to his or her de-selection." And it was clear from Baker, Ludlam, and Gamble's (1994) survey of Conservative politicians during the 1992–97 parliament that a large group of these MPs looked set to rebel. In the course of the 1997 general election, that rebellion occurred when more than 200 Conservatives defied explicit orders from the party leadership and published personal manifestos against the proposal for a single European currency, forcing the hand of the party leadership over the issue and ultimately contributing to the party's election defeat.

3

Discipline in the British Conservative Party: The Attitudes of Party Activists toward the Role of Their Members of Parliament

PAUL F. WHITELEY AND PATRICK SEYD

British parliamentary parties are renowned for their discipline and cohesion (Beer 1965). Since the development of the modern mass-based party system in the late nineteenth century, MPs have been elected to the House of Commons as representatives of a political party and, as such, have been very generally bound to their party's election manifesto. Their party loyalty, as measured by "whipped votes," has been high. Never, however, has party cohesion been absolute. Factions, tendencies, and cliques (Rose 1965) have prevailed within the parties, and opinions have often been expressed either through Early Day Motions (Berrington 1973) or, on occasion, by rebellions in the division lobbies (Norton 1978, 1980). When rebellion against party instructions has occurred in the division lobbies, both Conservative and Labour Party leaderships have possessed the ultimate sanction of withdrawal of the party whip as a means of maintaining party loyalty. Since the powers of both selection and reselection of parliamentary candidates reside with local party activists, for this sanction to be effective, either the party leaderships must have the power to order local party activists not to select a parliamentary rebel, or the local activists must share their leadership's views and refuse to reselect the rebel. As is well known, without party endorsement, an individual's chances of reelection to the House of Commons as an independent are almost negligible.

Nevertheless, Norton (1980) has noted the growth of intraparty dissent within the parliamentary parties during recent decades. This development might be partly explained by a rise in candidate-centered local parties, in which the local party activists are willing to sustain rebels under certain circumstances. For example, recent changes in the parliamentary selection procedures in the Labour Party, in particular the introduction of primaries or local ballots, may strengthen the position of local MPs vis-à-vis the party leadership. Another explanation may be that a shift has occurred in intraparty power relationships such that the parliamentary leadership has lost some of its authority in imposing its views on local parties. A third possibility is that since MPs are increasingly preoccupied with local constituency service (Cain, Ferejohn, and Fiorina 1986), this gives them a stronger local political base from which to defy the party leadership.

The purpose of this chapter is to examine the attitudes of local Conservative Party members toward the role of MPs in politics. The aim is to examine the extent to which party members are "localist" in their perceptions of the role of an MP. Clearly, if there is widespread support for the view that MPs are there primarily to serve their localities, as opposed to supporting the national party leadership, this creates the potential space for MPs to defy the leadership on a variety of political questions, providing they are serving these local needs.

Local parties in Britain, are thought to have, unlike those in the United States, a strong national political orientation, which would serve to undermine localism. However, this conventional wisdom is not based upon any systematic research of local party members. Accordingly, this question will be examined using data from the first national survey of Conservative Party members in Britain (see Whiteley, Seyd, and Richardson 1994). This survey makes it possible to address this important question for the first time with a representative sample of party members.

In the following section we review the literature on the role of MPs in the British political system, including work that discusses the relationship between local parties and MPs. This is followed by a model of the determinants of attitudes toward the work of MPs among party members in British politics. In a third section we examine some estimates of a model of the political orientation of local party members. Finally, we look at the implications of these findings for party cohesion in the House of Commons.

Members of Parliament and Local Parties

In both Conservative and Labour Parties, the powers to choose parliamentary candidates are decentralized. Although both party leaderships nowadays possess some powers to influence choice either by influencing the pool of eligibles (in the Conservative Party) or by vetoing the final choice (in the Labour Party), constituencies possess the crucial power of selection (Norris and Lovenduski 1995). When MPs have rebelled against their party leaderships' voting instructions, local party activists have often reinforced the powers of the party leaderships by disciplining the rebels. So, for example, the Labour Party dealt with its left-wing parliamentary rebels in the late 1940s by expelling them; although the MPs' constituency parties made some attempts to challenge these expulsions, they eventually acquiesced with the party leadership's decisions, and the parliamentary careers of these rebels were terminated (Ranney 1965, 155–59).

In the Conservative Party the position has been slightly more complicated because the party leadership has possessed less centralized powers. So when the whip has been removed from parliamentary rebels, there have been no attempts to expel them from the Conservative Party. Instead, the party leadership has relied on the constituency associations as "the true guardians of the orthodoxy of Conservative MPs" (Ranney 1965, 89). Their response to rebellion has varied. Seven Conservative MPs rebelled over the Conservative government's occupation of the Suez Canal Zone in 1956, and four of them were not readopted by their local associations as Conservative candidates at the following general election. By contrast, eight Conservative MPs rebelled against the Conservative government's abandonment of its embargo on the use of the Suez Canal, and none were refused readoption by their constituency associations.

The more formal structure and more centralized nature of the Labour Party have made it easier for its parliamentary leadership to curb rebellions than has been the case for the Conservative leadership. Nevertheless, after a thorough study of the selection processes between 1945 and 1960, Ranney concluded that "national leaders do not need to control local candidate selection in order to maintain party cohesion in Parliament; the local activists do the job for them" (1965, 281).

However, Norton (1980) has noted the growth of intraparty dissent within the Conservative and Labour parliamentary parties over recent decades. He suggests various reasons for this rising trend. He argues that Edward Heath's style of leadership played a significant part in the growth of parliamentary rebellions in the Conservative Party during the 1970–74 parliament. The measures that Heath introduced, the way in which he introduced them, and the way in which they were pushed through the House of Commons, along with Heath's failure to communicate with his party backbenchers and his failure to use his powers of patronage more effectively, contributed to party dissent.

Norton also suggests that there are other reasons for this growth in intraparty dissent that are specifically associated with changes in Parliament as an institution. Improved sources of information for backbenchers have made them less reliant upon government sources and therefore more prone to rebellion. Furthermore, the dispelling of the myth that a government defeat in a parliamentary vote leads automatically to its resignation has also contributed to greater rebelliousness.

Norton refers to one other factor that he considers to be of importance. He suggests that "local parties are not quite as ready and able to disown dissenting Members as was popularly believed" (Norton 1980, 466). So, for example, he notes that none of the Conservative Party's 20 rebels on the second reading of the European Communities Bill in 1972 were denied renomination by their constituency associations. Similarly, all the Labour rebels on the same bill were renominated, with the exception of Dick Taverne in Lincoln. In addition, the Labour MPs who opposed devolution for Scotland and Wales in the 1974–79 parliament first forced the abandonment of the Labour government's original policy, then imposed a requirement that 40% of the electorate should support devolution in a referendum on the issue in Scotland and Wales. The devolution issue eventually contributed to the Labour government's downfall in 1979, yet these MPs were all renominated by their local parties. Norton (1980, 467) concludes that "although constituency parties can and do act as constraints, strong ones, upon members considering entering the lobby against their own side, especially on an issue of importance, they are not quite as strong as was previously assumed."

Additional factors specific to the Labour Party may have contributed to this rising trend of dissension. In the mid-1970s, discipline in the party was eased once the extraparliamentary party was no longer tightly controlled by the right-wing parliamentary leadership of the 1950s (Shaw 1994). Furthermore, important changes have occurred in the selection and reselection procedures for Labour MPs. Increasingly, all individual members have been given the right to participate in the selection process. These changes in selection procedures are too recent to have produced any measured impact so far. It would seem likely, however, that the party leadership will find it more difficult to impose its views upon a reluctant MP if he or she has the support of the entire local membership. Thus, primary ballots may strengthen localist tendencies in the Labour Party.

It is within the Conservative Party, however, that parliamentary rebellion has been most prominent recently, particularly over the issue of European integration (Baker et al. 1994; see also chap. 4 of this volume). This issue eventually led to eight backbenchers losing the whip and a further one resigning the whip in early 1995. The party leadership's initial expectations were that these rebels would be forced back into line by the threat of the loss of their seats. It was assumed either that the local associations would willingly select an alternative Conservative candidate or that they might be coerced into selecting another candidate on pain of disaffiliation. There has been little sign of the former, however. Only one association has informed its MP publicly that it expects him to return to the Conservative whip as speedily as possible. Another two associations have been reported as wanting their MPs to retake the party whip (*The Guardian,* March 1, 1995). In general, however, the other associations seem happy to sustain their parliamentary rebels, in the belief that their Euro-skepticism is in line with the sentiments of Conservative members and voters. Thus, the fact that most Conservative Party members are Euro-skeptics has sustained the parliamentary rebels (Whiteley, Seyd, and Richardson 1994, 57–58).

The question of whether the National Union has the powers to disaffiliate a local association if it refuses to select a new candidate in place of the rebel is contentious. The correspondence columns of the *Daily Telegraph* have reflected this debate.[1] The party's Model Rules ensure that candidates on a constituency association's selection short list have to have been approved by a central office vetting procedure and that any association selecting an unapproved candidate will be disaffiliated. But the rules do not cover the case of the reselection of an MP who lacks the party whip. Furthermore, notwithstanding the legal position, there are clear electoral problems associated with any attempts to disaffiliate a local Conservative association in which the majority of members support the rebel MP.

In light of this discussion, in the next section we develop a model for explaining party members' perceptions of the role of an MP. The interesting question is whether they think that an MP should be primarily concerned with serving constituency or national political interests.

Local Party Members and Members of Parliament

The attitudes of local party members toward the role of MPs can be conceptualized in two ways. One possible interpretation of this role is to see it as a trade-off between national and local political orientations: thus, if local party members are inclined to think that the main role of their MP is to support the party leadership and to be a loyal backbencher, they are likely to attach little importance to the role of the MP in looking after constituents and keeping in regular contact with the local party. Similarly, party members who see the MP as primarily a constituency worker are likely to be indifferent to parliamentary party cohesion. If this is true, then party members who attach great importance to constituency service will be willing to support a perennially dissident MP, providing that he or she pays close attention to the needs of constituents and the local party. Thus, constituency service can be used to create political capital that can be "spent" rebelling against the party line in Parliament.

If party members in general are oriented toward national political issues, or "centralist" in their political orientations, then rebellious MPs are very likely to face reselection problems if they continuously dissent against the party leadership. By the same token, if most party members are oriented toward local political issues, or "localist" in their political orientations, then dissidence in Parliament is likely to be tolerated.

An alternative model is one in which perceptions of the role orientations of MPs are largely independent of each other. Thus, an MP might get into reselection difficulties for two quite different reasons: because he or she repeatedly rebelled against the party leadership in Parliament and thus ran into difficulties at the local level or because he or she failed to perform local constituency services that are expected to be part of the job of an MP. In this interpretation, performance in one area would not necessarily trade off against performance in another. An effective MP should perform well in both areas, and a member might get into difficulties if he or she ignored either aspect of the role of an MP. We examine evidence relating to these alternative models below.

Turning next to the determinants of the political orientations of the party members, we hypothesize that these will be influenced by two classes of factors: their political experiences and political attitudes. These will be examined in turn. In the case of political experiences, party members who are most involved in local party activities will be most likely to expect that MPs should focus on local representation rather than national politics. This is because the activists have more time and energy invested at the local level in comparison with inactive party members and consequently should see their MP as an ally in maintaining the local party organization. A corollary of this is that local party members who are officeholders within the local party organization should have the same views and should value the work of an MP at the local level. However, the same may not be true of local councilors, since they have extensive links with national government and are subject to nationally laid-down policies in much of their work. Accordingly, they are likely to attach considerable importance to the role of the MP in policy making.

It may also be the case that long-established members are more localist in their assessments of the role of MPs in comparison with recent recruits; the former have more invested in party membership than the latter, which may orient them more toward local politics.

One other type of political experience that should influence the attitudes of local party members toward the role of their MP is the party affiliation of that MP. Conservatives are likely to feel differently about the role of the local MP in supporting local party activities if he or she is a member of the Conservative Party. If the local MP is a member of the Labour Party or the Liberal Democrats, they are less likely to be interested in his or her role in supporting the local party organization.

With regard to political attitudes, members have views about the importance of local politics and the local party organization in influencing local politics. Clearly, party members who attach particular importance to local government or the autonomy of local parties are likely to be more "localist" than members who attach little importance to these matters. We develop a localist attitudes scale below and use this to model the relationships between such attitudes and views concerning the role of MPs.

In earlier work that focused on explaining party activism, we hypothesized that activism was promoted by various incentives for participation (Whiteley, Seyd, and Richardson 1994; Whiteley, Seyd, Richardson, and Bissell 1994). These included three types of "selective incentives" (see Olson 1965) for activism: process, outcome, and ideological incentives. These are incentives for political participation that accrue only to those individuals who actively participate.

It has long been noted that political leaders or "entrepreneurs" can be exempt from the paradox of participation, the proposition that rational actors will not participate in collective action (see Olson 1965), because they have such incentives as interesting, well-paid jobs and elective office (Salisbury 1969). One of the features of party activism in Britain that distinguishes it from protest behavior or participation in an interest group is that politicians have to serve an "apprenticeship" within their party organization before being chosen for elective office (Ranney 1965). From this perspective, activism can be regarded as an investment in a possible future career in politics. Thus, outcome incentives measure the private returns from participation associated with developing a political career. It is likely that local party members interested in building a political career within the party will be more "localist" in their political orientation than members who do not have such ambitions, since succeeding in politics primarily involves succeeding at the local level.

Process incentives and ideological incentives for participation are rooted, not in the outcomes of collective action, but rather in the process of participation itself. Different writers have referred to a number of motives that might be counted as process incentives: Tullock (1971) has written about the "entertainment" value of being involved in revolution; Opp (1990) has discussed the "catharsis" value of being involved in political protest. Process incentives refer to the extent to which party members enjoy participation, since it provides an opportunity to meet like-minded people and learn about the political process firsthand. We hypothesize that individuals who are strongly motivated to participate by process incentives are likely to be more localist than members in general, since their motivation to participate is driven by a desire for social interaction with local people and not by national policy concerns.

The ideological incentives variable is interpreted as another type of process motivation for participation. The so-called "law of curvilinear disparity" of political parties is the proposition that middle-level elites or rank-and-file activists in a political party are likely to be more radical than the party leadership or the voters (May 1973; Kitschelt 1989). In the case of the Conservative Party, it would imply that the activists are to the right of both the party leadership and Conservative voters (see also McKenzie 1963). This idea has been discussed mainly in relation to the question of defining party strategies; it implies, for example, that parties need to control their activists in order to pursue vote-maximizing strategies.

However, it also provides an interesting theoretical explanation of activism. Ideological radicalism should motivate party members to become more involved than the voters or inactive members if the reward for their involvement is the ability to give expression to deeply held beliefs along with other like-minded individuals. Their motives are similar to those of the regular churchgoer—church attendance allows them to give expression to religious convictions. In this case, however, ideological concerns are defined in relation to the national party organization, not just in relation to the local party. Accordingly, we would expect the national party to be the focus of ideological motives for involvement, making right-wing members more "centralist" in their political orientations than other members.

Finally, members vary in their strength of attachments to the Conservative Party or in terms of their expressive evaluations of the party. Such evaluations are rooted in the members' emotional attachments to the party and have long been discussed in the literature on party identification and voting behavior, since the early theorists saw partisanship as an affective orientation toward a significant social or political group (see Campbell et al. 1960). Again, as in the case of ideology, members identify with the party as a whole and not merely the party at the local level. Accordingly, we hypothesize that members who are strongly attached to the Conservative Party are likely to be less "localist" and more "centralist" in their attitudes toward the role of MPs in comparison with members who are relatively weakly attached to the party.

In the next section we consider some estimates relating to these models.

Modeling Attitudes toward the Role of MPs

The second wave of the panel survey of Conservative Party members contained a battery of questions that asked party members the question, "How important are the following parts of an MP's job?" They were

Table 3.1

The Attitudes of Conservative Party Members to the Role of an MP ($N = 1,604$)

Perceptions of the Role of an MP	Very Important	Fairly Important	Not Very Important	Not at All Important
Speaking in Parliament	34.7	47.3	16.8	1.2
Holding regular constituency surgeries	73.6	24.8	1.4	0.1
Attending local party meetings	53.1	41.5	5.1	0.3
Helping with individual problems	56.4	38.4	4.7	0.5
Supporting the party leader	59.9	32.9	5.8	1.5
Speaking to the national press and TV	23.1	44.1	27.6	5.2
Defending party policy	56.0	36.7	6.0	1.2

asked to comment upon seven different aspects of the work of a member of Parliament, and the responses to this battery of questions appear in table 3.1.[2]

It can be seen that three of these aspects are unequivocally related to the role of an MP as a local constituency worker: "holding regular constituency surgeries," "attending local party meetings," and "helping with individual problems." Similarly, three of these role perceptions relate unambiguously to the role of an MP as a national actor, in support of the national party organization: "speaking in Parliament," "supporting the party leader," and "speaking to the national press and TV." The final indicator, "defending party policy," can be interpreted in either way.

In view of the importance of the member's role in supporting the national party, it is interesting that the most important perception of the role of an MP was "holding constituency surgeries," which is very much a local matter. It is also noteworthy that majorities of party members regard the other two indicators of localism, "attending party meetings," and "helping with individual problems," as very important.

In contrast, party members were less likely to attach importance to the indicators of national orientation, with the exception of "supporting the party leader"; some 60% of members thought this was a very important function. Clearly, party members attach importance both to "localist" and to "centralist" political functions, but the former appear to be marginally more important than the latter. It is possible to investigate whether there is a single underlying "centralism-localism" scale in the

Table 3.2

Factors Underlying Attitudes to the Role of an MP

Perceptions of the Role of an MP	Centralism Factor	Localism Factor
Speaking in Parliament	0.53	—
Supporting the party leader	0.79	—
Speaking to the national press and TV	0.69	—
Defending party policy	0.80	—
Holding regular constituency surgeries	—	0.79
Attending local party meetings	—	0.78
Helping with individual problems	—	0.75
% variance explained	34.5	21

responses or more than one such scale by means of a factor analysis of these indicators. This appears in table 3.2.

The factor loadings in table 3.2 indicate that there are two distinct independent scales underlying the data.[3] The first scale, which is described as a "Centralism factor" loads on the nationally oriented indicators, which include the ambiguous measure "defending party policy." The second scale, described as a "Localism factor," loads highly on the three localism indicators. It is clear that supporting the national party and constituency service are two separate dimensions of the role perceptions of MPs and that they do not directly trade off against each other in the minds of party members. Given this, it is interesting to examine the relationship between these variables and the indicators of political experience and political attitudes discussed above. Measures of these different aspects of the determinants of attitudes toward the role of an MP are discussed in the appendix to this chapter.

Table 3.3 contains regression models of the Centralism and Localism factors, where the dependent variables are factor scores from the analysis in table 3.2. On the Centralism scale, a high score factor score denotes a belief that the role of an MP in national politics is unimportant, and a low score the reverse; similarly, a high score on the Localism scale means that respondents attach little importance to the local role of the MP, with a low score denoting the opposite. There are two models for each scale, the second model containing only statistically significant predictors from the first model.

The Activism scale in table 3.3 encompasses a number of high-cost activities such as canvassing, attending party meetings, and running for office within the party organization (see the appendix to this chapter).

Table 3.3

Models of the Centralism and Localism Factors

Predictor Variables	Centralism Scale	Centralism Scale	Localism Scale	Localism Scale
Activism scale	0.16***	0.18***	0.00	—
Year respondent joined the party	0.09***	0.09***	−0.03	—
Respondent local councillor	−0.08**	−0.07***	0.01	—
Respondent officeholder in party	0.01	—	−0.05	—
Constituency held by Conservatives	0.01	—	−0.01	—
Local government scale	0.04	—	0.06*	0.06*
Local party scale	−0.05	—	0.12***	0.13***
Outcome incentives for activism	−0.11***	−0.11***	0.11***	0.11***
Process incentives for activism	0.20***	0.20***	0.11***	0.11***
Left-right ideology scale for party	−0.09**	−0.09**	0.04	—
Strength of identification with party	0.16***	0.16***	0.11***	0.10***
% variance explained	0.12	0.11	0.07	0.06

$*p < 0.10$; $**p < 0.05$; $***p < 0.01$.

The relationship between the Activism and Centralism scales implies that the highly active members are less likely to attach importance to the national role of the MP than inactive members. The same point can be made about recent recruits to the party and party members motivated by outcome incentives: both types of members attach considerable importance to the local role of the MP. In contrast, right-wing members, strongly attached members, local councillors, and members who are motivated by process incentives all attach great importance to the nationally oriented role of their MP.

These findings all accord with expectations, except for the findings that members motivated by process incentives and those who have been long-standing members are more likely to support a centralist role for their MP. Process incentives for participation appear to behave like ideological incentives, and individuals motivated by such concerns are oriented toward the national rather than the local level. Similarly, since most of the long-standing members have little contact with the local party organization, this fact clearly orients them toward the national party leadership. Also, Conservative incumbency at the local level does not appear to influence attitudes toward the national role of the MP, nor do the various attitudes that make up the local government and local party scales.

Turning next to the Localism scale, in this case a high score on the factor implies that a respondent discounts the importance of the local role of the MP, and a low score has the opposite interpretation. Thus, members with a low score on this factor will attach considerable importance to the constituency work of the local MP. In this case, activism appears to have very little influence on attitudes, and the same is true for office holding, Conservative incumbency, and ideology. However, scores on this scale are significantly predicted by the two localist attitude scales that relate to attitudes toward the local provision of services and toward the autonomy of the local party organization and the locally elected council. Not surprisingly, party members who oppose the contracting out of local services to the private sector and the opting out of local schools from local authority control tend to attach particular importance to the constituency service role of an MP. The same point can be made about party members who attach importance to the autonomy of the local party organization and local government: they value constituency work by an MP.

In common with the Centralism scale, it is also the case that party members who are motivated by outcome incentives tend to favor a localist orientation to constituency service by MPs. However, the same is not true of members motivated by process incentives. It may be recalled that they tended to be procentralist on the Centralism scale, but in this case they tend to be prolocalist. Thus, the original hypothesis that members motivated by process incentives would be oriented to the local level is partially confirmed: this is true when they are evaluating constituency service but not true when they are evaluating the role of the MP in supporting the parliamentary party line. A similar point can be made about strongly attached party members: they are procentralist on the Centralism scale and prolocalist on the Localism scale. For both variables, a belief in the importance of constituency service does not rule out a belief in the importance of loyalty in supporting the government.

These differences in the two models of attitudes toward the role of MPs create the possibility for strategic decision making by MPs with regard to their relationships with local party members. If they choose to persistently rebel against the party whip in Parliament, this will upset strongly attached and process-oriented party members. But with these groups, they can "buy off" that discontent by being assiduous constituency workers who hold regular surgeries and look after the interests of their local party.

On the other hand, if an MP is a stalwart party loyalist in the House of Commons, this will not offset the unpopularity engendered by his or her neglect of constituency matters for those party members who attach considerable importance to local government and local party autonomy.

Their beliefs about the desirability of local autonomy influence their attitudes toward the constituency work of MPs but do not influence their attitudes toward the MP's role in the House of Commons. From the MP's point of view, good behavior in the House does not buy credit at the local level from this particular group of members.

In relation to the future of party cohesion in the House of Commons, the finding that activists are more prolocalist than other members on the Centralism scale is particularly important. It seems clear that activists, who are particularly influential in the recruitment of MPs, are less concerned about party loyalty in the House than the conventional wisdom suggests. In addition, they do not appear to be more concerned about constituency work than other less active members. This suggests that an MP can be a dissident without having to be an assiduous local constituency worker, at least as far as the activists are concerned. Given that for the average MP, the most important issue in their relationship with local parties is to keep the activists happy, this gives them considerable scope for dissension in the House.

Conclusions

In evaluating the future of party discipline in the House of Commons, researchers need to focus on the relationship between the "selectorate"—the local party activists—and MPs. An examination of party members' attitudes toward the role of MPs produces some predictable findings, such as that strongly attached party members value party loyalty in the House and that party members who value local autonomy attach particular importance to constituency service by their MP. However, the analysis also produces some surprising findings, particularly the fact that activists are not that concerned about their MP's willingness to toe the party line in Parliament. Moreover, a dissident MP does not have to be overly preoccupied with constituency service in order to keep them happy with his or her performance. It seems clear that the modern Conservative Party is different from the party discussed by Ranney (1965), in which the local activists were the enforcers of parliamentary discipline.

Some current trends in British politics are likely to promote a more "candidate-centered" type of politics in which the grip of the parliamentary whips is likely to weaken over time. One such development is the growth of the personal vote at the constituency level. Traditionally, the personal vote in Britain has been seen as rather small, but recent evidence suggests that it is rather larger than the conventional wisdom believes (Wood and Norton 1992). Given this fact, it seems plausible that MPs will increasingly seek to emphasize constituency work as a means of overcoming a national deficit in their party's popularity. This trend will reinforce the localist tendencies within constituency parties.

A second development is the weakening of local government, a trend that has been taking place over the last 15 to 20 years. As central government has reduced the power and influence of locally elected authorities, the incentives to participate have been weakened for those party members who want to build a career in politics. This builds resentment toward the center—both Parliament and, more particularly, the national party organization. The latter is no longer seen as being supportive of local parties, but rather as the agent of a national institution that has systematically devalued local party activity. This could, in part, explain why the members' strength of identification with the national party has declined significantly over time (Whiteley and Seyd 1995). It could also explain why some 51% of party members think that the leader should be elected by a system of one party member, one vote (Whiteley, Seyd, and Richardson 1994, 266). Again, this will tend to reinforce localism and make party activists less likely to support national imperatives such as sustaining backbench discipline in the House of Commons and donating money to the national party funds.

In light of this discussion, it appears that appeals to the grassroots by the parliamentary leadership for help in disciplining rebellious backbenchers are increasingly quite likely to fall on deaf ears. Of course, dissident MPs need to pay attention to localist attitudes among their party activists and also to the incentives that encourage members to participate at the local level. But at least in the case of the Conservative Party, an MP who gratifies local sensibilities and who does a reasonable amount of constituency service can persistently rebel in the House of Commons without being unduly concerned that this will lead to his or her deselection.

APPENDIX

The scales used in table 3.3 were constructed from various attitude indicators in the survey of Conservative Party members.

The Activist Scale

Members were told, "We would like to ask you about political activities you may have taken part in during the last five years:" The activities were "Displaying an election poster in a window," "signing a petition supported by the party," "donating money to Conservative Party funds," "delivering party leaflets during an election," "attending a party meeting," "helping at a Conservative Party function," "canvassing voters on the doorstep on behalf of the party," "canvassing voters on the telephone on behalf of the party," "standing for office in the party organization," and "standing for elected office in a local government or national parliamentary election." Possible responses were 1 = *not at all,* 2 = *rarely,* 3 = *occasionally,* and 4 = *frequently.* A principal-components analysis with a varimax rotation revealed two factors underlying the responses to these items. The first factor, which loads highly on all items, from delivering leaflets to standing for office in local government, is used in the present analysis.

Local Government and Local Party Scales

These scales were derived from a factor analysis of a set of attitude measures relating to the autonomy of local government and the local Conservative Party. Members were asked to respond to the following Likert-scaled items (1 = *strongly agree,* 2 = *agree,* 3 = *neither agree nor disagree,* 4 = *disagree,* and 5 = *strongly disagree*):

- "Contracting out local government services to private firms has not improved the quality of local services."
- "Elected local government should be protected from central government interference."
- "Schools should not be encouraged to opt out of local education authority control."
- "Conservative Central Office should have a more influential role in the selection of parliamentary candidates."
- "Party policies should be determined by party members."

The local government factor loaded highly on the first, third, and fourth of these items, and the local party factor loaded highly on the second, fourth, and fifth items.

Outcome Incentives for Participation

This scale was derived from two Likert-scaled statements:

- "A person like me could do a good job of being a Conservative Councillor."
- "The Conservative Party would be more successful if more people like me were elected to Parliament."

Both items loaded highly on a single factor.

Process Incentives for Participation

This scale was derived from three Likert-scaled statements:

- "Being an active party member is a good way to meet interesting people."
- "The only way to be really educated about politics is to be a party activist."
- "Getting involved in party activities during an election can be fun."

All three items loaded highly on a single factor.

Left-Right Ideology Scale

This was measured by a 9-point left-right scale, introduced with the following preamble:

> In Conservative Party politics, people often talk about the "left" and the "right." Compared with other Conservative Party members, where would you place your views on the scale below?

Strength of Identification with the Party

Members were asked, "Would you call yourself a very strong Conservative, fairly strong, not very strong, or not at all strong?" (coded from 1 to 4 respectively).

NOTES

1. See November 30, December 2, December 5, and December 8, 1994.
2. Membership data in the Conservative Party are held at the constituency level, so our survey of party members involved a two-stage stratified random-sample panel design. A 5% sample of constituency associations in Great Britain was selected and stratified by region, and a random sample of party members were surveyed in those constituencies in early 1992, just before the general election. The survey response rate was 63%, giving 2,467 individual respondents after weighting for gender and strength of partisanship. The second-wave panel was conducted in the spring of 1994 and had a response rate of 64.9%. Interlocking weights for strength of partisanship and gender were applied to ensure that this wave was representative of members in general. Further methodological details of the surveys can be found in Whiteley, Seyd, and Richardson (1994, appendix 1).
3. Table 3.2 contains the varimax rotated factor loadings from a principal-components analysis of the seven indicators.

REFERENCES

Baker, David, Steve Ludlam, and Andrew Gamble. 1994. "Mapping Conservative Fault Lines: Problems of Typology." In Patrick Dunleavy and Geoffrey Stanyer, eds., *Contemporary Political Studies 1994.* Exeter: University of Exeter Press.
Beer, Samuel H. 1965. *Modern British Politics.* London: Faber & Faber.
Berrington, Hugh. 1973. *Backbench Opinion in the House of Commons, 1945–55.* Oxford: Pergamon.
Cain, Bruce, John Ferejohn, and Maurice Fiorina. 1986. *The Personal Vote, Constituency Service and Electoral Independence.* Cambridge, MA: Harvard University Press.
Campbell, Angus, Philip E. Converse, Warren E. Miller, and Donald Stokes. 1960. *The American Voter.* Chicago: University of Chicago Press.
Kitschelt, Herbert. 1989. "The Internal Politics of Parties: The Law of Curvilinear Disparity Revisited." *Political Studies* 37: 400–21.
May, John D. 1973. "Opinion Structure of Political Parties: The Special Law of Curvilinear Disparity." *Political Studies* 21: 135–51.
McKenzie, Robert. 1963. *British Political Parties.* New York: St. Martin's Press.
Norris, Pippa, and Joni Lovenduski. 1995. *Political Recruitment, Gender, Race and Class in the British Parliament.* Cambridge: Cambridge University Press.
Norton, Philip. 1978. *Conservative Dissidents.* London: Temple Smith.

———. 1980. *Dissension in the House of Commons, 1974–79.* London: Oxford University Press.

Olson, Mancur. 1965. *The Logic of Collective Action.* New York: Schocken Books.

Opp, Karl-Dieter. 1990. "Postmaterialism, Collective Action, and Political Protest." *American Journal of Political Science* 34: 212–35.

Ranney, Austin. 1965. *Pathways to Parliament.* New York: Macmillan.

Rose, Richard. 1965. *Politics in England.* London: Faber.

Salisbury, Robert H. 1969. "An Exchange Theory of Interest Groups." *Midwest Journal of Political Science* 13: 1–32.

Shaw, Eric. 1994. *The Labour Party since 1979.* London: Routledge.

Tullock, Gordon. 1971. "The Paradox of Revolution." *Public Choice* 11: 89–99.

Whiteley, Paul F., and Patrick Seyd. 1995. "The 'Spiral of Mobilization': The Effects of a General Election on Political Participation in Britain." Paper presented at the Annual Meeting of the Political Studies Association, April, York, UK.

Whiteley, Paul F., Patrick Seyd, and Jeremy Richardson. 1994. *True Blues: The Politics of Conservative Party Membership.* Oxford, UK: Clarendon Press.

Whiteley, Paul F., Patrick Seyd, Jeremy Richardson, and Paul Bissell. 1994. "Explaining Party Activism: The Case of the British Conservative Party." *British Journal of Political Science* 24: 79–94.

Wood, David, and Philip Norton. 1992. "Do Candidates Matter? Constituency Specific Vote Changes for Incumbent MPs, 1983–1987." *Political Studies* 40: 227–38.

4

Backbenchers with Attitude: A Seismic Study of the Conservative Party and Dissent on Europe

DAVID BAKER, ANDREW GAMBLE,
STEVE LUDLAM, AND
DAVID SEAWRIGHT

In contrast to the U.S. system of government, British political parties place enormous weight on unity; parliamentary dissidence, especially in the Conservative Party, tends to be single-issue and short-lived in character. The conventional wisdom is that not only the electoral system but the very procedures of Parliament institutionalize strong single-party government. Consequently, in spite of deep and enduring internal disagreements, the Conservative Party has suffered only two major *splits* in the last 149 years.[1] Unlike the Liberals and Labour, the Conservatives have never split on domestic issues. There have, however, been numerous Conservative *divisions* over imperial and foreign policy: 80 Conservative MPs voted against the Government of India Bill in 1935, 74 against the Washington Loan in 1946, 50 against the Rhodesian sanctions in 1965, and—with the biggest postwar Tory rebellion in a whipped vote—116 on the same issue in 1978. In spite of these divisions, few splits have occurred. However, major strategic policy choices occasionally make it hard to sustain this facade of unity, and the two occasions when the party has split (1846 and 1906) emerged over just such strategic choices, namely Britain's future role in the world political economy. Such choices cannot easily be subsumed by the need to win elections or to placate declining sections of the economy. In 1846 it was the abolition of the Corn Laws and in 1906 disagreement over the necessity for Tariff Reform that split the party (Baker, Gamble, and Ludlam, 1993a; see Gamble 1974 for a fuller discussion of these two splits).[2]

Today, European integration has become exactly this sort of issue for the Conservative Party, since the decision to go on or to hang back (perhaps even to withdraw) has serious implications for the long-term future of the British economy and the sovereignty of national political institutions. As a result, the European issue has been responsible for a series of humiliating parliamentary defeats and U-turns. It has also played a major part in the loss of several members of recent Conservative governments, including two chancellors and Prime Minister Margaret Thatcher. It led to the withdrawal of the whip from eight MPs—the first time such action had been taken by a Conservative government since 1928.[3] So serious are the differences that arise over this issue that there has been inevitable speculation as to whether the party could be on the verge of another historic split like those over Tariff Reform and the Corn Laws (Baker et al. 1993a).

Yet in spite of the known severity of the divisions within the Parliamentary Conservative Party (PCP), this has not been reflected in the voting patterns of Conservative MPs. British parliamentary procedures and the strong single-party government system make the process of detecting the attitudes of MPs and ministers through their behavior patterns in Parliament all but impossible. The system gives no alternative home for most rebellious MPs, who must face the prospect of an election and replacement by the opposition if they place their beliefs above their party in crucial votes. The "iron law of backbench rebellions," attributed to former Labour Prime Minister Harold Wilson, states that the maximum number of rebels in any Commons vote of confidence is one less than the number needed to wipe out the government's majority (*Economist,* October 31, 1992). This was an "iron law" that the extraordinary circumstances surrounding the Maastricht Bill might have proved capable of breaking (Baker, Gamble, and Ludlam, 1994b).[4]

In addition, considerations of career and threats and/or inducements from the party whips make open dissent a dangerous game, particularly for members of the governing party. The whipping system (a formal party discipline mechanism based on the whips' office) is a very effective machine under most circumstances (Baker, Gamble, and Ludlam, 1993b). The rules of the parliamentary game as played by most MPs are loyal support for the government no matter what the private beliefs of the individual MPs, an attitude summed up in a phrase by Clemenceau: "A speech may often change my mind; my vote never." Few MPs habitually rebel. Enoch Powell's record of voting against the whips on 113 occasions between 1970 and 1974 was an enormous exception to this rule. Most MPs manage to be rather more loyal than that. Not surprisingly, Powell described the whips as "a prerequisite for civilization like a sewer." The whips are unnecessary as party conduits where ministers are concerned, since ministers are bound by cabinet collective responsibility to toe the government line, at least in Parliament, or to resign. Since Heath used his position as a whip as a springboard to high office, service as a whip has been recognized as a point of entry into higher ministerial ranks—William Whitelaw and John Major are also notable former whips.

The whips' offices are well-oiled political machines, with huge powers of patronage over career advancement, government jobs, membership of select committees, foreign trips, and so forth. Most of the warfare is purely psychological, as one whip remarked: "Eighty percent of all confessions to the Spanish Inquisition came when they explained what was going to happen to their victims and showed them the implements." Nor does pressure end with the vote: ministers and "loyalists" often demand that examples be made of those who defy the government line, usually in the form of removal of the whip, deselection, or demotion. The fact that a free-vote has to be called to allow MPs and ministers to vote according to their conscience is a sign of the strength of party discipline in the Commons.

Consequently, voting behavior is often a very limited way of telling what the real attitudes of most MPs of the governing party are, for what may appear as minor tremors detected through open parliamentary dissent can in fact be "seismic" traces of what is a potential major earthquake of dissent underneath. The problem is how we find out what is going on when observable behavior in Parliament may represent only a hint of the real levels of dissent existing underneath.

Logically, dissent should be most evident when a pressure-point issue emerges that divides the party deeply (Baker et al. 1993a). Postwar conflict over European integration used to be seen by political scientists as most damaging to Labour, but the Conservative Party also has a long history of division over Europe. Skillful party management in the 1960s and Labour rebels in the 1970s enabled successive Conservative leaders to conduct negotiations to join the European Economic Community (EEC) while marginalizing their own dissidents in Parliament. As a result, the issue received relatively little detailed academic attention apart from Ashford's study of the 1945-to-1975 period, which, significantly, concluded that the European issue required the party to be viewed more as a "managed coalition" than as a stable hierarchy (Ashford 1980, 123–24). The tensions beneath the surface of the party increased as the process of European integration deepened during the 1980s, but it was the lethal combination of the Maastricht Treaty, Britain's membership in and ignominious exit from the Exchange Rate Mechanism (ERM),[5] a government reliant on a small majority in the Commons, and Labour's new-found pro-European unity that undermined this party management strategy, revealing a growing ambivalence within the Conservative leadership about closer European integration (Lawson 1992, 71–76).

The Maastricht Minefield

The first Danish Referendum in June 1992[6] provoked the appearance of open dissent in the party, since it gave hope to the rebels that their case was shared elsewhere and that a Danish "no" vote would lead to the fall of the treaty. The Parliamentary Euro-Rebellion was launched by the anti-Maastricht "Fresh Start" Early Day Motion (EDM)[7] on June 3, 1992. The rebels' resolve was further reinforced by Britain's forced withdrawal from the ERM in September 1992. From now on, certain names would reappear in the opposition lobbies with monotonous regularity on Maastricht, most notably Bill Cash, Sir Teddy Taylor, and Anne and Nicholas Winterton. We have compiled a "league table" of the 50 Conservative MPs who voted against the government in one or more of 62 divisions on the European Communities (Amendment) Bill between May 1992 and May 1993 (table 4.1).

Three leading rebels voted against the government no less than 50 times, or 81% of all divisions. The top 22 names, all of whom rebelled between 25 and 50 times in the divisions, read like a "Who's Who" of the Maastricht rebellion. No fewer than 43 of the 50 dissenters signed both of Michael Spicer's "Fresh Start" EDMs in June and September 1992. From then on, the passage of the Maastricht Bill was dogged by "ducked" votes, humiliating U-turns, particularly on the Social Chapter[8] Amendment, and outright defeat on the composition of Britain's

Table 4.1

League Table of Conservative Dissent in Parliament on the European Communities (Amendment) Bill, 1992–1993

Name	No. of Dissenting Votes	% of Dissenting Votes in All Divisions	Name	No. of Dissenting Votes	% of Dissenting Votes in All Divisions
Cash, W.	50	81	Hawksley, W.	18	29
Taylor, Sir T.	50	81	Porter, D	17	27
Winterton, N.	50	81	Legg, B.	16	26
Winterton, Mrs. A.	48	77	Pawsey, J.	15	24
Gill, C.	46	74	Allason, R.	14	23
Knapman, R.	45	73	Carttiss, M.*	14	23
Jessel, T.	44	71	Boyson, Sir R.	12	19
Skeet, Sir T.	44	71	Duncan-Smith, I.	10	16
Gorman, Mrs. T.	42	68	Townend, J.	9	14
Walker, B.	41	66	Fry, P.	6	10
Marlow, T.	40	65	Hunter, A.	6	10
Budgen, N.	39	63	Moate, Sir R.	4	6
Shepherd, R.	39	63	Bonsor, Sir N.	3	5
Lawrence, Sir I.	38	61	Greenway, H.	3	5
Lord, M.	37	60	Bendall, V.	2	3
Spicer, M.	37	60	Clark, Dr. M.	2	3
Cran, J.	36	58	Devar, N.	2	3
Wilkinson, J.	34	55	Jenkin, B.	2	3
Body, Sir R.	32	52	Whittingdale, J.	2	3
Biffen, J.*	30	48	Dunn, B.	1	2
Tapsell, Sir P.*	28	45	Johnson Smith, Sir G.*	1	2
Gardiner, Sir G.	25	40	Luff, P.*	1	2
Butcher, J.	23	37	Robatham, A.	1	2
Carlisle, J.	22	35	Rowe, A.	1	2
Sweeney, W.*	21	34	Vaughan, Sir G.	1	2

Source: Information supplied to the authors by the Public Information Office, House of Commons, 1 Derby Gate, Westminster, London SW1A 2DG.

*Indicates that this individual failed to sign both of the "Fresh Start" Early Day Motions of June and September 1992.

delegation to the Committee of the Regions. What also marks this out as a serious disagreement within the PCP was the appearance, in September 1993, of the "Fresh Start Alliance"—a right-wing group within the party that campaigned on a range of European issues. They represented a well-organized alliance of anti-Maastricht rebels who supported both "Fresh Start" EDMs of June 3 and September 24, 1992, and were prepared to use any procedural device or alliance with the opposition to defeat the treaty. Lady Thatcher and Lord Tebbit supported this alliance from within the Lords. Significantly, the last such group appearing within the Conservative Party that threatened the over-all majority was also anti-European—the so-called "1970 Group" of Common Market entry dissenters (Norton 1978, chap. 3). Indeed, former Conservative Prime Minister Edward Heath suffered a defection of no less than 20 of his party on a vote of confidence on Europe in 1972 (see table 4.2, 1972i).

The rebellion strengthened during the Maastricht Bill's second reading—so much so that the combined efforts of the 1992 committee of backbench MPs to "ambush" its rebel members, strident ministerial denunciations, and appeals to constituencies to discipline rebels, on top of the efforts of the whips, all failed, as revealed by the government's defeat by 22 votes on a Committee of the Regions Amendment (in which 26 Conservative MPs rebelled and 18 abstained). Having forced damaging U-turns on Social Chapter Amendments, 41 Conservative rebels then voted against the third reading of the Maastricht Bill, along with five abstainers.

Had Major's majority been higher, more "Fresh Starters" might well have joined the rebels. Three tactics were employed by the rebels to defeat the bill. First, they sought to delay the bill in the hope of changes in the wider political environment—in particular, by submitting a huge volume of amendments (in all, there were 210 hours of debate and over 600 amendments by the third-reading vote). Second, they tried to force the government to hold a national referendum on Maastricht (particularly when the Danish Referendum raised hopes of a Maastricht defeat). After the Committee of the Regions Amendment defeat, the rebels repeatedly offered a truce on the grounds of the holding of such a referendum. As Teddy Taylor put it, "A referendum and the rebellion ends tomorrow." (But since Labour's frontbench were opposed to a referendum, there was no real prospect of defeating the government on this issue). Third, the rebels sought to pass an amendment or amendments that would wreck the whole treaty.

During the third reading, the government was forced into embarrassing tactical retreats, avoiding procedural votes and acquiescing in a set of amendments that it did not dare put to the vote, culminating in a humiliating Commons U-turn by Foreign Secretary Douglas Hurd, who suddenly climbed down on a number of hostile amendments. Maastricht ended in high drama. In the votes on the Social Chapter on July 22, 1993, the government was defeated by eight votes on the substantive motion. Since a positive vote was needed for ratification of the treaty, the government was forced to use its bluntest weapon—threatening to

Table 4.2

Key Conservative Parliamentary Rebellions against European Integration, 1961–1995

Year	Vote	Cross-Voters	Abstainers	Total Rebels	Rebels as % of Back-bench MPs	Notes
1961	Conservative government motion supporting EC entry application	1	24	25	9	Passed with Labour opposition support
1967	Labour government motion supporting EC entry application	26	0	26	10	Passed with Conservative opposition support
1971	Conservative government motion supporting EC entry application	39	2	41	16	Labour opposed (Conservative free vote)
1972i	Conservative government European Communities Bill second reading, Heath's vote of confidence	15	5	20	8	Labour opposed, government majority 8
1972ii	Conservative rebel proreferendum amendment	22	9	31	12	Only passed with Labour support
1972iii	Conservative government European Communities Bill third reading	16	4	20	8	Labour opposed
1975	Labour government motion accepting "renegotiated" entry terms	8	18	26	9	Conservative support (Labour free vote)
1978	European Assemblies Elections Bill third reading	9	0	9	3	Conservatives support Labour government
1986	European Communities Amendment (Single European Act) Bill third reading	7	0	7	2	
1992i	European Communities Amendment ("Maastricht") Bill second reading	22	4	26	10	
1992ii	European Communities Amendment ("Maastricht") Bill paving motion	26	6	32	13	Government majority 3, with Liberal-Democrat support

Table 4.2

Key Conservative Parliamentary Rebellions against European Integration, 1961–1995
continued

Year	Vote	Cross-Voters	Abstainers	Total Rebels	Rebels as % of Back-bench MPs	Notes
1993i	European Communities Amendment ("Maastricht") Bill Committee of the Regions amendment	26	18	44	17	Government defeated by 22 votes
1993ii	European Communities Amendment ("Maastricht") Bill referendum amendment	38	13	51	20	Government win by 239 votes
1993iii	European Communities Amendment ("Maastricht") Bill third reading	41	5	46	18	Government majority of 180
1993iv	Postponed Social Chapter vote, July 22	23	1	24	9	Government defeated by 8 votes
1993v	Major's confidence vote, July 23, on Social Chapter	0	1	1	0	Government Majority 40, whip removed from abstainer
1994i	Major's confidence vote, November 28, European Communities (Finance) Bill second reading	0	8	8	3	Labour abstain, Government majority 241, whip removed from 8 rebels, a ninth resigns
1994ii	Vote on Labour amendment to Finance Bill to abandon stage 2 of imposition of VAT on fuel	7	10	17	6	Government defeat by 8 votes; all but one of "unwhipped" Euro-rebels rebel

Source: Adapted from Ludlam (1996).

hold a "vote of confidence" in itself the following day, that, if lost, threatened defeat for the Conservatives in a subsequent general election. This threat brought all the Euro-rebels except one (Rupert Allison, who was otherwise engaged in Bermuda and who lost the whip for his pains) back into the government lobby. This graphically underlines the limits of dissidence in the PCP. As ever, party mattered more than principle on this occasion. One should remember, however, that the government was assisted by the fact that the opposition was more pro-European than it was, offering to incorporate the Social Chapter and raising an even "worse" specter of prointegrationist federalism if elected.

As it was, the bill only survived because the government postponed any vote on the Social Chapter until after it was enacted, leaving ratification of the treaty dependent on the separate votes that produced such drama on July 22 to 23, 1993 (in spite of an overwhelming Commons majority for the treaty).

Old Wine in New Bottles?

The reasons behind this outbreak of open civil war in the Conservative Party include the change in Labour's position on Europe. This has altered considerably since Edward Heath piloted Britain into Europe in 1972. In 1972 Labour was seriously divided over Europe, and "anti-Marketeer" Conservatives were under pressure to preserve party unity in order to maximize the Conservative Party's electoral advantage. In recent years Labour appears as a united pro-European party, and calls to unite behind a pro-European policy in order to defeat Labour on Europe are more easily resisted by today's Euro-rebels (Baker and Seawright 1997). Also, when electoral considerations and whip's pressure failed to discipline his rebels, Edward Heath could rely on dissenting Labour votes to ensure a majority; consequently, he never lost a vote on Europe. In contrast, John Major had to face a disciplined pro-European Labour opposition.

It is also noticeable that in both 1972 and 1993, Conservative governments had relatively small majorities, making threats to withdraw the whip from rebels largely empty. Events proved this, when eight Conservatives lost the whip and one voluntarily relinquished it without any major effect on their dissent, and they were subsequently accepted back into the fold without any of the usual disciplinary measures against them because of the drastic situation of a government majority down to one. Many hard-core rebels also occupied relatively safe seats. Of those rebelling on the Maastricht Paving Motion or the Committee of the Regions Amendment, three quarters enjoyed majorities of over 10%, more than half of over 20% (see also Norton 1978, 188–89, and chap. 3 of this volume).

Major's chief strategy during Maastricht was to hold the Conservative Party together and prevent it from splitting, both by fudging the issues wherever possible and by threatening to resign and take the party out of office with him where this failed (tactics reminiscent of Heath's in the early 1970s). The triumphant "opt-outs" from the Social Chapter and Economic and Monetary Union (EMU) negotiated at Maastricht were chiefly designed to hold the party together. Nevertheless, the Euro-skeptics were alarmed by this, since it highlighted the dangers of the process that had necessitated the opt-outs in the first place. Major's strategy and the problems he encountered in the process were best summed up in off-the-cuff remarks that he made to a television journalist, which were inadvertently recorded for posterity and later less than inadvertently leaked:

> The real problem is one of a tiny majority. Don't overlook that I could have all these clever decisive things which people wanted me to do—but I would have split the Conservative party into smithereens. And you would have said I acted like a ham-fisted leader. Just think it through from my perspective. You are the prime minister with a majority of 18, a party that is harking back to a golden age that never was, and is now invented. You have three right-wing members of the cabinet who actually resign. What happens in the parliamentary party? . . . I could bring in other people. But where do you think most of this poison is coming from? From the dispossessed and the never-possessed. You can think of ex-ministers who are going round causing all sorts of trouble. We don't want another three more of the bastards out there. (July 27, 1993)

If anyone has any doubts of the discrepancy between the private views of members of the Commons and their public utterances, they should contrast this with Major's answer to a Labour MP's question delivered during the Danish Referendum debate, on June 3, 1992: "On the Hon. Gentleman's 1975 illustration, as I recall the Conservative Party voted against a referendum in 1975. It was introduced only to cover up divisions in the [Labour] Cabinet of the day. No such divisions exist in my Cabinet" (*Hansard,* 6th ser., 208, col. 839).

Seismic Detection: How to Reveal the True Depth of Dissent?

In the British context, the figures of parliamentary dissent over Europe in both the 1971–72 and 1992–93 sessions are unprecedented under a Conservative government in this century. But given the huge pressures on Conservative MPs to conform, they may serve as only a "seismic" indicator of deeper tremors beneath the surface. Crucially, it is the persistence of the rebellion in Parliament, rather than its scale, that gives away the depth of division within the party.

When Norton emphasized the level of persistent dissent over the European issue in the 1970–74 Conservative government, he used Finer et al.'s quote in support of the idea that the "European issue" was more the exception than the rule: "The Conservative party is not divided into wings, with each wing espousing a line or tendency of policy affecting all departments of national life. This alone goes far to explain the resilience and unity of the Conservative party. By their very nature, the internal quarrels of the party are temporary. They subside as the issues which gave birth are resolved" (Finer, cited in Norton 1978, 244). But as we have discussed above, more than 20 years after Mr. Heath fought to take Britain into Europe, the issue has still not subsided within the Conservative Party. Norton himself continually emphasized that the incidence of dissent over the European issue, particularly in the session 1971–72, was without precedent in postwar British parliamentary history, both in terms of the number of divisions with dissenting votes and in terms of the persistent public dissent expressed on the floor of the House (Norton 1978, 61). The persistent dissension found by Norton in the parliamentary session 1971–72 is stronger for the parliamentary session 1991–92 (see table 4.3). The former session included 38 members rebelling on one occasion and 36 members rebelling on between two and nine occasions; but during the Maastricht Bill, no fewer than 53 MPs rebelled once and 117 MPs between 2 and 10 times.

Norton's findings also show that no more than nine Tory MPs were willing to oppose their government in the 1971–72 session on more than 59 occasions. Yet on 59 occasions during the European Communities Amendment Bill, between May 21, 1992, and May 20, 1993, an average of 19 Conservative members opposed their government on this issue alone. Also, in 10 of those incidents, we find only one or two MPs opposing the Maastricht Bill, mostly Bill Cash or Sir Teddy Taylor. If these incidents are not considered, the average Conservative "dissent" on just this bill rises to 22 members in each division for the 1991–92 session, compared to Norton's 10 MPs. Moreover, Norton (1978, 66) highlights the fact that 44 Conservatives registered their disapproval against entry to Europe in an EDM on July 23, 1970. However, on June 3, 1992, no less than 84 Tory MPs signed the "Fresh Start" EDM calling for the government to grasp the opportunity afforded it by the Danish Referendum—which effectively suspended Maastricht—to renegotiate Britain's position vis-à-vis Europe (see Appendix for full text).

Table 4.3
Conservative Dissent, 1971/72 and 1992/93

Session	No. of Dissenting Votes Cast	No. of Members
1971/72	1 only	38
	2–9	36
	10–19	4
	20–29	0
	30–39	4
	40–49	1
	50–59	2
	60–69	5
	70–79	0
	80 or more	2
Total		92
1992/93	1 only	53
	2–10	117
	11–20	7
	21–30	8
	31–40	7
	41–50	10
	51 or more	4
Total		206

Sources: Norton (1978, 63); Campaign Information Ltd. (1994).

If such dissent does persist, as it would appear to have done, it jeopardizes the very nature of British party government. Thus, Rose (1975, 129) states that "the government of Britain depends upon party organisation. The disciplined support of a parliamentary majority is a *sine qua non* of cabinet government as we know it." The British media have made great play over Mr. Major's lack of this indispensable asset. However, it is clear that the party in the legislature is still one of tendencies and not one of factions, as defined by Rose (1975). Recently a debate has arisen about Rose's definition of factions and tendencies (Brand 1989; Barnes 1994, 342–45). For instance, groups such as the No Turning Back Group and Conservative Way Forward are organized and active on a range of issues from a particular right-wing perspective. "The once conventional view of a Parliamentary Conservative Party (PCP) free of internal tendencies, factions and ginger groups has long been challenged, and from the perspective of 1995 it is hard to imagine how such a view was ever credible" (Ludlam 1996, 98–99).

The so-called "Fresh Start" alliance does not easily fit Rose's (1975, 313) definition of "consciously organised political activity on a broad range of policies" because it operates only on the European issue. However, there certainly is a faction in Rose's other use of the term—that is, an element of opinion within the party that has "persisted through time": "Because they persist through time, factions can be distinguished from the *ad hoc* combinations of politicians in agreement upon one particular issue or at one moment in time" (Rose 1975, 313).

But the only realistic method of revealing the true depth of division (factional or otherwise) is to discover in some way the actual beliefs of the PCP on the European issue in this period and to compare the figures of dissent on specific European issues with known attitudes in the parliamentary party. This is what this chapter is ultimately intended to achieve. But before we turn to our core analysis, it is salutary to review other approaches to the measurement of dissent.

British Parliamentary Behavior Studies

Studies of how MPs behave in Parliament have yielded a rich crop of qualitative insights but have often been hampered by the small number of quantitative measures available. The most fruitful examples of the latter have been records of voting, attendance, and speaking; membership of committees; and the signing of EDMs.

Because voting in the House is widely considered unreliable as an indicator of beliefs, an alternative method of studying MPs behavior is the analysis of EDMs, a methodology employed by Finer, Berrington, and Bartholemew (1961) and Berrington (1973). Berrington (1973, 3) quotes Feinburgh's definition of EDMs as "a recognized parliamentary gambit . . . a device whereby members advertise their views, and no one, neither whips nor frontbench, can prevent a member from using this channel," adding that "EDMs remain . . . one of the least controlled mechanisms for expressing opinions." But the problem here is that serving ministers do not sign such motions and that ambitious backbenchers are wary of revealing their attitudes even through this forum. Others may use it simply to align themselves with powerful elements in the party. One political commentator has remarked that EDMs "are a method not so much of influencing the government as of buying cheap and risk-free popularity from one's colleagues" (quoted in Berrington 1973, 16).

An alternative approach is to study ideological indicators of private belief through the analysis of MPs' membership in party and nonparty groups, speeches, memoirs, biographies, books, articles, and journalism.

The problem here is that these are all to some extent unreliable as indicators of Conservative MPs' real beliefs. For instance, membership of a group does not necessarily mean allegiance to all of its principles. Also, written or spoken expressions of belief by politicians may be simply for public consumption, to protect friends and colleagues, to blacken enemies, or to cover up past mistakes, and there is no easy way to filter out such bias.

Patterns of dissidence in the Commons, measured by votes against the party whip, were studied by Jackson (1968) and then comprehensively by Norton (1978, 1980). Norton used MPs' voting records and participant observation in his attempt to establish and assess these levels of dissent in the Conservative Party, concluding (as we saw above) that Europe was *the* divisive issue in the Conservative Party as early as 1970 to 1974 (Norton 1978). But Norton's study of the levels of dissent in the 1970–74 parliaments also encounters the problem that it measures only dissenting attitudes that are observable in Parliament. In fact, given our own evidence below on the discrepancy between current levels of private dissent and those willing to sign EDMs and/or to vote against the government on Maastricht, there could have been much wider disagreement within the party at that time than was measured by his model.

We have new evidence, in the form of a survey of Conservative parliamentarians on Europe, that shows that levels of dissent within the PCP in the post-1992–93 period far exceed the dissent registered in parliamentary rebellions. The methodology we have adopted here is to compare known dissent—percentages of the PCP voting against the government on Europe and signatories to anti-Maastricht EDMs—with the results of our own survey of MPs' private views, carried out in 1994, shortly after the Maastricht rebellion (Baker et al. 1995, 1996).

PCP Survey Evidence Compared with Known Parliamentary Behavior

Our survey of the private views of Conservative MPs, members of the European Parliament (MEPs), and candidates in the 1994 European Parliament election was compiled in the summer of 1994. The survey questionnaire contained 65 questions on European integration, designed to reflect a wide variety of standpoints. The questionnaire was sent to all Conservative MPs, MEPs, and EP candidates. In all, 38% of backbench MPs responded and 19% of ministers, an overall response

Table 4.4

Levels of Parliamentary Conservative Party Dissent with Official Party Line, as Manifested in Survey, Parliament, and Early Day Motions (%)

Issue	Survey of Backbenchers	Divisions in Parliament	EDMs
"Ultraskepticism"	32	9	26
EMU	61	9	
Central bank	64	9	
Single currency	68		33
ERM	52		19
VAT	76	8	
QMV	54	5	
Training	70	10	

Sources: Survey of Parliamentarians; Campaign Information Ltd. (1994).

Note: Percentage figures rounded for responses to survey questions and divisions of dissent in the House. See chapter appendix for survey questions and amendments.

rate of 33% for MPs. The questionnaire was anonymous, but three-quarters of respondents also returned a separate identity-coded post-card, enabling us to test the representativeness of our sample against Norton's ideological typology of Conservative MPs.[9] The results of our test leave us confident that there is a very close match between our respondents and the proportions of the party classified by Norton as "Thatcherites," "Loyalists," and "Damps/Wets" (Baker et al. 1995, 1996).

We also analyzed respondents in terms of their cohort: that is, which general election first brought them into Parliament or followed their entry in a by-election. Finally, we tested our known respondents by two measures of backbench parliamentary behavior over Europe. In rounded figures, our known respondents include 31% of all Tory back-benchers, 30% of the Maastricht Bill third-reading rebels, and 33% of the wider group of signers of the two 1992 "Fresh Start" EDMs[10] (Baker et al. 1996).

Table 4.4 offers an overview of eight key issues in which some of the results of our survey are compared with voting records and the signing of EDMs during the Maastricht and post-Maastricht period. We had great difficulty in matching the wording of our survey questions to those of the EDMs and amendments, although on these eight issues we have endeavored to match their spirit. The wording of an amendment is often obscure, to say the least, and in many cases a number of amendments are bundled together for the division vote. In addition, we had great difficulty in obtaining the actual wording of these amendments, since *Hansard* does not keep a record of them and since the Commons Information Service could not provide the wording either.[11] Consequently, this comparison does not represent a comprehensive set of data. However, on every issue, our figures show that backbench dissent was far greater than that measured by the other indicators, and on all of them the discrepancies are significant.

One of the most significant discrepancies is on the "ultraskeptical" issue. The survey question showed that 32% of respondents thought that any benefits of Britain's membership of the European Union (EU) were outweighed by the disadvantages. Yet only 9% of backbenchers were prepared to vote for an equally strong anti-integrationist amendment. On this issue the EDM was a much better indicator of backbench opinion, with 26% signing a motion calling for a halt to political union.[12]

However, on the vital economic indicators of pro and anti-Europeanism, there is a wide discrepancy between our survey findings and both voting and EDM indicators. On EMU and a Central Bank, only 9% of backbenchers were willing to defy the party leadership in the lobbies, but when asked for their private beliefs, 61% and 64% respectively were against such developments. Equally, while 33% and 19% respectively signed skeptical EDMs on the single currency and ERM, no less than 68% were hostile to the former and 52% to the latter in private.

On VAT we found that 76% of respondents were against its harmonization within the EU, but only 8% were willing to support an opposition Labour amendment that called for the deletion of the treaty provisions for the harmonization of indirect taxation. Similarly, on qualified majority voting, while a tiny 5% of Conservative MPs were willing to openly defy the government, over half those polled (54%) were for restoring the blocking minority in the Council of Ministers to preenlargement levels. On the final issue, that of an EU training strategy, only 10% were willing to register dissent on this issue in Parliament, while 70% registered their disapproval in our survey.

Conclusion

The above data, limited though they are, confirm for the first time by this method that backbench PCP attitudes cannot easily be inferred from behavior in Parliament, particularly under a Conservative government faced with the European issue. Other methods have to be used to tease out what is actually happening, and if these are used carefully, the true depth of dissent is revealed to be much greater than parliamentary dissidence would indicate.

Not only is the opposition to Europe within the PCP persistent, but the compliance of MPs with government opinion in contradistinction to their own privately held views on Europe is just as persistent. For example, we can see from table 4.1 that the 22 most rebellious MPs who dissented on between 25 and 50 occasions over Maastricht make up only 7% of the 329 elected Conservative MPs in Parliament on March 21, 1995.[13] But by viewing our survey and comparing it with similar EDM/division dissent, we see that many more Conservative MPs hold skeptical views.

The rebels believe that their positions on Maastricht and sovereignty have majority support in the Conservative Party, in the country, in Parliament, and in the electorate. The cabinets' pro-European majority and its supporters in the parliamentary party appear to believe the opposite. The 1994 European election punished the Conservatives, returning the smallest number of Conservative MEPs ever returned, but this does not indicate a general unhappiness with their Euro-policies, since the election was treated by many voters (encouraged by Labour's campaign) as a referendum on domestic handling of the economy rather than a European election as such. No one can be sure what would happen if the party was confronted with an unambiguous choice over Europe in the next few years. If an inner core of European states decided to push ahead with European integration and drive toward EMU (as now seems possible), this would present a Rubicon that a significant part of the Conservative Party is determined never to cross and could provoke an outright split in the party if it were in government at the time. Yet ironically, it could be said that the arch-Europhiles like Heath, Bottomley, Knox, and Currie, currently on the defensive within the party, are the ones most likely to split away from the party if it adopts an open and aggressive anti-European stance in the future.

APPENDIX

Ultraskepticism

Survey: Percentage disagreeing with the statement: "The disadvantages of EC membership have been outweighed by the benefits."

Division: Mr. Cash's amendment to the European Communities (Amendment) Bill: Deletion of Provisions for Amending the Treaty of Rome. (January 14, 1993)

EDM: That this House urges Her Majesty's Government to use the decision to postpone the passage of the European Communities (Amendment) Bill as an opportunity to make a fresh start with the future development of the EEC and in particular to concentrate its efforts on the chosen agenda of the British presidency which is to extend the borders of the EEC and to create a competitive common market. (June 3, 1992)

EMU

Survey: Percentage agreeing with the statement: "EMU is not desirable."

Division: Mr. Cash's Amendment to Clause 1 of the European Communities (Amendment) Bill: Deletion of Treaty provisions re. the third stage of EMU. (April 19, 1993)

Central Bank

Survey: Percentage agreeing with the statement: "Britain should never permit its monetary policy to be determined by an independent European Central Bank."

Division: Mr. Cash's Amendment to Clause 1 of the European Communities (Amendment) Bill: Deletion of Treaty provisions re: Central Banks. (April 19, 1993)

Single Currency

Survey: Percentage disagreeing with the statement: "Britain should join a single currency if it is created because of the economic consequences of remaining outside."

EDM: That this House congratulates the Prime Minister for making it clear on 8th January that it is not in the United Kingdom's interest to join a single currency in 1997 and for his confirmation that there are no proposals for legislation necessary for the purpose nor for the United Kingdom to accept any changes at the Inter-Governmental Conference which will impact on the constitution of the United Kingdom; and notes his rejections of the support for the principle for a single currency by the Leader of Her Majesty's Opposition and M. Jacques Santer. (February 8, 1995)

ERM

Survey: Percentage agreeing with the statement: "Britain should never rejoin the ERM."

EDM: That this House welcomes the Government's decision to leave the ERM; and urges a fresh start to economic policy, in particular the abandonment of fixed exchange rates and a commitment to sound finance, stable money and the right climate for steady growth. (September 24, 1992)

VAT

Survey: Percentage disagreeing with the statement: "VAT should be harmonised within the EU."

Division: Opposition Amendment to Clause 1 of the European Communities (Amendment) Bill: Deletion of Treaty provisions for the harmonization of indirect taxation. (January 29, 1993)

QMV

Survey: Percentage agreeing with the statement: "At the 1996 IGC, the QMV blocking minority should be restored to 23."

Division: Mr. Shore's Motion to grant a Second Reading to a new clause 2 to the European Communities (Amendment) Bill: Act of Parliament required to approve changes in voting procedure at Council of Ministers. (May 5, 1993)

Training

Survey: Percentage disagreeing with the statement: "In principle there should be a Union strategy on training."

Division: Opposition Amendment to Clause 1 of the European Communities (Amendment) Bill: European Community competence re. Vocational Training. (January 20, 1993)

NOTES

1. Splits need to be distinguished from divisions. Only occasionally will division of opinion in a party become a split, in which there is a formal break-

away by a substantial group, followed by the establishment of a new party or an alliance with an existing one (Baker et al. 1993a).

2. In 1846 the Corn Laws were supported by the old aristocratic and landed wing of the party and opposed by the manufacturing interests in order to lower the cost of production through lower food costs and wages. In 1906 Tariff Reform was an unsuccessful attempt by the populist Joseph Chamberlain and his supporters to protect national industry against those in the party who still advocated a free trade orthodoxy.

3. In 1978 Norton went so far as to state that "the power to withdraw the whip . . . has fallen into disuse in the Conservative Party" (129–30). Sir W. Wayland lost the whip after supporting an independent candidate in a 1931 by-election (Richards 1959, 151). In May 1957 eight Conservative MPs belonging to the "Suez Group" *resigned* the Conservative whip, and in 1942 one Conservative had the whip removed by the coalition government (see Norton 1978, 166).

4. The 1992–93 European Communities (Amendment) Bill, commonly called the Maastricht Bill, was the necessary parliamentary approval for the deeper European integration process, sparked by the agreement between all the heads of government at the Maastricht European Council in the Netherlands in December 1991.

5. The ERM, within which exchange rates could be adjusted to allow development toward a common currency and also a European Currency Unit (ECU), which some expected would become a single currency, the Euro. On so-called "Black Wednesday" (September 16, 1992), international speculation against the pound sterling forced Britain's withdrawal from the ERM, much to the delight of the Euro-skeptics in the Conservative Party.

6. A referendum was held over ratification of the Maastricht Treaty on June 2, 1992, and returned a narrow defeat of Maastricht by 50.7% to 49.3%. A subsequent referendum vote narrowly reversed this decision, however.

7. For a full discussion of the nature and importance of EDMs, see the section below on methodology. The actual wording of these EDMs can be found in the appendix.

8. The Social Chapter is the section of the Maastricht Treaty that governs workers' rights to representation on company boards and guarantees certain levels of social provision and working conditions across the EU. John Major negotiated an "opt-out" on this on the grounds that Britain preferred to operate with a free market in labor markets and believed that productivity and inward investment would suffer.

9. For our discussion of Norton's typology of Conservative MPs, see Baker, Gamble, and Ludlam (1994a). The typology can be found in Norton (1990).

10. The survey was funded as part of an Economic and Social Research Council Award Number R000231298 and was carried out by the Parliament

Project in the Department of Politics at the University of Sheffield in collaboration with Nottingham Trent University.

11. We eventually obtained the material from Campaign Information Ltd.

12. See the appendix for the exact wording of the Amendments and EDMs.

13. Courtesy of the Public Information Office, House of Commons. The reason for the wording of this is that nine MPs elected as Conservatives have lost the whip; eight have had it withdrawn (Budgen, Carttiss, Gill, T. Gorman, Marlow, R. Shepherd, Sir T. Taylor, Wilkinson), and one (Sir Richard Body) resigned the whip. It is interesting to note from table 4.1 that while all of these individuals are in the top 22 Maastricht rebels, several of the most rebellious remained inside the party and declined to "fall on their swords." As already stated, the eight MPs who lost the whip were allowed to return shortly afterwards without the usual thumbscrews being applied on their return because of the wafer-thin majority of the government.

REFERENCES

Ashford, D. 1980. "The European Community." In Zig Layton-Henry, ed., *Conservative Party Politics.* New York: Macmillan.

Baker, D., I. Fountain, A. Gamble, S. Ludlam. 1995. "Backbench Conservative Attitudes to European Integration." *Political Quarterly* 66: 221–33.

———. 1996. "The Blue Map of Europe: Conservative Parliamentarians and European Integration: A Survey." In C. Rallings, D. Farrell, D. Denver, and D. Broughton, eds., *British Elections and Parties Yearbook, 1995.* London: Frank Cass.

Baker, D., A. Gamble, and S. Ludlam. 1993a. "1846 . . . 1906 . . . 1996: Conservative Splits and European Integration." *Political Quarterly* 64(4): 420–34.

———. 1993b. "Whips or Scorpions? The Maastricht Vote and the Conservative Party." *Parliamentary Affairs* 46(2): 151–66.

———. 1994a. "Mapping Conservative Fault Lines: Problems of Typology." In P. Dunleavy and J. Stanyer, eds., *Contemporary Political Studies 1994: Proceedings of the Political Studies Association Annual Conference.* Belfast, Ireland: Queens University Belfast, U.K. Political Studies Association.

———. 1994b. "The Parliamentary Siege of Maastricht." *Parliamentary Affairs* 47(1): 37–60.

Baker, D., and D. Seawright, eds. 1997. *Britain for and against Europe: British Politics and the Question of European Integration.* London: Oxford University Press.

Barnes, J. 1994. "Ideology and Factions." In A. Seldon and S. Ball, eds., *The Conservative Century.* London: Oxford University Press.

Berrington, H. B. 1973. *Backbench Opinion in the House of Commons, 1945–55.* New York: Pergamon.

Brand, J. 1989. "Faction as Its Own Reward: Groups in the British Parliament 1945–1986." *Parliamentary Affairs* 42: 148–64.

Campaign Information Ltd. 1994. *Conservative Dissent, May 1992–November 1993.* Available from Mind House, 20 North Road, Inkwell, Biggleswade, Beds. SG18. 9ED.

Finer, S., H. B. Berrington, and D. J. Bartholomew. 1961. *Backbench Opinion in the House of Commons, 1955–59.* New York: Pergamon.

Gamble, A. 1974. *The Conservative Nation.* London: Routledge & Kegan Paul.

Jackson, R. J. 1968. *Whips and Rebels.* New York: Macmillan.

Lawson, N. 1992. *The View from Number 11: Memoirs of a Tory Radical.* London: Bantam Press.

Ludlam, S. 1996. "Backbench Rebellions: Europe, the Spectre Haunting Conservatism." In S. Ludlam and M. J. Smith, eds., *Contemporary British Conservatism.* New York: Macmillan.

Norton, P. 1978. *Conservative Dissidents: Dissent within the Parliamentary Conservative Party 1970–74.* London: Temple Smith.

———. 1980. *Dissension in the House of Commons 1974–79.* Oxford, UK: Clarendon.

———. 1990. "'The Lady's Not for Turning': But What about the Rest? Margaret Thatcher and the Conservative Party 1979–89." *Parliamentary Affairs* 43(1): 41–58.

Richards, P. 1959. *Honourable Members: A Study of the British Backbencher.* London: Faber

Rose, R. 1975. *The Problem of Party Government.* New York: Macmillan.

PART III

Established Continental European Systems

In Part II we saw two examples of a growing body of work that shows the United Kingdom as less monolithic than has tended to be assumed. In this part we move further afield. While debates on party cohesion can swiftly become locked into U.S.-U.K. comparisons, relatively little is known about parliaments elsewhere. Moreover, as the U.K. chapters suggested, the electoral system and rules on candidate nomination at the local level can have important effects in terms of aiding and abetting backbench indiscipline. To the extent that the electoral system does matter, the comparison between the United States and the United Kingdom—both of which share the single-member simple-plurality system—may well hide this. The chapters in this part address this point, assessing the experience of party cohesion in other (continental European) parliamentary systems and examining the impact of different electoral systems.

The three chapters provide a good mix of cases, ranging from the highly cohesive Norwegian system, archetypical of the Scandinavian model that John Fitzmaurice has described as one of "iron party discipline in parliament" (cited in chap. 6), to the far less cohesive Swiss system, which, as described by Lanfranchi and Lüthi, bears many similarities to the U.S. separated system, where there is "no institutional incentive for [MPs] to vote cohesively." Roll call analysis, reported in chapters 5 and 6, confirms these respective trends, and in the Norwegian case, despite the rise of volatility at the electoral level in recent years, parliamentary voting discipline remains high and rising.

Between the two extremes we have the Spanish case, as a relatively recent entrant to the family of West European democracies, where great effort has been made to enforce strong party discipline in Parliament. In chapter 7, Sánchez de Dios stresses such features as the imposition of rules to attempt (not entirely successfully) to dampen down faction hopping; the requirement for individual MPs to have permission before they can put down amendments to bills; and the imposition of fines for absenteeism. A particularly interesting feature of the Spanish case is the role of the *portavoz* (whip): unlike the Westminster model, this is an elected office, which, rather than seeking to turn out individual MPs to vote, actually votes, on a weighted basis, for the parliamentary group as a whole.

All three cases share the list system of proportional representation, and the authors stress the important role played by this electoral system in encouraging parliamentarians to conform with the wishes of their party leadership. A feature of the Swiss case relates to the differences between the two chambers: the National Council, which is elected by proportional representation, and the Council of States, which for the most part is elected by majoritarian systems in each of the cantons.

5

Cohesion of Party Groups and Interparty Conflict in the Swiss Parliament: Roll Call Voting in the National Council

PRISCA LANFRANCHI AND RUTH LÜTHI

The Swiss Political System

This chapter deals with the voting behavior of members of the Swiss parliament (National Council). Our central question is: Do members of the same party vote cohesively? Mathew D. McCubbins and Terry Sullivan (1987, 3) tell us that "different institutions lead to different patterns of individual behavior." Thus, if we are interested in the voting behavior of MPs, we need to know the institutional context in which they operate. We therefore first must gain insight into the political system of Switzerland.

Students of Swiss politics like to point out that it is "special," even a "deviant case" of democracy. As a matter of fact, some interesting, unique qualities characterize the Swiss political system. But even if Switzerland cannot easily be designated as either a parliamentary or a presidential system (see Riklin 1977), there exist some similarities with the political systems of other countries. Winfried Steffani (1983, 394), for example, in contrast to most Swiss scholars, classifies the Swiss political system clearly as a presidential system. Using the terminology of Terry Moe and Michael Caldwell (1994), we suggest below that the Swiss case can be described as a separation-of-powers system. A number of institutional features appear to affect Swiss legislative behavior.[1]

First, Swiss federalism consists of three levels: the federation, the 26 cantons, and the more than 3,000 communes. Communes and cantons are given a large degree of autonomy and play an important role in Swiss political life. The cantons not only enjoy great autonomy but also participate in an intensive way in the decision-making process of the federation, which allows them to prevent any uncontrolled growth in its powers. The most important federalist element in the decision-making process of the Swiss Federation is the bicameral legislature: the National Council and the Council of States. The two councils are absolute equals in all matters of legislation. Every proposition or bill destined to become a federal law has to be approved by a relative majority in both chambers. There are, however, different electoral systems for the two chambers that reflect different ideas of representation.

The National Council consists of 200 members representing the Swiss people. Each canton constitutes an electoral constituency, where seats are allotted in proportion to the resident population. Constituency size varies markedly: Zurich elects 35 MPs, while in the five smallest cantons, the citizens elect just 1. With the exception of those five constituencies, the National Council is elected by a system of proportional representation (PR) and has been since 1919.

The Council of States has 46 members representing the Swiss cantons. Each canton elects two members, and each half-canton elects one, regardless of their size. Election procedure is determined by cantonal law and varies from canton to canton. Only one canton uses PR; the others use a majority system.

The different electoral systems lead to different compositions in the two chambers. The PR elections to the National Council result in the greater representation of small parties (see table 5.1). On the other hand, in the Council of States, 34 of the 46 seats are shared between just two parties, and the Social Democrats, who hold 42 of the 200 seats in the National Council, have only 3 seats in the Council of the States.

A second institutional feature affecting legislative behavior is direct democracy. Not only do Swiss citizens elect their representatives to Parliament; they are also the ultimate decision makers on many important issues. Swiss direct democracy consists of three instruments: the *obligatory referendum,* in which all proposals for constitutional amendment and important international treaties are subject to a vote of the people; the *optional referendum,* in which 50,000 citizens may, within 90 days, demand the holding of a popular vote on laws passed by Parliament;

Table 5.1

Distribution of Seats in the National Council and the Council of States, 1991–1995

	Votes (%)	National Council Seats	Council of States Seats
Governmental Parties	69.5	147	41
Radicals	20.9	44	18
Social Democrats	19.0	42	3
Christian Democrats	17.8	35	16
People's Party	11.8	25	4
Nongovernmental Parties	30.5	53	5
Green Party	6.4	14	—
Automobile Party	5.1	8	—
Alternative Left	4.0	3	—
Liberals	3.0	10	3
Swiss Democrats	2.8	5	1
Independents	2.7	5	1
Protestant Party	1.9	3	—
Others	4.6	5	1
Total	100	200	46

Source: Linder (1994, 45).

and the *popular initiative,* in which 100,000 citizens may request a total or partial revision of the Constitution. Our main interest here is in the impact of direct democracy on the political system, especially its impact on Parliament and party groups (for more general discussion and an extensive bibliography, see Linder 1994). One of the most important results of direct democracy is another institutional feature of the Swiss political system, namely power sharing.

As described so far, Swiss politics is similar in many ways to the U.S. system, where federalism also plays an important role in the decision-making process and where, in several states, there are elements of direct democracy. But there is one fundamental difference, and this relates to the third institutional feature that we need to mention. The United States has a two-party system with winner-take-all elections, whereas Switzerland has a power-sharing system (see Steiner 1990). Direct democracy has had impacts on the composition of Swiss federal government. A large political group that is in opposition to the government is able to block the political decision-making process by using the referendum as a weapon. Because of this, the major parties have been forced to cooperate. Since 1959, the four major parties have together formed the executive. According to the so-called magic formula, the executive consists of two members each of the Radical Party, the Christian Democrats, and the Social Democrats and one member of the People's Party.

Central to our concerns is the fact that there is no powerful opposition in the Swiss parliament comparable to what exists in Westminster systems (see chaps. 3 and 4 of this volume). The Social Democrats as the major left party are "integrated" into the government of the three "bourgeois" parties (Radicals, Christian Democrats, and People's Party). However, the government parties are not bound by a coalition contract containing a set political program.

In the Swiss system, unlike most parliamentary systems, the legislature cannot stage a vote of no confidence, and the executive does not resign when outvoted in Parliament. The executive, on the other hand, cannot dissolve the parliament or veto its bills. Therefore, Switzerland may be described as a separation-of-powers system, having many similarities to the U.S. system. However, there are some differences, the most important of which is that the executive in Switzerland is elected for a four-year-term by Parliament and not by the people.

Previous Research on the Voting Behavior of MPs

Before reviewing Swiss research on the voting behavior of MPs, and to place this chapter in its international context, it is worthwhile to take a look at the comparative literature, especially the literature on the U.S. case.

As Melissa Collie points out in her survey (1984, 5), the bulk of analyses have concerned the U.S. Congress: "While the American context has traditionally generated studies of this type, analysts of non-American legislatures have not devoted nearly as much attention to the topic, largely because consistently high levels of party cohesion and conflict in these legislatures have made such investigations appear superfluous." She distinguishes two schools of research on legislative voting behavior: one focusing on collective behavior, with particular attention to cleavage and alignment patterns, and the other focusing on individual behavior, with studies of individual decision-making patterns. In the early 1980s, Collie (1984, 33) notes that "in the American setting, the primary object and unit of analysis has shifted gradually and erratically from the study of collective behavior to the study of individual behavior."

Recent studies stress the importance of institutional factors affecting legislative behavior (e.g., Rieselbach 1990; Searing 1991; McCubbins and Sullivan 1987). The member of Congress is no longer described as an individual free rider but is said to be constrained by a set of institutional arrangements (such as committee membership). In this chapter, we suggest that institutional factors are interesting for analyzing collective as well as individual legislative behavior.

In Switzerland, parliamentary research is a relatively young field. Political scientists were not, however, the first ones to be interested in voting behavior. Early research on Swiss legislative voting behavior in the 1950s by a student of law, Marco Vasella (1956), was mainly focused on the normative question of whether strict party discipline is a good thing. The first research by a social scientist on the voting behavior of Swiss members of Parliament was carried out by Hans-Peter Hertig (1980). His study belongs to the tradition of individual voting behavior research. He was interested in whether the party, the electors, or the interest groups were the primary factors in determining the voting behavior of members of the National Council, and his research was based mainly on interviews with MPs.

The study by Adrian Vatter (1994) also falls into the category of individual voting behavior research. However, his main interest was not the influence of party or interest groups but the question of district representation. He tried to explain the behavior of MPs on the cantonal level, exploring the extent to which the MPs' votes were influenced by constituency concerns. His findings show that the district-voting approach seems to be important in explaining individual voting behavior, at least for members of cantonal parliaments and on issues concerning infrastructural projects.

Most recently, the Institute of Political Science at the University of Berne established a data bank in 1989 where roll call votes could be collected. This now contains all roll call votes held in the National Council since December 1983. In 1991 Ruth Lüthi, Luzius Meyer, and Hans Hirter published the results of their research based on these data. Their primary interest was to document and to explain intraparty cohesion and interparty conflict. Additionally, they measured voting cohesion of MPs belonging to the same interest groups.

This chapter is in the tradition of *collective behavior research:* that is, we are interested in cleavage and alignment patterns. In this sense, the study is a continuation of the research of Lüthi et al. (1991). Inspired by the discussion in recent U.S. studies about the importance of institutional factors, we also explore the assertion that voting behavior is influenced by committee membership.

Empirical Evidence of Intraparty Cohesion and Interparty Conflict in the Swiss National Council

This section will give some impression of the importance of party groups in structuring floor voting in the Swiss National Council, as shown by the levels of intraparty cohesion and interparty conflict. This measure is generally used to test the strength of parties in the U.S. Congress (e.g., Ward 1993), though the strict U.S. definition of party strength—high party influence when cohesion within the parties and conflict between the parties are both high—must be adjusted in our case for several reasons. First, fundamental characteristics of the Swiss political system (outlined above), such as multiparty government, must be taken into account. Second, as this section will show, roll call votes are the exception in Swiss parliamentary life, being used by party groups in the National Council as a specific "political weapon." They do not reflect the whole range of party behavior in the Swiss federal parliament. Therefore, instead of measuring and depicting party importance in the strict American sense, we give first impressions, which will have to be deepened in future research.

Roll Call Votes in the National Council

Unlike "Congress watchers," Swiss parliamentary researchers cannot rely on an extensive database for analyzing voting behavior. Until the beginning of 1994, when an electronic voting system was installed in the National Council (see below), voting in both chambers of Parliament was in most cases carried out by the MPs standing up from their seats. Although voting behavior was thus not secret, it was not wholly transparent either, at least not for ordinary people or political scientists without the time or possibility to sit in Parliament day after day recording the voting behavior of the MPs. However, there was, and still is, an exception to this standard way of voting, the so-called votes by calling the names (roll call votes).

In the National Council, this way of voting has been known since the first statute of the chamber in 1850 and has been modified several times over the last hundred years (Lüthi et al. 1991). According to the present rule, 30 members of the National Council may request in written form that a vote on a bill, or on particular sections of it, be carried out by calling the names of the MPs. In those cases, the voting of each MP is recorded and published in the official *Bulletin of the Federal Assembly*.

In the Council of States, where 10 members may ask for the same procedure, this possibility of recorded voting has so far hardly ever been used (Lüthi et al. 1991). This may be explained in part by the fact that party membership and its constraints on behavior are linked to proportional representation (Loewenberg and Mans 1988, 170). Unlike members of the National Council, members of the Council of States are elected by a majority system and are thus more independent of the parties to which they belong. In addition, the majority electoral system produces a rather homogeneous composition of this chamber (domination by the "bourgeois" parties and underrepresentation of the Social Democrats), and members of the dominant parties are obviously not interested in making their votes public by asking for a roll call vote.

Thus, the empirical basis of this chapter consists of roll call votes carried out in the National Council. Although an electronic voting system was introduced at the beginning of 1994, the National Council decided in 1995 to restrict use of this instrument, thereby shattering the hopes of political scientists for easy availability of voting records. First, it was decided that individual voting decisions are only to be published in specified cases.[2] Second, the recorded data on roll call votes—although published in the official bulletin—are not handed over to political scientists on disks. Therefore, researchers interested in these votes still have to collect the relevant information in a database by themselves to be able to analyze the voting behavior of Swiss MPs.

The Political Significance of Demanding a Roll Call Vote

As Lüthi et al. (1991) point out, there is a deep feeling of distrust among most MPs concerning roll call votes. It is widely feared that they are then "classified" and somewhat hindered from expressing their individual choice of vote. This feeling of distrust is rooted in the liberal idea of representation by "free mandate" as explicitly embodied in the Swiss Constitution.[3] In the classical liberal view, MPs are assumed to represent the overall interests of society, being independent of all kinds of special interests like regions, organizations, groups, or even parties.[4] However, this normative view of totally independent MPs does not stand up to parliamentary practice. As a matter of fact, party groups in the National Council have an important instrument at their disposal to influence individual voting behavior. To ask for a roll call vote is actually to use a "political weapon" to enforce voting discipline in their own ranks or to reveal voting behavior of the MPs of other party groups (Vasella 1956; Lüthi et al. 1991).

The specific political significance of requesting a roll call vote has effects on our empirical findings, in the sense that our database predetermines in some ways the results that we obtain. Because we do not have data on all floor votes in the National Council, and because roll call voting is usually demanded in cases of important and contested issues, our findings are biased. We would get lower indices of party cohesion as well as less evidence of interparty conflict if we had data on all the votes at our disposal because the bulk of the unpublished votes concern minor issues or issues on which the parties do not oppose one another.

We use the standard Rice Index of Party Cohesion for measuring intraparty cohesion in the Swiss National Council (Rice 1928). This index is calculated by computing the difference between the proportion of the majority of $group_i$ and the proportion of the minority of the same $group_i$. If the Rice Index is zero, then $group_i$ was completely divided: i.e., 50% voted "yes" and 50% voted "no." As the Rice Index increases, $group_i$ votes more and more cohesively.

Various methodological problems are attached to this way of measuring party cohesion. First, the Rice Index fails to take into account the size of the units, or party groups. Deviant voting by MPs belonging to a smaller party has a larger impact on the index of cohesion of this group than deviant voting in a larger parliamentary party. Second, using the standard Rice Index means neglecting the MPs who abstain. However, abstaining seems to play a minor role in the National Council (see Lüthi 1989).[5] Third, our measuring method also neglects the MPs who decide not to participate in the voting. It may be argued that nonparticipation is a means of evading a vote so as not to offend the party (Müller 1994). But since there are other plausible "nonpolitical" interpretations of nonparticipation in a vote, and because it is not possible to detect the real reasons with our database, we will stick to the standard Rice Index of party cohesion, thereby neglecting nonparticipating MPs.

Party Cohesion in the National Council:
Longitudinal Trends (1920–1994)

Figure 5.1 shows the number of roll call votes in the National Council since 1920. There is a marked increase of requested roll call

Figure 5.1   Roll Call Votes in the National Council, 1920–1994

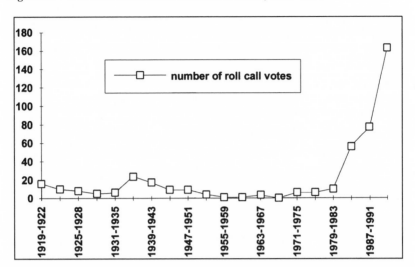

votes in the last 12 years. This trend has been explained by Vatter (1997) as a reflection of the growing interparty conflict between the different political groups—between the conservative/liberal ("bourgeois") majority and the Social Democrat/Green minority—on important decisions over such policy fields as finance, environment, and energy.[6] To be more precise, the failure to elect an official candidate of the Social Democrats to the federal government by the so-called bourgeois majority in Parliament marked an important turning point. The party group of the Social Democrats announced shortly after this "insult" in 1983 that they intended to ask for more roll call votes in the future to make parliamentary decisions and voting behavior of MPs more transparent to the public (Forschungszentrum für schweizerische Politik 1985). But the Social Democrats were not alone in rediscovering the use of roll call votes as a political weapon. The "bourgeois" MPs in recent years have also increasingly used this instrument to show, for example, the "antiarmy" spirit of the Social Democrats (Lüthi et al. 1991).

The marked increase in roll call votes has not been caused only by the polarization in the National Council. Figure 5.1 shows an almost "explosive" increase in roll call votes in the most recent legislative period (1991–95). We suggest that this may be partly explained by the fact that, due to the technical innovation of an electronic voting system in 1994, MPs are able to ask for a roll call vote without causing a major waste of the precious and restricted time of the plenary sessions.[7]

Intraparty cohesion in the national council. Winfried Steffani (1991) distinguishes between two types of political systems, the presidential and the parliamentary. The separation of powers in the U.S. presidential system is based on independence between the executive and the legislative branch: that is, there are no votes of no confidence, and the parliament may not be dissolved by the president. In parliamentary systems, on the other hand, where the possibility of a no-confidence vote and dissolution of the parliament exists, there is a sort of "separation of powers" between the party in government and the party in opposition. In presidential systems the legislature can check the power of the executive; in parliamentary systems the opposition checks the party in government. Here, if the majority party is to stay in government, it is necessary that its members vote cohesively on crucial issues, whereas the U.S. president does not depend on the votes of his or her party to stay in office (see also Epstein 1980, 340–42).

As pointed out above, Switzerland may be classified as a separation-of-powers system (absence of a vote of no confidence and absence of the possibility of dissolution of Parliament). Thus, there exists no institutional incentive for members of the Swiss National Council to vote cohesively. For every bill, each party group designates a speaker to report the opinion of the party concerning that bill to the floor, but the members of the party groups are not forced to vote accordingly. Therefore, we assume that—as in the U.S. case—there is no evidence of strict party discipline on roll call votes in the National Council.

To test this assumption empirically, we computed the Rice Index of Party Cohesion in the National Council, based on a total of 426 roll call votes from 1920 to 1994. The results are shown in table 5.2; four trends are worth stressing. First, the Rice Index is in most cases higher for nongovernmental party groups than for the three "bourgeois" governmental parties (Radicals, Christian Democrats, People's Party). Second, among the governmental parties, the Social Democrats vote most cohesively in all periods of time (Rice Index around 90). To what extent this finding may be explained by the minority status of the Social Democrats in Parliament and in government and/or by the prevailing understanding of representation in this party must be the subject of further research. Third, the lowest Rice Index of party cohesion among the governmental parties since 1971 is found for the Christian Democrats. The most convincing ad hoc explanation for this is given by the rather heterogeneous composition of this party group. On some issues (e.g., social

Table 5.2

Rice Index of Party Cohesion in the National Council, 1920–1994

	1920–53	*1971–83*	*1983–87*	*1987–91*	*1991–94*
Governmental Parties					
Radicals	68.9	74.7	73.4	70.5	79.2
Social Democrats	95.4	91.3	89.1	92.9	96.3
Christian Democrats	75.5	63.0	60.1	70.4	68.3
People's Party	80.5	84.4	74.0	77.8	80.7
Nongovernmental Parties					
Green Party				92.1	94.9
Liberals		78.2	97.9	96.2	90.4
Independents/Protestant Party*		79.0	79.5	83.1	85.5
Swiss Democrats			69.0		85.5
Automobile Party					98.2
N	108	22	56	77	163

Sources: Lüthi et al. (1991); Institute for Political Science of the University of Berne.

Note: No data available for 1953–67.

*The Rice Index for 1971–83 and 1987–94 is limited to the Independents and does not include the Protestant Party.

policy), it is likely that MPs on the "right" of the party hold different views than MPs on the "left." Therefore, it would be fruitful to take into account policy content in future research on roll call votes (see below). Finally, there seems to be no overall trend toward increased party cohesion over time, as was asserted by Vatter (1997) on the basis of former data. While some party groups (nongovernmental parties, Radicals) in 1991–94 do have increased scores compared to earlier periods, the results for other party groups fluctuate or are more or less stable over time (Christian Democrats, Social Democrats, People's Party).

Without seeking to oversimplify, we find some similarities with the U.S. case. For instance, as in the U.S. Congress (see Ornstein, Mann, and Malbin 1990), party cohesion in the National Council differs over time and on the whole (i.e., not taking account of differences between the parties) is relatively low, probably lower than in most parliamentary systems of western Europe (see Epstein 1980, 315–17, who, however, does not deliver empirical evidence for his assertions).

Interparty conflict in the national council. According to Lijphart's (1984) distinction between types of democracies, Switzerland can be labeled as consensual. Among the different elements that characterize democracies of this type, Lijphart cites the principle of executive power

Table 5.3

Voting Alliances among the Government Parties

Large Alliance	Bourgeois Alliance	Left-Green Alliance	Left-Green-Christian Alliance	Other Alliances
At least two "bourgeois" party groups (Radicals, Christian Democrats, People's Party) and the Social Democrats	At least one of the two "core bourgeois" party groups (Radicals, People's Party)	Social Democrats, Green Party	Social Democrats, Green Party, Christian Democrats	Nongovernmental party/ies

One of the "core bourgeois" party groups and the Social Democrat |
| (Optional, nongovernmental parties) | (Optional: Christian Democrats, nongovernmental parties) | (Optional: other nongovernmental parties) | (Optional: other nongovernmental parties) | |

sharing, or grand coalitions. As we saw above, executive power in Switzerland has been shared since 1959 between the four largest parties. In view of this principle of executive power sharing, it might be assumed that the coalition of the four largest parties also structures floor voting in Parliament. To test this assumption, we have analyzed the composition of voting alliances on 162 roll call votes in the most recent legislature (1991–94), defining a voting alliance as occurring when the majorities of two or more party groups vote in the same direction. Table 5.3 distinguishes five different forms of voting alliance with regard to the *government* parties: large, bourgeois, left-Green, left-Green-Christian, and other.[8]

We might expect that, in view of the composition of the Federal Council (executive), the "large alliance" would be the most frequent voting alliance type to be found in the National Council. But as figure 5.2 reveals, of the total of all counted alliances (324), only 27 or 8.3% were "large alliances," formed by the majorities of at least two "bourgeois" party groups and the Social Democrats. By far the most frequent alliances on roll call votes were formed by at least one of the "core bourgeois" party groups (People's Party or Radicals), without the Social Democrats.

So far we have not distinguished between winning and losing alli-

Figure 5.2 Frequency of Different Alliances on Roll Call Votes in the National Council, 1991–1994

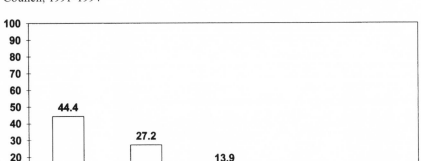

ances, a distinction that would seem to be of major interest, especially since observers of the National Council have asserted that the last 15 years have been marked by growing polarization on important decisions: the traditional model of consensus democracy is shifting to a politics of majorities with rigid "bourgeois" majorities and Social Democrat/Green minorities (Linder 1988, Vatter 1997). Figure 5.3 shows whether this assertion of a rigid constellation of losers and winners holds true for roll call votes in 1991–94.

As might be expected in view of the composition of the National Council, "large" alliances have the highest success rate. All of the 27 voting alliances belonging to this category have been on the winning side. In view of the assumption of a rigid politics of majorities mentioned above, the results for the types of alliance labeled "bourgeois" and "left-Green" are of special interest. Whereas alliances of the former type won in two-thirds of the 144 cases in which they voted together, the "left-Green" alliances, formed by majorities made up of Social Democrats, the Green Party, and other nongovernmental party groups, won in only 6 out of 88 relevant cases (6.8%). Although the large difference in the success rates of these two voting alliances seems to support the thesis of a polarized situation for our period, the next point puts this conclusion into context.

Figure 5.3 Winning and Losing Alliances on 162 Roll Call Votes in the National Council, 1991–1994

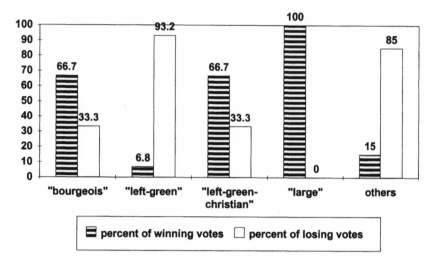

The third most frequent alliance type is formed by the Social Democrats, the Green Party, and the Christian Democrats (and optionally, other nongovernmental party groups). This type of voting alliance has been as successful as the "bourgeois alliance," winning 66.7% of its roll call votes in 1991–94. Among the "bourgeois" governmental parties, then, the Christian Democrats not only have the smallest index of party cohesion but also vote to a considerable extent with the Social Democrat/Green minority, thus enabling the "eternal losers" to gain a majority in two-thirds of the 45 roll call votes where they are voting in an alliance. For future research, it will be fruitful to link these findings to the policy dimensions of the bills in order to sort out the topics on which these three party groups form voting alliances (see below).

A Further Research Question: Committees as Competitors to Party Groups?

Parliamentarians are not only members of party groups but also members of legislative committees. From an institutional point of view, one could question, therefore, if committee membership is also important for voting behavior. To date, there has been no research on this question in Switzerland, although it can be found in U.S. studies (see below).

The U.S. Research: Party Government versus Committee Government

The alleged weakness of parties in Congress is a dominant theme in U.S. research (see Cox and McCubbins 1991). The assumption of decline and weakness of congressional parties has gone hand in hand with studies of the rising power of committees. Some scholars speak of committees as autonomous units, which operate quite independently of such external influences as legislative party leaders, chamber majorities, and the president (e.g., Fenno 1973). Gary Cox and Mathew McCubbins (1993) have analyzed the relations between parties and committees, arguing that parties are more important than was maintained in previous studies. They underpin this with considerable empirical tests—for example, on the influence of parties over the appointments to committees or on the representativeness of a party's committee contingents. Of interest to us are their findings about the difference between the voting behavior of a party's committee contingent and the voting behavior of the rest of the party on committee-specific roll calls. They use a method that would seem interesting for future Swiss research. By considering the example of the Agriculture Committee, they explain their procedure as follows: "As it turns out, a total of twenty-three roll-calls pertinent to bills were reported out by the Agriculture Committee in the Ninety-eighth Congress. . . . First, for each of the twenty-three roll-calls we compute the difference between the proportion of the contingent voting yes and the proportion of the rest of the party voting yes. Second we take the absolute value of each of these twenty-three differences and average them. This approach yields a straightforward statistic, the mean absolute difference (MAD). . . . If MAD is zero, then the contingent and the rest of the party never differed . . . ; as MAD grows larger, the contingent appears more and more distinctive in its behavior vis-à-vis the rest of the party" (Cox and McCubbins 1993, 220).

The authors computed MAD scores for the Democrats' committee contingents to be between 2.3% and 17.9%, with most of the committee contingents clustering in the range of 7 to 13% (Cox and McCubbins 1993, 222–23). They use the difference between the contingent's voting behavior and the voting behavior of the respective party as a test for the representativeness of committees. At the same time, they point out some problems in using MAD this way, since members of Congress may also vote not according to their preferences, but strategically: "To what extent do differences between how committee contingents and their party colleagues vote reflect logrolling within committees rather than distinct preferences?" (223).

This methodological problem is not relevant in our case, since our primary concern is not the representativeness of committees but the potential impact of committee membership on floor voting behavior. Our question is: Are there any differences in the voting behavior between members of the committee who prepared the bill and their party colleagues? For this purpose, MAD seems to be a useful measure. If MAD is zero, committee membership is assumed to be of no importance for floor voting; as MAD grows larger, committee membership may be expected to be another explanatory variable for voting behavior.

Contingent versus Party Behavior in the Swiss National Council: First Empirical Results

At the beginning of 1992, a system of 12 standing committees was introduced in both chambers of the Swiss parliament. Each committee is responsible for a specific policy field. Before the 1992 reform, most of the important bills were treated by ad hoc committees, which were then dissolved when the bill had been passed in both chambers. Since the system of standing committees of the Swiss parliament is only two years old, one may describe it as being less institutionalized than the U.S. House of Representatives, which has been described as "the most institutionalized in the world" (Shaw 1990, 258). According to Shaw, the level of institutionalization of a committee system is a significant factor among others in the importance of the committees in a legislature. Furthermore, the more important committees there are, the more committee membership may compete with party membership: that is, the more committee members are assumed to vote differently from their party colleagues. Following this, it may be expected that even if members of committees in the National Council vote differently from their party colleagues on committee-specific roll calls, these differences will be lower than in the U.S. case.

In an exploratory test, we calculated MAD—as Cox and McCubbins have done for the Democratic Party and its committee contingents in

Table 5.4

Mean Absolute Difference (MAD) in Percentage Voting "Yes" between Committee and Noncommittee Members, 1992–1994

Committee	MAD (%)	Roll Calls (N)
Christian Democrats		
SGK (social security and welfare)	15.9	17
WAK (economy and tax)	12.9	23
RK (legal issues)	8.5	24
SPK (political institutions)	9.6	15
APK (foreign affairs)	1.6	7
UREK (environment and energy)	10.6	7
Radicals		
SGK (social security and welfare)	4.9	17
WAK (economy and tax)	9.1	23
RK (legal issues)	8.7	24
SIK (military security)	11.4	9
Social Democrats		
SPK (political institutions)	2.6	15
FK (finance committee)	3.7	34

Congress—for the three major parties and some of their committee contingents in the Swiss National Council in the period 1992–94. Some caveats are in order. First, the committee contingents—even the ones from the three largest parties—are much smaller than their respective parties. Four to six members form a committee contingent. So the percentage voting "yes" may change considerably if only one member of the contingent deviates. Second, the number of roll call votes pertaining to bills reported out by the committees in the three years considered is also rather small; the committees we analyzed reported out 7 to 34 bills during this period. Furthermore, we have taken into account only the contingents whose composition did not change in the course of the three years considered.

As table 5.4 indicates, our results do not differ significantly from those obtained by Cox and McCubbins. Thus, although the committee system of the Swiss National Council is not as institutionalized as that of the U.S. Congress, members of the committees considered do vote differently from their party colleagues. In particular, in a few cases we found rather high differences between committee members' voting behavior and the behavior of the other members of the party group. However, table 5.4 does reveal differences between the party groups considered. It is not surprising that the Christian Democrats, who have relatively low indexes of party cohesion, have a higher MAD score than the Social Democrats, who vote more cohesively (see table 5.2). Thus, we suggest that among the three governmental party groups considered, committees most likely constitute a competing factor for the Christian Democrat Party.

For the Social Democrats, we find that in most cases the committee contingent did not differ from the rest of the party. However, there were a few interesting cases in which a big difference actually did occur. It obviously happens sometimes that the committee contingent defends a solution achieved in committee even if the party group is against this solution. For example, on a vote over whether the prohibition of gambling should be abolished, the majority of Social Democrats voted against this for social reasons (people losing their money at gambling tables): only 14.3% of the noncommittee members voted for the abolition. On the other hand, 80% of the Social Democrat members of the Finance Committee, which had prepared the bill, voted in favor of this abolition (presumably because the owners of gambling tables would have to pay taxes according to the new bill, thereby increasing the state's revenue). This resulted in a MAD score of 65.7 for this roll call.

There are interesting cases found for other party groups too. Take, for example, a roll call vote on the purchase of army airplanes. The question was whether the state should make advance payments *before* the popular vote on the airplane purchase was held. The Radical members of the Committee of Military Security were all in favor of these advance payments because they wanted a quick purchase of the airplanes. More than half of the other members of the Radical Party, however, voted against these advance payments, with a resulting MAD score of 56 in this case.

Prospects for Further Research on Voting Behavior in the Swiss Parliament

This chapter has isolated three main findings. First, party cohesion on roll call votes in the Swiss National Council differs across the party groups, with the Social Democrats achieving higher scores than the three other government parties. Although there exist assumptions in the Swiss literature about an increase of party cohesion over time, we have found no empirical evidence of an overall trend toward increased party cohesion. Second, we have found that many different alliances occur on roll call votes in the National Council. In spite of what one may expect in view of the Swiss power-sharing system, voting alliances involving all government parties appeared only rarely in the period that we analyzed. The two most frequent alliances on roll call votes were "bourgeois alliances" (with the highest success rate) and "left-Green alliances" (with the lowest success rate). The third most frequent voting alliance was formed by the Social Democrats, the Green Party, and the Christian Democrats. These alliances were as successful as the "bourgeois alliance"; thus, the Christian Democrats may be described as "majority makers" in the National Council. Third, we have presented initial results on the assumed difference between the voting behavior of committee members and noncommittee members, showing that in some cases such differences do exist, as in the U.S. Congress, although the committee system of the Swiss parliament is not as institutionalized as that of the U.S. Congress.

In closing this chapter, we suggest two areas for future research: collective behavior and individual decision-making patterns.

With regard to collective behavior, first, it would be interesting to put the Swiss case into comparative perspective in order to test the theoretical assumption of intraparty cohesion being determined by the political system (parliamentary versus presidential system). Second, we suggest analyzing the course of interparty conflict from a longitudinal view: Is the thesis of a growing polarization in the Swiss National Council and the shifting of the traditional model of consensus democracy to politics of majorities (with rigid "bourgeois" majorities and Social Democrat/Green minorities) really supported by empirical evidence? Third, we propose taking into account the dimensional aspect, a focus on the policy areas affected: On which issues and under what circumstances do members of a party group vote cohesively, and when do they differ? Which alliances between the different party groups are formed, and for which issues? A fourth research question is the relation between parties and committees. On the one hand, it would be useful to collect more data in the coming years in order to have a better base for quantitative analysis; on the other hand, single case studies could lead to interesting results as well.

With regard to individual decision-making patterns, different factors that presumably affect the voting behavior of individual MPs will have to be empirically tested: party and committee membership, the constituency factor, membership in interest groups, gender, and—especially interesting in the Swiss context—regional and language factors. Do French- or Italian-speaking members of the Swiss National Council vote differently from German-speaking members? We suggest analyzing the relative influence of these different institutional and noninstitutional factors on legislative voting with multivariate regression in order to test different theories of individual voting behavior.

NOTES

We would like to thank Hans Hirter for putting the data he collected at our disposal and for helping us on various research problems.

1. For further insight into the workings of Swiss democracy, see Linder (1994).

2. Since the beginning of 1994, in addition to requested roll call votes, the following votes are also being recorded and published: voting on the whole of a bill (*Gesamtabstimmung*), final voting after both chambers have decided on a bill (*Schlussabstimmung*), and voting on bills to be treated as urgent. Consequently, the bulk of voting on particular parts of a bill, which is especially interesting in terms of analyzing the way in which voting alliances are formed (i.e., logrolling), is still not made wholly transparent.

3. The Constitution, article 91, states that the MPs vote without instructions.

4. This way of perceiving the parliamentary mandate is reflected in the results of a comparative study by Loewenberg and Mans (1988). On the basis of interviews held with MPs from 1975 to 1976, the authors find that Swiss MPs consider partisan loyalty as constraining their behavior.

5. On the basis of data from 1983 to 1988, Lüthi (1989) showed that the abstention rate was generally low (about 2%) and that the same party group that voted most cohesively also had the highest abstention rate.

6. Lüthi et al. (1991, 64) point out that the increased number of roll call votes may be an expression of a politically polarized situation; at the same time they emphasize that a lack of those votes in former periods does not automatically mean that there were not any conflicts between the parties at that time. They stress, however, the fact of the changed political meaning of roll call votes.

7. In 1994, 75 roll call votes were held in the National Council on request by at least 30 MPs, compared to 39 in 1993.

8. This reduction proved to be necessary, since parliamentary life is in fact marked by a wide variety of different alliances if one treats governmental and

nongovernmental parties equally. For the period in question (1991–94), 60 different voting alliances were counted.

REFERENCES

Collie, Melissa P. 1984. "Voting Behavior in Legislatures." *Legislative Studies Quarterly* 9: 3–50.

Cox, Gary W., and Mathew McCubbins. 1991. "On the Decline of Party Voting in Congress." *Legislative Studies Quarterly* 16: 547–70.

———. 1993. *Legislative Leviathan: Party Government in the House.* Berkeley: University of California Press.

Epstein, Leon D. 1980. *Political Parties in Western Democracies.* New Brunswick, NJ: Transaction Books.

Fenno, Richard F. 1973. *Congressmen in Committees.* Boston: Little, Brown.

Forschungszentrum für schweizerische Politik. 1985. *Année Politique Suisse 1984.* Bern: Universität Bern.

Hertig, Hans-Peter. 1980. *Partei, Wählerschaft oder Verband? Entscheidfaktoren im eidgenössischen Parlament.* Bern: Francke.

Lijphart, Arend. 1984. *Democracies: Patterns of Majoritarian and Consensus Government in Twenty-One Countries.* New Haven, CT: Yale University Press.

Linder, Wolf. 1988. *Politische Entscheidung und Gesetzesvollzug in der Schweiz.* Bern: Haupt.

———. 1994. *Swiss Democracy: Possible Solutions to Conflict in Multicultural Societies.* New York: St. Martin's Press.

Loewenberg, Gerhard, and Thomas C. Mans. 1988. "Individual and Structural Influences on the Perception of Legislative Norms in Three European Parliaments." *American Journal of Political Science* 32(1): 155–77.

Lüthi, Ruth. 1989. *Die Fraktionsdisziplin im eidgenössischen Parlament 1984–1988: Eine Analyse aufgrund von 76 Namensabstimmungen.* Bern: Seminararbeit im Nebenfach Politologie.

Lüthi, Ruth, Luzius Meyer, and Hans Hirter. 1991. "Fraktionsdisziplin und die Vertretung von Partikulärinteressen im Nationalrat." In Parlamentsdienste, ed., *Das Parlament: "Oberste Gewalt des Bundes"?* Bern: Haupt.

McCubbins, Mathew, and Terry Sullivan. 1987. *Congress: Structure and Policy.* Cambridge: Cambridge University Press.

Moe, Terry M., and Michael Caldwell. 1994. "The Institutional Foundations of Democratic Government: A Comparison of Presidential and Parliamentary Systems." *Journal of Institutional and Theoretical Economics* 1: 171–95.

Müller, Michael. 1994. *Zwischen Parteimeinung und Eigenveranwortung: Die Fraktionsdisziplin im bernischen Grossen Rat zwischen 1984 und 1991.* Bern: Seminararbeit im Nebenfach Politologie.

Ornstein, Norman J., Thomas E. Mann, and Michael J. Malbin. 1990. *Vital Statistics on Congress 1989–1990.* Washington, DC: Congressional Quarterly.

Rice, Stuart A. 1928. *Quantitative Methods in Politics.* New York: Knopf.

Rieselbach, Leroy N. 1990. "Institutional Factors, Legislative Behavior, and Congressional Policymaking: Developments in the 1980s." *Annual Review of Political Science* 3: 160–97.

Riklin, Alois. 1977. "Die Stellung des Parlaments im schweizerischen politischen System: Beitrag für den Schlussbericht der Studienkommission der Eidgenössischen Räte 'Zukunft des Parlaments'." *Forschungsstelle für Politikwissenschaft, Beiträge und Berichte,* No. 55. St. Gallen: Hochschule St. Gallen.

Searing, Donald D. 1991. "Roles, Rules, and Rationality in the New Institutionalism." *American Political Science Review* 4: 1239–60.

Shaw, Malcolm. 1990. "Committees in Legislatures." In Philip Norton, ed., *Legislatures.* London: Oxford University Press.

Steffani, Winfried. 1983. "Zur Unterscheidung parlamentarischer und präsidentieller Regierungssysteme." *Zeitschrift für Parlamentsfragen* 3: 390–401.

———. 1991. "Regierungsmehrheit und Opposition." In Winfried Steffani, ed., *Regierungsmehrheit und Opposition in den Staaten der EG,* 11–35. Opladen: Westdeutscher Verlag.

Steiner, Jürg. 1990. "Power-Sharing: Another Swiss 'Export-Product'?" In Joseph V. Montville, ed., *Conflict and Peacemaking in Multiethnic Societies.* Lexington, MA: Lexington Books.

Vasella, Marco. 1956. *Die Partei- und Fraktionsdisziplin als staatsrechtliches Problem.* Zurich: P. G. Keller.

Vatter, Adrian. 1994. *Eigennutz als Grundmaxime in der Politik?* Bern: Haupt.

———. 1997. "Parliament of Switzerland." In G. T. Kurian, ed., *World Encyclopedia of Parliaments and Legislatures.* New York: Congressional Quarterly Press.

Ward, Daniel S. 1993. "The Continuing Search for Party Influence in Congress: A View from the Committees." *Legislative Studies Quarterly* 18: 211–30.

6

Electoral Systems, Parliamentary Committees, and Party Discipline: The Norwegian Storting in a Comparative Perspective

BJØRN ERIK RASCH

Over the last two or three decades, a certain unrest has been observed at the voter level in several West European countries. This includes Norway (and the other Nordic countries), where the party loyalty of voters has become weaker, party identification has decreased, and volatility has increased (Lane et al. 1993). The reduced loyalties of voters do not seem to be mirrored at the level of legislative representatives (in the Storting). Parliamentary party groups in Scandinavia are known to act as highly cohesive and disciplined units of legislators. Fitzmaurice (1986, 274) even speaks of the "iron party discipline in parliament" in these countries. With respect to Norway, Laver and Schofield (1990, 237) state that political parties "function more as unitary actors than do those in most of the other West European systems."

This chapter comments on the Norwegian case and relates it to some more general hypotheses concerning party discipline. There is no reason to believe that unrest among voters should have a negative effect on party discipline in the legislative assembly; instead, I indicate other types of mechanisms—primarily centrifugal forces—of relevance in the parliamentary context. One of these is associated with the electoral system, potentially making the district, or constituency, highly significant to legislators' actions. The internal organization of the parliament and organizational features of the parliamentary parties are other sources of accounting for disciplined behavior. For instance, if parliamentary committees are prestigious and powerful, they may threaten the unity of the party groups or their ability to command the loyalty of their legislators.

It is relevant to consider several different mechanisms when trying to explain the degree of discipline of parliamentary party groups. Such mechanisms may not necessarily work in the same direction: some might be expected to weaken party discipline, others to strengthen it. To my knowledge no broad theory (or lawlike explanation) has yet been developed in this field to show how the various mechanisms are related and when they are, so to speak, switched on and off.

It seems reasonable to make a distinction, building on other authors, between party cohesion and party discipline (e.g., Ozbudun 1970; chap. 1 of this volume). Cohesion is regularly associated with a certain consensus in values and attitudes, or a clear "affinity" of preferences. Party discipline, of course, is related to cohesion but refers primarily to legislative behavior. Typically, a party is regarded as disciplined to the extent that its representatives vote in similar ways in the assembly. The reasons for uniformity in voting may be diverse: one possibility is that party members have similar preferences and values; another is that they abide by party decisions (the majority binds the minority) or follow the will of the party leadership.

The chapter starts, in the next section, with a rudimentary sketch of a rationale for parties, referring to the general effects of electoral systems and parliamentary organization on party discipline. The second section is devoted to the measurement of party discipline in Norway; roll call data still demonstrate a remarkable cohesiveness in legislative behavior (despite the electorate's becoming more and more fluid). In the third section I mention one type of strategic party voting found in legislatures that potentially reduces the pressure generated by the centrifugal mechanisms discussed earlier.

Mechanisms Affecting Party Discipline

A Rationale for Parties

In all modern parliaments the overwhelming majority of legislators belong to organized party groups. In most parliaments, the parties play an important role in selecting presiding officers, in allocating legislators to committees and to leadership positions within committees, and in shaping the agenda for consideration of bills and other measures.[1] Why are such organizations—which create hierarchical relations among formally equal representatives—established and maintained? A very general answer has been developed recently by rational choice theorists (see Cox and McCubbins 1993, 83–135, 1994; Kiewiet and McCubbins 1991, 22–38; Aldrich 1995; see also chap. 2 of this volume). The basic idea is that "parties are invented, structured, and restructured in order to solve a variety of collective dilemmas that legislators face" (Cox and McCubbins 1993, 83). There are three basic types of collective dilemma—free-rider problems, difficulties in achieving coordination, and the arbitrariness of social choice instability—and these dilemmas would prevail, easily leading to suboptimal outcomes, in a hypothetical, completely unorganized legislative setting.[2] The main task of legislators, of course, is to act as representatives of those who have elected them and to engage in processes of passing legislation by majority rule or some stronger requirement. The legislative task is collective in nature, and collective dilemmas will readily emerge. The same can be said with respect to the task of getting reelected in mass electorates; collective dilemmas are inherent in such situations and need to be solved in some way so as to avoid suboptimal outcomes.

In general, *central authority*—attained by the formation of attractive elective leadership positions—represents a solution to collective dilemmas.[3] Party groups are organized—that is, networks of principal-agent relationships are established, and authority is delegated from individual legislators to a central agent—in order to realize benefits of collective action as seen from the perspective of self-interested, individual legislators. The central agent will monitor compliance and try to prevent defection from group-regarding action. According to the theory of political entrepreneurship, central agents (in this context, the party leadership) have to possess three essential features to facilitate collective action: "(1) They bear the direct costs of *monitoring* the community faced with the collective dilemma; (2) they possess *selective incentives* (individually targetable punishments and rewards) with which to reward those whom they find cooperating or punish those whom they find 'defecting'; (3) they are *paid,* in various ways, for the valuable service they provide" (Cox and McCubbins 1993, 91).

Selective incentives in the parliamentary arena include such things as staff support, attractive committee (and rapporteur) assignments, and access to mass media as the spokesperson of the party on certain types of issues. The ideas that Cox and McCubbins use are also known from other institutional contexts, such as the Hobbesian view of the state as a means to overcome the "war of all against all" and the theory of the firm.

Most parliamentary parties in western Europe are institutionalized—for instance, in the sense that they have formal statutes. Typically, the parties favor majority rule on internal matters, although actual voting seldom takes place.[4] With respect to Norway, all parties but one—the right-wing Progress Party (FRP)—vote only on issues where internal disagreement has been strong. The Progress Party is the only one requiring a qualified majority (two-thirds of the votes) to bind the group members to a party line; all other parties may in principle tie up their legislators by simple majority.

Parliamentarism

Before turning to centrifugal forces, an important centripetal force often mentioned in scholarly debate should be outlined. Clearly, the constitutional system of a country may significantly affect legislative party discipline.[5] In particular, the relationship between the legislature and the executive—presidentialism versus parliamentarism—is a factor often discussed. In presidential systems the chief executive is elected directly by the people for a fixed term of office. The president typically commands a more or less circumscribed veto to guard against legislative trespass and is empowered to initiate legislation and to issue decrees (Shugart and Carey 1992). In parliamentary systems, on the other hand, the head of government and the ministers operate on the basis of confidence from the legislative branch. The majority of the legislative assembly has the power to form and, at any time, remove the government. The instrument of censure in the hands of parliamentary majorities is normally balanced by the government's right to dissolve parliament and arrange early elections.[6]

In parliamentary systems, two dimensions are relevant for each legislator on the occasions when votes are taken (except for motions of no confidence, which only involve one dimension): legislators vote to support or oppose some policy or bill (usually proposed by the government) and, at the same time, to support or oppose the present government (Huber 1992). At least on bills regarded as sufficiently important by the group controlling government offices, a vote against the governmental policy position would be equivalent to a vote against the government;

such action can contribute to replacing the government. The possibility that roll calls are easily transformed into a question of confidence in the government provides incentives for disciplined party voting. MPs of the governing party or coalition may contribute to the fall of their own government by voting contrary to the party line on a bill, thereby losing their share in the various benefits of executive power. They also risk being punished later, since reelection fortunes and parliamentary committee assignments may be at least partly controlled by party groups. Opposition parties may also have incentives to act unitarily in their struggle to try to win governmental office.

Sartori sums this up as follows: "Putting all in a nutshell, parliament-dependent government implies party-supported government; a support that in turn requires voting discipline along party lines" (Sartori 1994, 193). Undeniably, however, there is some variation within the parliamentary context: for instance, Japan and Italy have until recently been mentioned as countries with relatively fragmented dominant-party systems.

Preferences, Institutions, and Voting Behavior

Party discipline, as stated above, refers to congruence in voting behavior. Parliamentary voting behavior, furthermore, is always guided by formal rules and norms defining majority requirements, the right to table amendments, the order of voting, and so forth. A simple example shows that *institutional details of agendas and voting in parliaments may also be relevant to an understanding of party discipline.* Disciplined (and undisciplined) behavior may have subtle institutional sources and does not have to reflect underlying partisan preferences (the degree of cohesion) very directly. In this example, let us assume a one-dimensional policy space, as shown in figure 6.1. The legislators have Euclidean (or "Downsian") preferences, meaning that alternatives become less attractive as they move away from a legislator's ideal point and that a legislator is indifferent between proposals of equal distance from the ideal point. All MPs of party A have ideal points in the shaded area of the figure. Now, assume that a vote is taken between the bill B_1 and SQ (status quo, or no bill at all). Clearly, all legislators of party A will prefer B_1 to SQ and will vote as a unitary bloc in favor of this piece of legislation. The party is coherent, and voting is disciplined without any system of sanctions or any crack of a party whip. If we instead, for whatever reason,[7] assume that the MPs face a choice between B_2 and SQ, the behavioral implications are less straightforward. In one sense, party A

Figure 6.1 Distribution of Ideal Points in One Dimension

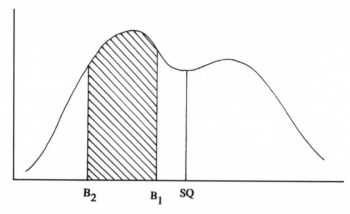

has to be *no less cohesive* this time, since *preferences are unchanged*. The altered location of the bill along the relevant policy dimension will, however, cause a division. Some of the MPs of party A will prefer B_2 to SQ, while some others will have the reverse preference. Unity in voting this time has to rest on some kind of enforcing mechanism (or long-term self-interest).

Centrifugal Forces: Electoral System and Committees

Electoral systems can be classified in various ways (e.g., Blais 1988; Taagepera and Shugart 1989, 19–37; Bowler and Farrell 1993). A major distinction is between systems based on single-member districts, systems based on multimember districts, and various combinations of both, as in Germany. Huge variations can be observed with respect to districts electing more than one legislator. Some countries operate with the entire nation as one district (Israel, Netherlands), while other countries are divided into relatively small districts electing only a handful of legislators in each. This variation can be shown by calculating the *district magnitude* of a system (i.e., the [average] number of seats in a district).[8] If district magnitude is (very) low (equal to 1 if all districts elect one MP each), we should expect party discipline in the parliament to be affected negatively. As district magnitude decreases, a real home district—and a distinct segment of district voters—becomes more and more clearly defined to the representative. A need to cultivate the district emerges, potentially leading the representative into conflicts with the party line.

A second, related, distinction concerns ballot structure, in particular whether the elector votes for *candidates* or for *party lists.* Typically, single-member districts use the former type of ballot, while both variants may be found in the multimember context. The existence of party lists means that someone has to arrange them. If the placement on party lists is centrally controlled or is controlled by the party branch of large regions, the representatives have an incentive to cultivate the party leadership. This may introduce an additional impediment to voting contrary to the party in Parliament and thus may affect party coherence positively. As such, it is not the list systems that generate this type of effect (e.g., if the local party is exclusively in charge of nominations in small constituencies); the essential question is who controls list access.

A third element separating electoral systems is their decision rule(s), or *electoral formulas.* As the literature shows, there is a vast range of formulas in single-member districts (e.g., plurality, alternative vote, second ballot) and multimember districts (e.g., quota methods, divisor methods, single transferable vote, single nontransferable vote). For my purpose, an important distinction is between "d'Hondt-like" (and more disproportional) rules applied regionally (i.e., not with the nation as a single district) and other, more proportional rules.[9] It is well known that the plurality formulas in single-member districts imply a system with two dominant parties.[10] D'Hondt-like approaches also may encourage the formation of alliances—or at least there are no incentives to party splits (a party would get fewer seats if it split into two parties). With respect to party discipline, we should expect parties operating under the more disproportional electoral formulas to be broader, more factionalized alliances (than parties operating under conditions of perfect proportionality and low thresholds of representation). Thus, the parliamentary parties—all else being equal—should be less disciplined entities.

Let us move to internal organization and suggest some possible linkages to party discipline. First, *staff* resources may be linked to individual legislators, to the parliamentary institution, or to each of the parties. If the staff are organized and controlled primarily by the parliamentary party groups, the level of party coherence will most likely be higher than in situations where these resources are affiliated to individuals or to the parliament. Second, committee members may serve on short-term contracts (ad hoc committees) or long-term contracts (standing committees). Stability in committee contracts and membership encourages the development of expertise. Over time, legislators learn to know certain policy fields quite well, and the information advantage may generate differences in opinion between the party representatives. Such differences of opinion also potentially affect party discipline. Third, legislators are allocated to committees in different ways. Three approaches are followed, often in combination: legislator "self-selection," allocation by the plenary of the parliament, or allocation by the parliamentary party groups themselves (at least on the decision of who should serve on what committee). The more central the role of the party in committee assignments, the stronger we should expect party discipline to be.

In this section we have looked at some general mechanisms likely to affect the behavior of parliamentary parties. Clearly, parliamentarism strengthens party discipline, compared to presidential forms of government. However, characteristics of the electoral system as well as the internal organization of the assembly might contribute to a weakening of party discipline.

Party Discipline in Norwegian Roll Call Voting

The Norwegian party system has exhibited some signs of turbulence in the last few decades. Two elections—in 1973 and 1993—have significantly reshaped the political landscape. As we can see from figure 6.2, the relative strength (in seats) of the various parliamentary parties has changed during the post–World War II period. Labor has lost seats, and the Liberals (Venstre) have been completely erased. In the 1970s new parties emerged on both the left and right. The Conservatives (Høyre) are no longer the clearly dominating force of the nonsocialist camp.

It is difficult to bypass the parties. Only once during the entire period since 1945 has an independent representative been elected to the parliament, in 1989. Fraction hopping has also been very rare. Two MPs moved from Labor to the Socialist Left (and one of them was reelected from the list of the new party). Some MPs have left the right-wing Progress Party to act as independents (one before the 1993 election and four after). Only one major party split has occurred: the Common Market issue caused the Liberal Party to split into two party groups (with eight and five representatives) in 1972.

Let us now move to the question of party discipline. There has been little analysis of party voting in the Storting. This is not surprising, first, because everyone (correctly) believes party discipline to be very high and, second, because until recently there have been no comprehensive

Figure 6.2 Distribution of Seats in the Norwegian Parliament (Storting), 1945–1997

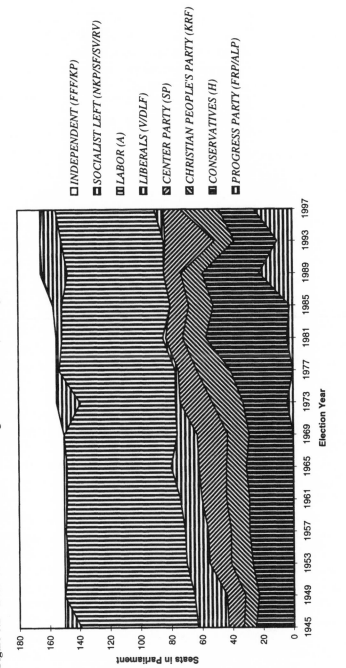

☐ INDEPENDENT (FFF/KP)
■ SOCIALIST LEFT (NKP/SF/SV/RV)
▥ LABOR (A)
■ LIBERALS (V/DLF)
▨ CENTER PARTY (SP)
▨ CHRISTIAN PEOPLE'S PARTY (KRF)
■ CONSERVATIVES (H)
■ PROGRESS PARTY (FRP/ALP)

sets of roll call data. At the outset it should be added that there is no obvious way to measure (intra)party cohesion or party discipline; several approaches have been suggested in the literature (e.g., Collie 1985; Brady, Cooper, and Hurley 1979). Here I present a range of different measures, but, as we shall see, they all lead to the same conclusion: highly disciplined parties.

One approach is to rely on an index, such as Stuart Rice's (1928) Index of Party Cohesion. For a given vote by a party i, the index is simply calculated as follows:

$$I_i = (\%_{YES} - \%_{NO})$$

The measure ranges from 0 (in the case of a party divided into two fractions of equal size) to 100 (in the case of complete party unity). The index is simple, and the results are fairly easy to interpret. Table 6.1 shows the Rice Index for all the main parties in the Storting and the Odelsting from 1979 to 1994 (a total of 11,393 roll calls).[11] The data include all ballots carried out electronically, which means that only unanimous or nearly unanimous votes are excluded from the data set. The actual index values range from 93.3 to 99.2 (both extremes are found in the agrarian Center Party, SP). There is no consistent pattern indicating more (or less) cohesive parties as a new election approaches. However, during the period covered, there has been a marked increase in the number of roll calls. This is due to the fact that opposition parties formulate amendments to government proposals more and more frequently.

On the basis of a relatively large number of roll calls in the Storting and the Odelsting, Bjurulf and Glans (1976) analyzed voting behavior in the period from 1969 to 1974. During these years there were governments of different size and party composition; the years cover the European Community referendum (1972) and the "earthquake" election of 1973. In other words, the political situation was one in which we might expect party unity to be put under considerable pressure. The voting pattern reported by Bjurulf and Glans was, however, unambiguous: in all parties the overwhelming majority of MPs voted the same way on most issues. One of the measures that the authors used in their analysis was the degree of individual, pairwise agreement in voting. For every pair of MPs it was calculated how often they voted the same way (yes-yes or no-no) before the representatives were grouped into parties and

Table 6.1

Intraparty Agreement in Storting and Odelsting Voting, 1979–1994: Main Parties, Election Results (Seats), and Rice's Index of Cohesion

Session	N Roll Calls	SV	A	SP	KRF	H	FRP
Election 1977		(2)	(76)	(12)	(22)	(41)	—
1979–80	285	98.9	98.2	96.9	93.4	96.8	—
1980–81	412	98.8	98.9	95.7	95.3	96.8	—
Election 1981		(4)	(66)	(11)	(15)	(53)	(4)
1981–82	293	98.7	95.8	93.3	94.6	97.5	96.2
1982–83	502	97.2	98.1	97.1	97.0	99.0	98.0
1983–84	375	98.4	97.9	98.1	97.4	99.0	98.2
1984–85	456	98.3	98.7	96.5	98.0	98.9	97.4
Election 1985		(6)	(71)	(12)	(16)	(50)	(2)
1985–86	449	98.0	98.3	98.9	98.0	98.3	98.2
1986–87	329	98.6	97.5	96.4	95.8	96.4	97.2
1987–88	549	98.7	98.3	96.8	94.4	97.3	98.6
1988–89	784	97.0	98.2	95.8	94.2	96.7	99.6
Election 1989		(17)	(63)	(11)	(14)	(37)	(22)
1989–90	1,315	98.3	98.9	99.2	98.7	98.4	98.6
1990–91	1,711	98.1	98.8	98.6	98.0	98.1	98.4
1991–92	1,459	98.0	98.4	97.2	98.1	98.0	98.1
1992–93	1,296	96.8	95.9	95.9	95.7	95.9	95.2
Election 1993		(13)	(67)	(32)	(13)	(28)	(10)
1993–94	1,178	98.3	99.2	98.1	97.4	98.1	94.1[a]

Source: Norwegian Social Science Data Service (NSD Bergen).

Note: SV = Socialist Left; A = Labour; SP = Centre Party; KRF = Christian People's Party; H = Conservatives (Høyre); FRP = Progress Party.

[a]Including those 4 representatives leaving the Progress Party (FRP) in April and May of 1994 to serve as independents (they formed their own parliamentary group).

averages taken. A summary of the results is shown in table 6.2. For most parties the internal agreement reached well above 90% over the entire time period. In general, there were no marked differences in party cohesion between the two largest parties, Labor and Conservatives.

A decade later, Shaffer (1991) found an equally high level of intraparty cohesiveness in the Storting. He studied the 1985–86 parliamentary session and found that "on approximately 84 percent of the Storting votes (336/402) analyzed in this research *every single representative* voted with his or her party. On the remaining measures, usually only

Table 6.2

Intraparty Agreement in Storting and Odelsting Roll Call Voting, 1969–1974

	A	V	KRF	SP	H	ALP	SV
1969–70	97	97	95	97	97	—	—
(N = 188)							
1970–71	98	97	97	99	99	—	—
(N = 114)							
1971–72	95	93	88	87	94	—	—
(N = 105)							
1972–73	94	80	93	93	94	—	—
(N = 166)							
1973–74	98	81	95	97	98	95	98
(N = 362)							

Source: Summary of table 2 in Bjurulf and Glans (1976, 239).

Note: See table 6.1.

Table 6.3

Contested Party Votes in the Storting, 1989–1993

	A	H	FRP	KRF	SP	SV
Size of party in % of seats	38.2	22.4	13.3	8.5	6.7	10.3
% contested party votes of all roll calls (N = 4,301)	13.8	10.5	6.6	6.6	4.3	5.8
Average no. of party members in minority on contested party votes	3	3	2	2	2	6

Source: Norwegian Social Science Data Service (NSD Bergen).

Notes: From the last parliamentary year 1992–93 of the election term, data include only the fall session (not spring 1993).

For acronyms, see table 6.1.

one or two members broke with party ranks. In fact, a minuscule 0.2% of all the *individual* votes cast on the 402 roll call votes broke with party position" (65).

Table 6.3 shows the extent of party unity in roll call voting, using data from recent parliamentary sessions. The data include all roll calls using the electronic voting device of the Storting (not the Odelsting), meaning that most unanimous decisions are excluded as well as some of the roll calls in which less than a handful of representatives opposed. A large portion of the data concerns budgets and appropriations; the

Table 6.4

Intraparty Agreement in Storting Voting, 1989–1993

	SV	*A*	*SP*	*KRF*	*H*	*FRP*
1989–93	98.5	99.0	99.1	98.7	98.4	98.8
($N = 4,301$)						

Source: Norwegian Social Science Data Service (NSD Bergen).

Notes: From the last parliamentary year 1992–93 of the election term, data include only the fall session (not spring 1993).

For acronyms, see table 6.1.

Odelsting and Lagting decisions on formal laws are not included. With respect to party cohesion, however, we should not expect systematic differences between the Storting and the Odelsting. Table 6.3 reveals, first, that on most roll calls the parties act as unitary actors. The fraction of roll calls where at least one representative breaks with party lines ranges from around 4% to almost 14%. The greatest number of divided votes is found in the largest party (Labor), whereas the smallest parties exhibit the fewest nonunitary votes. Second, the minorities voting contrary to party positions are very tiny (in absolute terms) in all parties. On average, only some two to six representatives constitute the party minority on divided votes, and the "largest" minorities are to be found in the Socialist Left Party (but it should be added that the party seldom splits—251 divided votes out of a total of 4,301). The overall impression is one of tight party discipline; the parties to a remarkable extent still act as unitary actors on the floor of the Storting.

The same message can be read from table 6.4, which uses the measure employed by Bjurulf and Glans (1976). Party voting is no less dominant today than two decades ago. There are some problems associated both with the roll call data and with the measures, however. First, all kinds of roll calls are mingled; the data set does not distinguish between unimportant or small issues and important or major issues. The really interesting question is the degree of party discipline on significant policy proposals. Second, if the parliament votes in a situation where three or more alternatives are formulated, voting proceeds in stages. Proposals are voted one by one in some predetermined order, and normally $n - 1$ ballots are needed if n alternatives exist (the successive voting procedure). In the data set, all ballots are treated the same way; it does not matter whether the vote concerns one proposal in a larger sequence of ballots or whether only one proposal is formulated to be voted up or down. Votes taken early in a larger sequence, typically on extreme proposals that nobody believes has any chance at all of adoption, are less interesting (or actually irrelevant) from our perspective. Third, the measures being used neglect abstention. In Storting voting, participation at the voting stage is mandatory in principle. Furthermore, it is not possible to express indifference by using blank votes (or by being present and refraining from voting); each and every MP should form preferences either for or against any proposal. From time to time, however, some legislators from a party may "disappear" just before votes are taken to avoid voting contrary to their conscience (e.g., avoiding the choice between "pest and cholera"), the party line, or the constituency.[12]

Strategic Party Splits

On what kind of issues is party discipline most likely to be relaxed? Two instances have been acknowledged as especially vulnerable to intraparty disagreement. First, on issues of regional interest, party-line voting from time to time breaks down. Such issues that may generate serious conflicts within all parties are the choices of sites for large public institutions and infrastructure, such as airports and roads, or even private ones, such as oil exploration bases, which require parliamentary permits. Here it might be accepted that coalitions would form across party lines. Second, on issues concerning the moral and ethical beliefs of the individual member (e.g., abortion), the individual members are often free to vote according to their conscience—particularly if they have already made their viewpoints known when nominated. In general, free votes normally involve matters of regional interest or individual conscience on issues cross-cutting the party lines and not threatening the standing of the government.[13]

Janda (1980, 123) mentions one type of factionalism that he calls *strategic* or *tactical:* "Members of political parties may agree on ideology and issues but disagree seriously on the strategy that the party ought to use in achieving its goal or perhaps on particular tactics that the party ought to follow within a given strategy." Disagreement in this case has a particular basis. One example probably is the left-wing activism seen in some Labor parties, where activists want to follow other (more radical) reform strategies than moderates, thereby reducing coherence in party behavior.[14]

I will point to a very different kind of *strategic* party division in voting and will use an incident from the Storting for illustrative pur-

Figure 6.3   Voting on Location of New Airport, the Storting, 1988

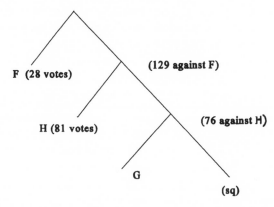

poses (Rasch 1990). In 1988 the Storting had to decide where in the Oslo area to locate a new main airport. Three solutions were discussed: (1) to build a completely new airport to the south of Oslo (at Hurum), (2) to upgrade an existing airport north of Oslo (at Gardermoen), and (3) to continue using the existing airports in the Oslo area in combination (Fornebu and Gardermoen; actually a formal status quo proposal). Let us call the proposals H, G and F, respectively. Communities in and around the capital of Oslo, of course, had very strong interests in the Storting decision and differed sharply with respect to the favored solution.[15] Disagreement among MPs from this area of the country did not follow party lines.

The Labor minority government in power proposed G as their alternative, and the government soon received support from most of the Labor MPs. However, the government needed additional votes to get its proposal adopted. As the vote approached, it seemed clear that a majority would support G—after the elimination of first F and then H. To the surprise of most MPs, H was adopted by a tiny majority *before* the assembly got the opportunity of voting on the governmental proposal G.

Figure 6.3 shows the results of voting, indicating that the government would have been supported by a majority if 14 of its 71 representatives had not voted in favor of proposal H (voted on earlier than G in the voting sequence).[16] In the case of H being voted down (as almost everyone expected), these Labor MPs would have voted *subsidiarily* in favor of G (as their second preference). Although the impact of the party split was rather dramatic for the government, none of the 14 MPs partly responsible for the governmental defeat seems to have been "punished" in any way after the vote. On the contrary, they all strengthened their position and reputation in their constituency and local party branch, and some of them later advanced to attractive positions in the Storting or on the committees.[17] Advancement is not possible without support from the parliamentary party leadership and majority.

The airport saga leads us to the following assertion: given the voting institution as outlined (the successive procedure), a free-rider strategy may be attractive to parliamentary parties if opinions diverge. The party may find it in its interest to let some MPs vote in favor of alternative proposals—important to their constituency, their local party, or some ideological segment—*before* the main proposal of the party is voted upon. The intention, of course, is not to contribute to the adoption of the alternative proposal; the party acts on the assumption that the alternative proposal has no real chance of getting through. In this way, deviant views are explicitly expressed, and the party line is at the same time supported—as either the first or second preference—by each legislator of the party. Thus, the party is able to serve both intense minorities in some constituencies and the majority views. The problem with this free-rider strategy is that it occasionally misfires: the alternative proposal, voted upon early, gets adopted (as in the airport case).

If the strategic approach to voting outlined above is used with some frequency to ease the pressure on issues where party preferences are divided, actual party discipline in Norway is most likely even higher than reported in the analysis of all roll calls.

Conclusion

Parties in the Norwegian parliament act in a highly disciplined fashion, as we have demonstrated by using recent roll call data and various measures of party coherence (the Rice Index and frequencies of pairwise agreement among legislators). Party discipline has increased rather than decreased in recent years. This is the reverse of the tendencies observed in the electorate: voters have become more fluid and "disloyal," while party loyalty among MPs seems to be stronger than ever.

The fact that parties are extremely disciplined in Norway will come as no surprise to any observer. The more difficult—and more interesting—question is to explain why behavior is uniform. In this chapter I have only hinted at some mechanisms assumed to be relevant if we want to account for variation in party discipline. Parliamentarism will tend to make parties more disciplined, whereas candidate-centered electoral systems and strong parliamentary committees work in the opposite direction. The measurement of party discipline is still quite inaccurate, as voting rules (e.g., order of voting effects) and voter strategies (e.g., strategic party splits) are not taken into consideration.

NOTES

This chapter is based partially on data provided by the Norwegian Social Science Data Service (NSD).

1. Several of the chapters in Döring (1995) stress the importance of parties.

2. More formally, Cox and McCubbins (1993, 87) define a collective dilemma as a situation "that can be modeled by a game possessing Pareto-inefficient Nash equilibria."

3. Cox and McCubbins (1993, 90) illustrate the idea of central authority by an example of Chinese riverboat pullers. This is the collective dilemma: "In prerevolutionary China large gangs of men would tug fair-sized boats up Yangtze. The problem was that each man was tempted to slack off a bit. After all, if enough others were pulling, the boat would still progress; if too few others were pulling, it did not matter how hard one pulled anyway." As a solution to the free-rider problem, the workers agreed to hire someone to whip them. This ensured that everyone pulled.

4. Based on unpublished information about voting in West European parties, collected as part of a research project led by Professor Herbert Döring at the University of Potsdam (see Döring 1995).

5. See the discussion in Ozbudun (1970), which deals with federalism and parliamentarism. The author convincingly argues that federalism is not able to explain why some countries have undisciplined parties.

6. Although such a balance of threats is found in most parliamentary systems, the actual decision rules involved vary considerably. See Strøm (1994) and Strøm and Swindle (1995) on regulations concerning dissolution of parliaments and De Winter (1995) and Bergman (1995) on decision rules regulating government formation and removal. See also Rasch (1995).

7. For instance, there could be a party with members' ideal points to the left of B_2. A proposal B_2 from this party will do better than any other proposals to the left, and such a proposal may also be tabled simply because it may generate problems for the legislators belonging to the competing party, A.

8. District magnitude is not easily calculated for all countries because the electoral system may contain different "levels" of representatives. For instance, in some countries a pool of additional or compensatory seats is allocated nationally (8 out of 165 seats in Norway, 39 out of 349 in Sweden, 40 out of 179 in Denmark, at least 58 out of 386 in Hungary, 328 out of 656 in Germany, etc.).

9. It is possible to reformulate the d'Hondt divisors in terms of a quota (or actually an interval). This quota will always be close to the Droop and Hagenbach-Bishoff quotas, implying equivalence between these electoral approaches. Furthermore, Cox (1991) has shown that, under certain assumptions, applying the plurality rule in multimember districts (i.e., the single nontransferable vote) gives results similar to the d'Hondt method. I refer to regional d'Hondt or stronger formulas because d'Hondt applied nationally may function quite proportionally.

10. See Duverger's law. Behind the consolidation into two broad parties is a "mechanical effect" (nonlinear relationship between seats and votes, harming small parties) and a "psychological factor" (voters do not want to waste their vote and therefore vote strategically for one of the two top runners). See Riker (1982).

11. The Storting is elected as a single body but divides into two chambers—the Odelsting (lower chamber with three-fourths of the MPs) and the Lagting (upper chamber with one-fourth of the MPs)—when passing (nonfinancial) legislation. Bills need acceptance by both chambers. The party composition of the Storting and the Odelsting (and Lagting) has been (almost) identical. (The allocation of members to the Lagting is controlled by the Storting majority; members not appointed to the Lagting belong to the Odelsting.)

12. Although against the letter of the parliamentary rules of procedure, this practice is not normally viewed as illegitimate (as long as the assembly is quorate and outcomes are not changed). It has, however, happened that government proposals have been defeated because more than one representative, not aware of each other's preferences and intentions, have left the plenary hall through different doors just before voting.

13. This is not very different from what we find in other parliamentary democracies. For the British case, see Mughan and Scully (1995).

14. See, for example, Tsebelis (1990) on the approach of British Labour Party activists.

15. Some wanted the airport in their district because it would reduce unemployment and strengthen the economy of the affected municipalities. Others opposed an airport in their neighborhood because of noise and pollution.

16. If at least three Labor MPs had not voted in favor of H, the government proposal would not have been defeated. In this sense, the party needed 3 out of the 14 nonparty votes. As the result of the vote came as a surprise, the Labor Party did not know in advance that more votes were required to win.

17. One of the 14, Tom Thoresen, was in fact elected as leader of the parliamentary party group in the fall of 1996.

REFERENCES

Aldrich, J. H. 1995. *Why Parties? The Origin and Transformation of Party Politics in America.* Chicago: University of Chicago Press.

Bergman, T. 1995. *Constitutional Rules and Party Goals in Coalition Formation. An Analysis of Winning Minority Governments in Sweden.* Research Report No. 1. Umeå, Sweden: Umeå University.

Bjurulf, B., and I. Glans. 1976. "Från tvåblockssystem till fraktionalisering: Partigruppers och ledamöters röstning i norska stortinget 1969–1974." *Statsvetenskaplig Tidskrift* 79: 231–53.

Blais, A. 1988. "The Classification of Electoral Systems." *European Journal of Political Research* 16: 99–110.

Bowler, S., and D. M. Farrell. 1993. "Legislator Shirking and Voter Monitoring: Impacts of European Parliament Electoral Systems upon Legislator-Voter Relationships." *Journal of Common Market Studies* 31: 45–69.

Brady, David, Joseph Cooper, and Patricia A. Hurley. 1979. "The Decline of Party in the U.S. House of Representatives, 1887–1968." *Legislative Studies Quarterly* 4: 381–408.

Collie, Melissa P. 1985. "Voting Behavior in Legislatures." In Gerhard Loewenberg, Samuel C. Patterson, and Malcolm E. Jewell, eds., *Handbook of Legislative Research.* Cambridge, MA: Harvard University Press.

Cox, G. W. 1991. "SNTV and d'Hondt Are 'Equivalent.'" *Electoral Studies* 10: 118–32.

Cox, G. W., and M. D. McCubbins. 1993. *Legislative Leviathan: Party Government in the House.* Berkeley: University of California Press.

———. 1994. "Bonding, Structure, and the Stability of Political Parties: Party Government in the House." *Legislative Studies Quarterly* 19: 215–31.

De Winter, L. 1995. "The Role of Parliament in the Formation and Resignation of Governments in Western Europe." In H. Döring, ed., *Parliaments and Majority Rule in Western Europe.* New York: St. Martin's Press.

Döring, H., ed. 1995. *Parliaments and Majority Rule in Western Europe.* New York: St. Martin's Press.

Fitzmaurice, J. 1986. "Coalitional Theory and Practice in Scandinavia." In G. Pridham, ed., *Coalitional Behaviour in Theory and Practice: An Inductive Model for Western Europe.* Cambridge: Cambridge University Press.

Huber, J. 1992. "Restrictive Legislative Procedures in France and the United States." *American Political Science Review* 86: 675–87.

Janda, K. 1980. *Political Parties: A Cross-National Survey.* New York: Free Press.

Kiewiet, D. R., and M. D. McCubbins. 1991. *The Logic of Delegation: Congressional Parties and the Appropriations Process.* Chicago: University of Chicago Press.

Lane, J. E., T. Martikainen, P. Svensson, G. Vogt, and H. Valen. 1993. "Scandinavian Exceptionalism Reconsidered." *Journal of Theoretical Politics* 5: 195–230.

Laver, Michael, and Norman Schofield. 1990. *Multiparty Government: The Politics of Coalition in Europe.* London: Oxford University Press.

Mughan, A., and R. M. Scully. 1995. "Explaining Parliamentary Change: Free Votes in the British House of Commons." Paper presented at the 53rd Annual Meeting of the Midwest Political Science Association, Chicago, April 6–8.

Ozbudun, E. 1970. *Party Cohesion in Western Democracies: A Causal Analysis.* Beverly Hills, CA: Sage.

Rasch, B. E. 1990. "Lokket av Pandoras krukke: En voteringsteoretisk analyse av Stortingets Hurum-vedtak." In Knut Midgaard, ed., *Oppstyr og styring rundt flypass: Hurum, Fornebu, Gardermoen?* Oslo: Dreyer.

———. 1995. "Parliamentary Voting Procedures." In H. Döring, ed., *Parliaments and Majority Rule in Western Europe.* New York: St. Martin's Press.

Rice, Stuart A. 1928. *Quantitative Methods in Politics.* New York: Knopf.

Riker, W. H. 1982. "The Two-Party System and Duverger's Law: An Essay on the History of Political Science." *American Political Science Review* 76: 753–66.

Sartori, G. 1994. *Comparative Constitutional Engineering: An Inquiry into Structures, Incentives and Outcomes.* New York: Macmillan.

Shaffer, William R. 1991. "Interparty Spatial Relationships in Norwegian Storting Roll Call Votes." *Scandinavian Political Studies* 14: 59–83.

Shugart, M. S., and J. M. Carey 1992. *Presidents and Assemblies: Constitutional Design and Electoral Dynamics.* Cambridge: Cambridge University Press.

Strøm, K. 1994. "Oppløsningsrett og parlamentarisme: Et internasjonalt perspektiv." In B. E. Rasch and K. Midgaard, eds., *Representativt demokrati: Spilleregler under debatt.* Oslo: Universitetsforlaget.

Strøm, K., and S. Swindle. 1995. "Political Parties, Agenda Control, and the Electoral Incumbency Effect." Paper presented at the 53rd Annual Meeting of the Midwest Political Science Association, Chicago, April 6–8.

Taagepera, R., and M. S. Shugart. 1989. *Seats and Votes: The Effects and Determinants of Electoral Systems.* New Haven, CT: Yale University Press.

Tsebelis, G. 1990. *Nested Games: Rational Choice in Comparative Politics.* Berkeley: University of California Press.

7

Parliamentary Party Discipline in Spain

Manuel Sánchez de Dios

Spain provides an example of a new democracy based on well-structured and disciplined parties, where party stability is directly related to party discipline and to the control of party leaders. Spanish parties are essentially parliamentary parties. This is not only because, as elsewhere, the parliamentary group dominates the whole organization but also because, as in the United States, party membership is not significant. Compared to elsewhere in western Europe, Spanish parties have exceptionally small memberships (Gallagher, Laver, and Mair 1995, 247).

As a new democracy, the Spanish case fits Attila Ágh's thesis of "party parliamentarization" (chap. 8 of this volume): the parliamentary group has been the basis of party institutionalization. This process was stimulated in Spain by an initial "consensus" among the groups that provoked the transition to democracy in the 1970s: it has also been facilitated by the constitutional structure of the system. In Spain the process of party parliamentarization implies that a group of leaders take control over the whole party, imposing strong discipline by means of organizational rules and by deciding on who the party's candidates will be. In essence, the parties that have been created in Spain are parties of government.

After 20 years of democratic government, however, we can differentiate two periods in the Spanish party system. The first period, before 1982 (see table 7.1), is consistent with Laver and Shepsle's notion of parties emerging from "the primeval slime" (chap. 2 of this volume). Here we see various groups and factions ceding strategic autonomy in

Table 7.1

Spanish Parliamentary Parties, Number of Legislature Seats, 1977–1996

	C[a] 1977	I 1979	II 1982	III 1986	IV 1989	V 1993	VI 1996
N	350	350	350	350	350	350	350
Popular[b]	16	9	106	73	107	141	156
Centrista	165	168	12				
CDS				19	14		
Socialista	105	98	202	184	175	159	141
Soc. de Cat.	13	17					
Soc. Vasc.		6					
M. Cat.	11	8	12	18	18	17	16
Vasco	8	7	8	6	5	5	5
Comunista/IU[c]	20	23			17	18	21
Andalucista		5					
C. Can.						4	4
Mixed: Agrupaciones				39[g]			
Mixed: Rest	12[d]	9[e]	10[f]	11[h]	14[i]	6[j]	7[k]

Sources: Memorias de Legislatura; data from the Archives of the Congreso de los Diputados.

Note: See chapter appendix for key to party acronyms.

[a]Constituent assembly. The subsequent legislatures are indicated by roman numerals.
[b]AP in 1977, CD in 1979.
[c]Communists from 1977 to 1982; IU from 1986 to 1996.
[d]PSP (6), UDC (2), ERC (1), EE (1), P. Arg. (1), I. Cast. (1).
[e]UN (1), HB (3), ERC (1), EE (1), PAR (1), UPN (1), UPC (1).
[f]CDS (2), PCE (4), HB (2), ERC (1), EE (1).
[g]Dem. Crist. (21), P. Liberal (11), IU (7).
[h]HB (5), EE (2), PAR (1), AIC (1), CG (1), UV (1).
[i]HB (4), P. And. (2), UV (2), EA (2), EE (2), PAR (1), AIC (1).
[j]HB (2), ERC (1), PAR (1), EA (1), UV (1).
[k]HB (2), BNG (2), ERC (1), EA (1), UV (1).

the expectation of generating a disciplined party of government. An example of this is provided by the centrist party, UCD, which was little more than a coalition of leaders that finally dissolved. A further example is provided by the socialist party, PSOE, which won the 1982 election by a huge majority. Its electoral success was based on the fact that a group of leaders had taken control of the party. At this early stage in Spanish electoral politics, we also see the formation of a coalition of groups under the banner of the Popular Party (PP).

According to Cotarelo (1992, ix), the next phase in the development of the party system was marked by the consolidation of Spanish democracy after 1979. By 1982 the party system was structured around two basic dichotomies, right-left and center-periphery. Only when the Popular Party was refounded in 1990 and when new leaders took control of the party was the dilemma resolved about which center-right group was going to direct the conservative forces. The situation was even more clear after the 1996 election, which saw the alternation in power between the PSOE and the PP. Nowadays Spanish parties are very well differentiated by their programs, by their leadership group, and by their MPs: they have clearly left the "primeval slime."

The Spanish case can be considered also from the viewpoint of parliamentary government, which places stress on party discipline as one of its basic principles, particularly in Europe. Stable governments are those supported by a disciplined majority of a strong party or a coalition, and only a homogeneous and unified opposition can aspire to take control of the government.

Sometimes party discipline is imposed; at other times it is due to group cohesion. What is clear in all cases is that the practice of European parliamentary democracy is based on the existence of large and disciplined voting blocs. As a matter of fact, when we compare European parties with their U.S. counterparts, we see that their voters tend to vote for parties rather than for individual candidates and that individual parliamentarians think of themselves first and foremost as members of their party's parliamentary group (Gallagher et al. 1995, 52).

The Spanish case is entirely consistent with the European pattern of parliamentary government: the government is responsible to the legislature, and both the government and the parliament are dominated by parties. The party in government is supported by its parliamentarians on all issues, while the MPs of the different opposition groups support their party lines when voting in Parliament. Party discipline is a clear feature of Spanish parties.

Although on first impression Spain appears as a consensual system because of its written constitution, multiparty system, proportional representation electoral system, bicameralism, and regional autonomy, if we pay closer attention to how some of these characteristics operate, it is clear that things are not so straightforward. First, there is the "rationalization" of the system giving the prime minister power over the government.[1] Second, there is the weakness of the senate, which has no say in electing the prime minister and cannot place a vote of no confidence against the executive. Third, as the most important feature, there is the electoral system, which, although formally proportional, has some modifications that make it close to the majoritarian rule: notably, small electoral districts and the d'Hondt rule for dividing seats among parties. In consequence, the electoral system works in favor of having a small number of big and polarized parties, against multipartyism, and in favor of strengthening the power of ruling party leaders and party discipline at the highest level.

This chapter seeks to explain how party discipline works in the Spanish parliamentary system. Due to the secondary position of the senate— its representative function is quite similar to that of the chamber (*Congreso de los Diputados*)—the focus in on discipline in the parliamentary parties of the *Congreso*. The chapter starts, in the first section, with a consideration of constitutional rules, with particular reference to electoral and financial rules. I examine how these strengthen parties and the party leaders. Additionally I analyze turnover as an indicator of the degree of party discipline. Next, I consider the effects of parliamentary standing orders on the parliamentary party system, observing how these affect the structure and activity of groups, as well as the mobility of MPs between groups. The last section assesses party discipline from the point of view of the internal organization of groups, looking at mass and parliamentary group statutes and at disciplinary procedures.

The Constitutional Formula

Although parliamentary parties are fundamental actors in the system, the Spanish 1978 Constitution has only the briefest of references to them, in article 78.1, which states that parliamentary groups have to send representatives to the *Diputación Permanente,* a constitutional organ in charge of the Congreso's powers when it is not in session. But if the Constitution does not pay attention to parliamentary groups, it does affirm clearly that parties have a powerful role in the system. Article 6 states that parties are "fundamental instruments for political participation."

On the other hand, the Constitution ensures the freedom of MPs from being mandated (art. 67.2), and it states that MPs cannot delegate their vote to anyone (art. 79.3), since it is personal. In theory, at least, both these rules enable MPs to break party discipline without losing their seats. However, as we shall see, the practice of party discipline overrides this freedom, and one can talk of a pseudoimperative mandate of parties over MPs.

In Spain the main source of party power is the electoral system, regulated for the Congreso by the Constitution (art. 68), which establishes proportional representation based on closed party lists.[2] Moreover, the use of the d'Hondt formula,[3] together with small districts, has some extremely distorting effects that benefit the two major national parties (socialists and centrists or conservatives), as well as the Basque and Catalan minorities, which are the largest parties in their regions. These majority elements work against small parties and any splinters from the big ones. The electoral rules also enforce the power of party leaders because it is the leaders who determine the lists. This is the main source of party discipline: MPs wanting to be placed high on the electoral lists must accept the instructions and proposals set by the leadership.

As elsewhere in Europe, there are no American-style primaries, though in contrast to many of the older European parties, the leadership group of each Spanish party has a dominant role in candidate selection. More precisely, in the PP there is a national electoral committee, linked to the national executive committee of the party, that must approve the electoral lists for the *Cortes Generales*. In the PSOE there is a "committee on lists," elected by the party's federal committee, that controls the content of electoral lists. In the left coalition, IU (United Left), the federal political council approves the lists proposed by each federation. The same practice occurs in the Basque nationalist party, PNV, where the national executive organ (*Euzkadi Buru Batzar*) proposes the parliamentary list to the national assembly of the party.

In addition to the electoral rules, party leadership is also strengthened by the 1987 law on party finance.[4] Much as elsewhere in Europe, the bulk of Spanish party revenue comes from the public budget—about 80%—and goes directly to party headquarters (del Castillo 1990, 86). For this reason individual parliamentarians cannot oppose party leaders if they want to be economically protected by the party—for example, when financing electoral campaigns.

Parliamentary Party Turnover

When we take into account the effects of the electoral system on party structure, parliamentary turnover can be seen as a good measure of party discipline: the stronger the party discipline, the more stable the parliamentary representation, and vice versa. In this analysis, a "normal" rate of turnover is taken to mean that 70% of MPs (of a given group) from the previous parliament remain in office. This is the case for the PP in 1996 (68%) and the PSOE in 1993 (72%) and 1989 (74%). Whenever a parliamentary group's size grows after an election, the "normal" rate can be calculated on the basis of that proportion of MPs who were also members of the previous parliament. This is the case for PSOE in 1982 (85 of 121), PP in 1993 (74 of 107) and 1996 (107 of 141), and CIU (Catalan nationalist party) in 1986 (8 of 12) (see table 7.2).[5]

The PSOE and CIU are the most stable during the period (table 7.1).

Table 7.2

Parliamentary Turnover in Spanish Parties

AP-CD-CP-PP* (Conservative)	1977	1979	1982	1986	1989	1993	1996
1996	9	11	14	25	59	107	**157**
1993	16	18	22	45	74	**141**	68% (76%)
1989	17	16	26	57	**107**	74% (70%)	38%
1986	16	15	40	**105**	54%	32%	16%
1982	13	18	**106**	38%	25%	16%	9%
1979	4	**9**	17%	14%	15%	13%	7%
1977	**16**	44%	12%	15%	16%	11%	6%

Note: The table should be read as follows: Of the 157 MPs in 1996, 107 (or 68%) of them were MPs in 1993, 59 (or 38%) in 1989, and so on. The percentage figures in brackets show the reverse: i.e., 76% of MPs in 1993 remained in the parliament in 1996.
*AP in 1977, CD in 1979, CP in 1982 and 1986, PP from 1989.

UCD-CDS* (Liberal)	1977	1979	1982	1986	1989
1989	2	1	4	11	**14**
1986	2	4	2	**19**	79%
1982	8	10	**14**	11%	29%
1979	92	**168**	71%	21%	7%
1977	**165**	55%	57%	11%	14%

Note: The table should be read as follows: Of the 14 MPs in 1989, 11 (or 79%) of them were MPs in 1986, 4 (or 29%) in 1989, and so on.
*UCD in 1977, 1979, and 1982; CDS in 1982 to 1989.

PSOE (Socialist)	1977	1979	1982	1986	1989	1993	1996
1996	14	22	42	49	59	78	**141**
1993	26	40	76	95	114	**159**	55%
1989	34	49	102	129	**175**	72%	42%
1986	39	62	128	**184**	74%	60%	35%
1982	52	85	**202**	70%	58%	48%	30%
1979	75	**121**	42% (70%)	34%	28%	25%	16%
1977	**118**	62% (64%)	26%	21%	19%	16%	10%

Note: The table should be read as follows: Of the 141 MPs in 1996, 78 (or 55%) of them were MPs in 1993, 59 (or 42%) in 1989, and so on. The percentage figures in brackets show the reverse: i.e., 70% of MPs in 1979 remained in the parliament in 1982.

Table 7.2

Parliamentary Turnover in Spanish Parties *continued*

PCE-IU* (Communist)	1977	1979	1982	1986	1989	1993	1996
1996	1	2	3	0	6	11	**21**
1993	0	0	0	3	9	**18**	52%
1989	1	2	1	4	**17**	50%	26%
1986	2	3	0	7	24%	17%	0
1982	2	4	**4**	0	6%	0	1%
1979	17	**23**	100%	43%	12%	0	1%
1977	**20**	74% (85%)	50%	29%	6%	0	1%

Note: The table should be read as follows: Of the 21 MPs in 1996, 11 (or 52%) of them were MPs in 1993, 6 (or 26%) in 1989, and so on. The percentage figures in brackets show the reverse, i.e., 70% of MPs in 1979 remained in the parliament in 1982.
*PCE from 1977 to 1982; IU from 1986 to 1996.

CIU (Nationalist)	1977	1979	1982	1986	1989	1993	1996
1996	0	2	2	5	5	8	**16**
1993	1	3	4	11	11	**17**	50%
1989	1	6	7	17	**18**	65%	31%
1986	2	6	8	**18**	94%	65%	31%
1982	2	7	**12**	44% (67%)	39%	24%	12%
1979	5	**8**	58%	33%	33%	18%	12%
1977	**11**	63%	17%	11%	6%	6%	0

Note: The table should be read as follows: Of the 16 MPs in 1996, 8 (or 50%) of them were MPs in 1993, 5 (or 31%) in 1989, and so on. The percentage figures in brackets show the reverse: i.e., 67% of MPs in 1982 remained in the parliament in 1986.

PNV (Nationalist)	1977	1979	1982	1986	1989	1993	1996
1996	0	0	0	2	2	3	**5**
1993	0	0	0	2	4	**5**	60%
1989	0	0	0	3	**5**	80%	40%
1986	0	1	2	**6**	60%	40%	40%
1982	2	2	**8**	33%	0	0	0
1979	6	**7**	25%	17%	0	0	0
1977	**8**	86%	25%	0	0	0	0

Sources: See table 7.1.
Notes: The table should be read as follows. Of the 5 MPs in 1996, 3 (or 60%) of them were MPs in 1993, 2 (or 40%) in 1989, and so on.

See chapter appendix for key to party acronyms.

PSOE stability can be explained by the fact that it was a ruling party until 1996. Before 1982, when the PSOE was in opposition, the party strengthened its centralism (and stability) in order to fulfill its aim of being a party of government. Around 1996 the PSOE faced a big crisis over problems of corruption and of a "dirty war" against terrorism while it was governing. (There was also a crisis of leadership.) The stability of CIU—which is a coalition of nationalist parties—is due to the fact that it has been a governing party in its home region.

The nationalist Basque party (PNV) was very stable until the mid-1980s. In the 1989 election it separated into two different groups, and since then it has remained stable. What also explains the stability of the PNV is that it has been the ruling party in the Basque region. (On many occasions high turnover in the nationalist parties is due to the fact that MPs consider it more important to take part in regional institutions than in the national parliament.)

The PCE (Communist party) was stable, reflecting its strong position in Parliament through to the early 1980s. But its successor, IU, has been in constant difficulty, changing its parliamentary leaders very frequently. IU was formed when the PCE was unsuccessful in 1982, the leftist vote having gone to the PSOE. After that election, the PCE (which had been the best organized opposition to Franco's dictatorship) was in crisis, and many of its leaders joined the PSOE ranks. In 1986 the Communists set up the coalition IU, and the PCE is still the main group in control of it. The regular changing of leadership by IU stopped in 1989 when an orthodox group took control of the PCE. Since then, IU's stability has consistently increased.

On the right there have been two groups (national parties) competing between each other not only—or even primarily—for votes but also for MPs. The UCD is a centrist party based on a coalition of "families" (factions) ranging from liberals to social democrats and including Christian democrats (Esteban and López 1982, 88). UCD won the first and second elections with a relative majority. Due to disputes among internal groups, the party faced a big crisis in 1981 when the resignation of the prime minister and party leader, A. Suarez, was followed by the departure of some of its parliamentary party members. The party disintegrated after big losses in the 1982 election. Suarez founded a new centrist liberal party, CDS, with the aim of being a possible government coalition partner. Despite becoming the third largest national party in 1986, its plan was unsuccessful, and CDS disappeared after 1993.

The conservative party, AP (*Alianza Popular*), was founded by Francoists. It was unsuccessful in the two first legislatures, even though some liberals joined it before the 1979 election. UCD's difficulties helped conservative party development, and in 1982 AP set up a new coalition, *Coalicion Popular* (CP), which had a very good electoral result. CP became the main opposition party and a potential governing party. Some of UCD's MPs joined this group, though the figure was not really that significant, only about 16% (table 7.2). The rate of centrist deputies going over to the conservative group remained about the same in the subsequent parliaments, as can be seen when we consider how many MPs of the conservative group of 1986 had been in Parliament in 1977 and 1979 (15% and 14% respectively).

From 1982 onward, CP has had a big turnover. In 1986 only 38% of its deputies had been in the 1982 parliament. In 1989 the proportion increased to 54%. Before the 1989 election, the party changed leadership and name—to the Popular Party (PP)—and began a process of power centralization. In 1990 it held a party congress of "refoundation and renovation," which resulted in the party becoming firmly under the control of a new group of young leaders. This explains the stability of the party in 1993, when it held onto 70% of its MPs from 1989. In 1996 the PP achieved a huge majority and became a governing party. (The rate of PP turnover was higher in 1996 than in 1993 because many of its MPs had gone to take part in many regional institutions.)

To sum up, in the Spanish case, being a party of government makes for a stable and disciplined party. At the same time a stable party involves the existence of a group of leaders who control candidate selection. Thus, the leadership is structured under an autocratic regime. Finally, a party turnover of about 30% in every election is the normal rate for a stable party of government.

Parliamentary Parties in the Standing Orders of the Congreso

The parliamentary parties are well defined and structured by the standing orders of the Congreso. That is as a result of the main role that parliamentary groups play.

The Parliamentary Party System from 1977 to 1996

MPs must be integrated in a parliamentary group from the beginning of the legislature, or from the first time that the MPs arrive in Parliament (at the beginning of the session) (art. 23). There is the so-called *grupo mixto,* formed of MPs who cannot form a group in their own right and have to act through this.

From 1982 onwards, when new standing orders were adopted, it was specified that forming a parliamentary group required at least 15 MPs, or 5 if the party (or coalition) obtained either 5% of the total vote at the national level or 15% in the electoral districts where the party (or coalition) presented candidates. As a result of this rule, not only must MPs be part of a group, but they must be part of a strong group.[6] Another rule is that MPs cannot form an alternative parliamentary group to the one that included them in its electoral list. A consequence of this is that the Spanish parliament must have one of the smallest and most stable number of parliamentary groups. Before 1982, the rules were more lax: parties needed just five MPs (with no minimum vote requirements) to form a parliamentary group. This was the case with the Andalusian Socialist Party (PSA) in 1979. At that time it was also possible to form separate parliamentary groups of deputies of the same party, as was the case with the Catalan and Basque socialists (table 7.1).

In 1986, when the number of deputies in the *grupo mixto* increased because of a crisis in *Coalicion Democrática,* the President of the Congreso permitted the formation of *agrupaciones* (small parliamentary groups) in the *grupo mixto.* Christian democrats and liberals abandoned the *grupo popular* and formed two *agrupaciones.* The communists, with 4.7% of the vote at national level, could not form a parliamentary group, so they also set up an *agrupacion.*

Party Discipline According to the Standing Orders of the Congreso

According to the standing orders, the Spanish parliament is a "parliament of groups." Parliamentary parties are the main agents of the Congreso: they form the *Junta de Portavoces* (council of party representatives in the chamber), which is in charge of organizing parliamentary work (distribution of time). They also decide on the composition of parliamentary committees, which is based on a quota that every group has according to size.

The most important point of the standing orders is that groups are considered as unified actors with only one voice, so when a parliamentary group acts through a representative, its vote is worth exactly the number of members of the group (*voto ponderado*). This means that the representative of a group (*portavoz* or whip) votes on behalf of the entire group of deputies (the vote weighted according to the size of the group) in every parliamentary commission or in the main organs of the Congreso. The power of parliamentary parties is even more impressive when we consider how MPs can act in the Congreso. For instance, in the legislative process, individual deputies can present total or partial amendments to legislative bills, but all amendments must be signed by the chief whip of the parliamentary party (*Portavoz del grupo*) (art. 110). Legislative proposals (*proposiciones de ley*) can be tabled both by groups or by MPs. However, legislative proposals of deputies must be signed by at least 15 MPs (art. 126.1). In this case it is clear that only if the group supports the proposal will it be debated.

In the case of checking on executive power, we also find a strong hold of the groups over MPs. Because in parliamentary debates the only speakers are the representatives of the parliamentary parties, motions that end in a debate are controlled by groups, as are interpellations (which can be tabled both by groups or members), since they can give rise to a debate. In addition, because each parliamentary party has a limited number of interpellations in each session, it is a responsibility of the group leaders to decide when to table an interpellation. Only questions are totally reserved to MPs (art. 185), but even here there is a limited number for each group that the leaders administer.

Clearly, deputies are so controlled by the groups that one can conclude, with López Aguilar (1988, 205), that the only scope for MPs to speak freely is in the so-called *turno por alusiones*. This is when in a debate an MP refers to another where this reference is not central to the debate. In this situation the MP who has been referred to has a right of reply without any intervention by the group.[7]

Finally, the standing orders establish that financial and personal resources are in the hands of groups, which are in charge of distributing them. The resources of each group are proportional to size. The result of all this is the weakness of the individual parliamentarian, who has little room for autonomous initiative.

Interparty Mobility

The standing orders of the Congreso regulate faction hopping in a restrictive way. An MP who wants to change his or her group must be accepted by the chief whip of the target group, and the MP can ask for a change of group only in the first five days of a parliamentary session; otherwise the deputy has to remain until the end of the session in the *grupo mixto.* In spite of the restrictive regulation, interparty move-ment in the Spanish Congreso has been relatively frequent, as table 7.3 shows.

According to Ágh (chap. 8 of this volume), "migrations among the factions" are characteristic of the new democracies. The Spanish case differs from eastern Europe, and particularly from Hungary, in that the parties have always been very homogenous internally. This Spanish sin-gularity is due, first, to the fact that from the outset, the process of democratization in Spain entailed the establishment of two main parties on the right-left spectrum and, second, to the fact that leadership com-petition has tended to take place more in the electoral arena than in the parliamentarian one.

At a very early stage, PSOE dominated the center-left. The center-right, however, was disputed between two groups, and it is here that faction hopping tended to predominate (Montero 1989, 505), though in fact, in the fourth and fifth legislatures there were no significant moves because the PP won the race among right-wing groups. In the constit-uent legislature (1977–79), there was a big move from the Popular So-cialist Party (PSP)—which was in the *grupo mixto*—to PSOE, but this could be considered a normal process of integration of socialists into a single party. However, abandonment of the centrist group in the first legislature was due to a crisis in the party quite similar to that of the first Hungarian parliament as described by Ágh.

Moves to the popular group in the third legislature were produced by the addition of MPs from the Christian democratic and liberal groups that were members of the same electoral coalition in 1986 (CP). These changes took place at the end of the legislature, with the aim of rebuilding the electoral coalition. In the third legislature there were also moves to the centrist party, CDS, which at that time was being predicted as a possible pivotal party in the fourth legislature.

In conclusion, it is evident that the standing orders regulating parlia-mentary parties fit completely with the constitutional formula favoring the existence of a small and powerful group of parties in the Spanish democracy. The standing orders strengthen party discipline by further-ing strong leadership in each group, by constraining the free activity of individual backbenchers, and by making faction moves by MPs difficult.

Table 7.3

Intergroup Mobility (*Transfugismo*) in Spanish Parliamentary Parties, 1977–1996

	Beginning of Legislature	End of Legislature	Change to
Constituent legislature, 1977–79			
Group Centrista (GC)	165	157	8 GMx
Group Socialista (GS)	105	106	
Group Soc. de Cat. (GSC)	13	17	
Group Min. Cat. (GMC)	11	10	1 GMx
Group mixto (GMx)	12	15	4 GSC, 1 GS
I legislature, 1979–82			
Group Centrista	168	150	13 GMx, 4 GCD, 1 GA, 1 GMC
Group Socialista	98	97	1 GMx
Group Soc. de Cat.	17	16	1 GA
Group Coal. Democ. (GCD)	9	12	1 GC
Group Min. Cat.	8	9	
Group Comunista	23	22	1 GMx
Group Andalucista (GA)	5	7	
Group mixto	9	24	4 GSC, 1 GS
II legislature, 1982–86			
Group Centrista	12	11	1 GP
Group Popular	106	104	3 GMx
Group mixto	10	13	
III legislature, 1986–89			
Group Socialista	184	182	2 GMx
Group Popular	73	89	2 GCDS, 3 GMX, 1 GMC
Group Min. Cat.	18	19	
Group Vasco	6	4	2 GMX
Group CDS	19	27	1 GMX
Agrupácion Dem. Crist.	21	0	15 GP, 3 GMx, 3 GCDS
Agrupácion P. Liberal	11	0	6 GP, 3 GCDS, 2 GMx
Agrupácion IU	7	6	1 GCDS
Group mixto	11	23	
IV legislature, 1989–93			
Group Popular	106	105	1 GMx
Group CDS	14	12	2 GMx
Group mixto	15	18	
V legislature, 1993–96			
Group Coal. Canaraia	5	4	1 GMx
Group mixto	5	6	

Sources: See table 7.1.

Note: See chapter appendix for key to party acronyms.

The Internal Organization of Parliamentary Parties

Party discipline is structured by the internal organization of parties and primarily by party rules and statutes. As Katz and Mair (1992, 7) have pointed out, party rules offer a fundamental and indispensable guide to the character of a given party, "affording an insight into its internal conceptions of organizational power, authority and legitimacy." For this reason, to explain how Spanish parliamentary parties are organized, we have to take into consideration both mass party and parliamentary party statutes, as well as practices and ways of proceeding.

Mass Party Statutes

Some of the rules governing how parliamentary parties function are located in the mass party statutes: they are the basic principles. First, these party statutes set up a link between the party and the parliamentary group. For example, in the case of the PP, the president of the party is at the same time the president of the group. In the case of *Izquierda Unida* (IU), the party statutes state that the president and the *portavoz,* both elected by the parliamentary group, must be ratified by the federal council of the coalition (executive committee). This is the same for the Basque group. The PSOE statutes simply state that the parliamentary group elects its own leaders and that the president of the group is a member of the federal executive committee of the party.

The statutes of the PP, IU, and PNV establish that the parliamentary groups can write their own statutes but that these must be finally approved by the mass party leadership (executive committees). In the PSOE statutes there is a rule of unity of action and vote for MPs, who can be sanctioned if they do not act in accord with the set position. Similarly, the PP states that MPs must act according to instructions by the party leadership.

A clear difference among parties relates to the financial relationship between party and MPs. In the PP the parliamentary group is autonomous when administering its resources, so that deputies receive their salary directly from the Congreso. But for socialists, communists, and Basques, it is the mass party—through a special fund in which the deputies' salaries are deposited—that decides the wage of each MP.

The PSOE statutes state that parliamentarians who abandon the party should resign as MPs. This can be understood only as a moral requirement because no party can legally force an MP to resign. On the other hand, the PSOE accepts that members of its parliamentary group can be independents—though not socialist militants—as has happened several times. In such cases discipline has been difficult to demand, especially in the area of voting.

The Internal Statutes of the Parliamentary Parties

The general structure of parliamentary parties is stated in their internal statutes (*reglamento interno*). In each case it is specified that there is a *portavoz* of each group in the chamber who is a member of the *Junta de Portavoces*. This function is also defined in the Constitution and in the standing orders of the Congreso. The *portavoz* usually is the "chief whip"—according to the British pattern—and he or she is elected. The *portavoz* plays a very important role: it is the main representative of the group and the person who organizes and directs the whole group (Solé and Aparicio 1984, 138).

In the PP the president is different from the *portavoz*. When the PP was in opposition, the *portavoz* was the second leader of the party and substituted for the president in the council of direction (executive committee). When the PSOE was in government, the *portavoz* was also the president of the group. When the PSOE was in opposition, the president of the group was the party leader—and the leader of the opposition, as in Britain. In this case, the chief whip is a different person and is given the title of general secretary of the group. Both can act as the *portavoz* of the group, but usually the *portavoz* is the general secretary.

The PP party leaders propose the candidate to be the *portavoz;* in the PSOE, this position is elected by the group. The PSOE was homogenous and unified before the 1993 election, but since then two main factions have been competing in the parliamentary group (and in the mass party): "renovators," who are the majority, and "guerristas" (Guillespie 1992, 8–10). That is why in 1993, for the first time, PSOE MPs had to choose by secret ballot between two candidates for president of the group. And in 1994 and 1996, whenever the PSOE had to elect a new president or a general secretary, again there was an internal division in the group.

The mass party chooses the *portavoz* of the Basque group and of the Catalan minority. In the IU group there is a president, a vice president, and a *portavoz* elected by the group. Only the *portavoz* of the IU is in charge of having formal relations with other groups.

The two major parliamentary parties in the Congreso (PSOE and

PP) are organized along similar lines. Both meet in a general assembly (*pleno*) of all backbenchers who belong to the party. The PSOE general meeting takes place three times a month: that is, before each general assembly of the Congreso. The PP meet just once a month. Party leaders use these meetings to give information to backbenchers; PSOE also uses the occasion to have political debates. When the party is in government, ministers participate and inform backbenchers about their proposals.

Members of IU also meet regularly before each plenum of the Congreso to have a political debate. In the assembly of the IU group, different proposals or initiatives from MPs are taken into consideration before being tabled, and conflicts between MPs and committee coordinators are resolved.

Both the PSOE and PP are governed by an executive committee elected by the MPs. In the PSOE group, candidates to the direction committee (*comité de dirección*) can be proposed by the party's federal executive committee—which has been the usual practice—or by five members of the parliamentary group. The direction committee is responsible to the general assembly of the group, and in each session a vote of confidence in the committee must be held. The committee coordinates the activity of the whole group within the government.

The PSOE group has a second executive committee called the permanent committee (*comite permanente*). This is larger than the first one, with about 30 members, consisting of the entire direction committee and all the coordinators of commissions (i.e., the whips who are in charge of coordinating socialist MPs in each parliamentary commission). The permanent committee monitors legislative initiatives as well as the parliamentary activities of MPs.

The PSOE parliamentary group has a third committee that controls participation and voting by MPs: this is the committee on discipline. It has three members, and its president is a member of the permanent committee. The committee on discipline is helped by the whips, who give information about failings by MPs. The committee can propose sanctions that can be imposed by the direction committee.

The PP parliamentary group has just one formal executive committee: the council of direction. It is very large, consisting of leaders of the parliamentary party and others from the mass party. However, in its weekly meetings, only the main leaders of the parliamentary group meet under the presidency of the *portavoz*. When the PP was in opposition, there were meetings between the party president (who at the same time was president of all the party's parliamentary groups) and the chief whips of the parliamentary parties of both chambers and the European Parliament, held each week to coincide with the plenum of the Congreso, to prepare party strategy. A meeting of the council of direction of each parliamentary party was held afterwards. There was a second meeting at the end of the week to consider proposals or amendments that were coming up.

The council of direction studies different legislative proposals and initiatives by PP MPs before they are tabled. It designates members of the group for the parliamentary commissions. The council also takes decisions about party discipline. The general secretary of the group, who is also a member of the council, takes care of the discipline of the group and informs the council about absences by MPs. Finally, the popular group has a "coordinator of commissions," a member of the council who coordinates and monitors the parliamentary activity in commissions by popular MPs. The "coordinator" meets regularly with the *portavoz* or representatives of the party in each parliamentary commission.

Discipline Proceedings

Each parliamentary party has procedures for dealing with MPs who do not follow party discipline. In the case of the PSOE and PP, this is regulated in their statutes. For the IU group there is only a minor reference to this question. Usually it is the executive committee of the group who penalizes MPs. The statutes refer to the kind of penalties that can be imposed on deputies, depending on what they have done. If, for example, there is a very important vote requiring a qualified majority and an MP is absent without any justification, the executive committee can impose a fine of up to 25,000 pesetas in the PSOE group or 40,000 pesetas in the PP group. While in the PSOE group the money is easy to take because MPs receive their salary through the party, in the case of the PP group, deputies have to pay the fine by themselves.

The executive committee of each group can penalize other kind of acts by MPs, such as voting contrary to party instructions. Under party statutes it is usually the mass party leaders who are charged with monitoring the behavior of MPs and, if necessary, expelling recalcitrants from the party. The executive committee of each party acts as a high court with competence to judge on the appeals of MPs against such decisions. From this viewpoint we can analyze how party discipline works in practice, taking into consideration two variables—voting, in which we pay particular attention to levels of dissension, and substitution of MPs—examining to what degree these are due to poor relations between MPs and the party.

Dissension in voting has not been significant across the whole period. Research by Capo (1990, 99) on votes during the first four legislatures shows that there has been a general consensus among parties. In the 568 cases in which there has been a final vote on the entire legislative act (*leyes* and *decretos-leyes*), the average was 223 votes in favor, 28 against, and 14 abstentions. Moreover, there was more support for the proposed law in the case of minority governments than with majority ones; this means that UCD governments gained support from part of the opposition. It means also that we have to distinguish between UCD and PSOE governments. Before 1982, not only did every bill have to be negotiated among the different families that made up UCD, but also the government had to make deals with other parliamentary groups because it did not have an absolute majority (Capo 1990, 108). In the case of PSOE governments (the second, third, and fourth legislatures) the socialist parliamentary party provided a "rubber stamp" to government proposals (Guillespie 1989, 420). Abstentions are significant because prior notice is given of final votes, but it is difficult to link abstentionism with dissent because usually it is not made explicit.

Table 7.4 provides data on the numbers of substitutions of MPs—when an MP retires from the house midterm and is replaced by a substitute on the party list—showing a global number of 35 to 40 for each legislature. The particularly large amount in the first legislature was due to the fact that many MPs left to represent their parties in the brand-new regional parliaments that were being established. On average, three to four replacements are due to deaths in each legislature. Of the rest, only about 10% of substitutions are actually due to a crisis between the MP and the party.

In sum, from the point of view of the parliamentary party organization, we find in each group real integration among its members based on a strong direction that coordinates the group with the mass party, and, where applicable, with the government. There is also a unified representation of the whole group through the *portavoces* in the Congreso and in each parliamentary committee. In addition, in each main parliamentary group, there is a web, structured by the *portavoces,* that serves to transmit instructions to backbenchers as well as monitor them. Finally, in the Spanish case, party rules and statutes not only protect leaders by ensuring their legitimacy but also help enforce their power.

Table 7.4

Substitutions of MPs in Spanish Parliamentary Parties, 1977–1996

	C	*I*	*II*	*III*	*IV*	*V*
Group Centrista	5	9	2			
Group CDS				2	3	
Group Popular			7	9	12	6
Group Socialista	1	13	26	21	12	12
Group Soc. de Cat.	1	6				
Group Soc. Vascos		2				
Group Comunista-IU	2	4		1		
Group Min. Cat.		7	2	4	2	2
Group Vasco	1	3	2	1	3	1
Group Mixto	1	1			5	1
Group Andalucista		2				

Source: See table 7.1.

Note: C = Constituent legislature; I–V = first through fifth legislatures. See chapter appendix for key to party acronyms.

Concluding Remarks

In Spain, party discipline is very strong, to the point that we can affirm how in practice the constitutional principle of free mandate of deputies is ineffective. Spanish MPs always act according to party instructions. The reason for this is the electoral law, which places in the hands of party headquarters the capacity to decide who appears on the electoral lists. Moreover, party discipline is helped by the principal role that parties have in the parliamentary system: parliamentary groups are the main actors in Parliament.

Among the parliamentary parties, the PSOE group has the most extensive set of rules on party discipline, ensuring that it has been more cohesive and stable than any other group. There are different explanations for this: first and most important, it has been a government party (with a qualified majority) for several parliaments; second, it is a center-left party that takes party discipline seriously; and finally, it has been organized as a mass party with the highest rate of membership affiliation in Spain.

By contrast, the conservative and liberal groups have been less stable, as reflected by a high turnover of deputies. These parties are primarily electoral parties with weak organizations: a lack of professionalism among the MPs is evident. The most important cause of instability in the conservative parties was the nonexistence of a unique political organization; there have always been two competing parties with MPs moving between them. Nevertheless, since 1990 the PP has been moving in the right direction. A new leadership has strengthened its organization, and by 1996 it had become the only national center-right party and the majority party in government.

APPENDIX

Abbreviations for Parties

AIC	Agrupaciones Independientes de Canarias
AP	Alianza Popular
BNG	Bloque Nacionalista Galego
C. Can.	Coalición Canaraia
CIU	Convergencia i Unió
CD	Coalición Democrática
CDS	Centro Democrático y Social
CG	Coalición Galega
Coal. Can.	Coalición Canaria
CP	Coalición Popular
Dem. Crist.	Democracia Cristiana
EA	Eusko Alkartasuna
EE	Euskadiko Eskerra
ERC	Esquerra Republicana de Cataluña
HB	Herri Batasuna
I. Cast.	Independientes de Castellon
IU	Izquierda Unida
M. Cat.	Minoria Catalana
P. And.	Partido Andalucista
PAR	Partido Aragonés Regionalista (in 1996 part of Group Popular)
P. Arg.	Partido Aragonés
PCE	Partido Comunista de España
P. Liberal	Partido Liberal
PNV	Partido Nacionalista Vasco
PP	Partido Popular
PSOE	Partido Socialista Obrero Español
PSP	Partido Socialista Popular
Soc. de Cat.	Socialistas de Cataluña

Soc. Vasc.	Socialistas Vascos
UCD	Unión de Centro Democrático
UDC	Union Democrática de Cataluña
UN	Unión Nacional
UPC	Unión del Pueblo Canario
UPN	Unión del Pueblo Navarra (from 1992 part of Group Popular)
UV	Unión Valenciana

NOTES

1. According to articles 99 and 113 of the Spanish Constitution, the vote of confidence (investiture) and the vote of no confidence (censure motion) of the *Congreso de los Diputados* are given only to the prime minister—as president of the government—and not to the entire government. In addition, the prime minister is charged with the formation and leadership of the government as well as the coordination of its members (art. 98). The prime minister has a virtual free hand over the structure of and appointments to cabinet (Heywood 1991).

2. Senate elections are under a majority rule, which usually produces the same majorities as in the chamber.

3. Real Decreto-Ley de 18 de marzo sobre Normas Electorales 1977; Ley Orgánica 5/1985 de 19 de junio, sobre el Régimen Electoral General 1985.

4. Ley Orgánica 3/1987, de 2 de julio, sobre Financiación de los Partidos Políticos 1987.

5. The stability of a group can be also understood if we take into consideration the fact that the total number of MPs of each parliament is about 45% of the total of two parliaments before.

6. Sometimes a party helps another to form a parliamentary group by lending an MP just for its formation. This happened in 1993 and in 1996 with Partido Aragonés Regionalista (PAR) and Coalición Canaraia. Shortly thereafter, there was a faction change between both groups (see table 7.3).

7. There is another possibility for MPs to act freely from group control. This is when the cabinet provides information to the Congreso and MPs ask for complementary information.

REFERENCES

Capo, Jordi. 1990. *La legislación estatal en la España democrática: Una aproximación politológica.* Madrid: Centro de Estudios Constitucionales.

Castillo, Pilar del. 1990. "La financiación pública de los partidos políticos y su impacto en las instituciones representativas." In Angel Garrorena, ed., *El parlamento y sus transformaciones actuales.* Madrid: Tecnos.

Cotarelo, R., ed. 1992. *Transición politica y consolidación democrática: España 1975–1986.* Madrid: Centro de Investigaciones Sociológicas.

Esteban, Jorge, and Luis López. 1982. *Los partidos políticos en la España actual.* Barcelona: Planeta.

Gallagher, Michael, Michael Laver, and Peter Mair. 1995. *Representative Government in Modern Europe,* 2d ed. New York: McGraw-Hill.

Guillespie, Richard. 1989. *The Spanish Socialist Party.* London: Oxford University Press.

———. 1992. "Factionalism in the Spanish Socialist Party." In *Institut de Ciènces Politiques i Socials Working Paper. No. 59.* Barcelona: ICPS.

Heywood, Paul. 1991. "Governing a New Democracy: The Power of the Prime Minister in Spain." In G. W. Jones, ed., *West European Prime Ministers.* London: Frank Cass.

Katz, Richard, and Peter Mair, eds. 1992. *Party Organizations.* Newbury Park, CA: Sage.

López Aguilar, J. 1988. *La oposición parlamentaria y el orden constitucional.* Madrid: CEC.

Montero, José R. 1989. "Los fracasos políticos de la derecha española: Alianza Popular." In José F. Tezanos, R. Cotarelo, and A. de Blas, eds., *La transición democrática española.* Madrid: Sistema.

Solé, Jordi, and Miguel A. Aparicio. 1984. *Las cortes generales.* Madrid: Tecnos.

ADDITIONAL SUGGESTED READINGS

Abellán, A. M. 1994. "Los representantes y el derecho de participación en el ordenamiento jurídico español." *Revista de Estudios Políticos* 84: 199–215.

Alda, Mercedes, and Lourdes Lopez. 1993. "El parlamento español 1977–1993." *Revista de Estudios Políticos* 81: 241–64.

Capo, Jordi, Ramón Cotarelo, and Diego López Garrido. 1990. "By Consociationalism to a Majoritarian Parliamentary System: The Rise and Decline of the Spanish Cortes." In U. Liebert and M. Cotta, eds., *Parliament and Democratic Consolidation in Southern Europe.* London: Pinter.

Saiz, Alejandro. 1989. *Los grupos parlamentarios.* Madrid: Congeso de los Diputados.

Sánchez de Dios, M. 1995. "Las cortes generales." In Paloma Román, ed., *El sistema político español.* New York: McGraw-Hill.

———. 1995. "La esencia del régimen: El control parlamentario del gobierno." *Politica y Sociedad* 20: 35–53.

PART IV

Newly Emerging Systems

The chapters in Part III examined three non-Anglo parliaments in which, among other factors, electoral rules were identified as important components of party cohesion. But, as we noted in chapter 1, the chamber itself provides a whole series of incentives—carrots and sticks—that can aid efforts to impose party discipline. Moreover, the legislatures we have examined so far are all well established (with the partial exception of Spain), with electoral and institutional arrangements that have been in place for some time. In this part we change perspective once again, this time to examine newly forming legislative settings, where—to paraphrase Laver and Shepsle (chap. 2)—parties and party discipline are emerging from the "primeval slime." In the chapters that follow, we see parties moving quickly into center stage, and we also see how procedural arrangements inside the chamber concerned make an important contribution to developing party cohesion.

Europe has seen two recent developments that provide a perfect means to observe the emergence of parliamentary party discipline from "the primeval slime." The first and most dramatic of these has been the process of democratization in eastern and central Europe since the late 1980s. The second, more gradual development (and starting far earlier) has been the process of European integration, which started with the Treaties of Paris and Rome in the 1950s and has been steadily building up steam in recent years. The three chapters in this part provide some useful insights into both of these developments.

Attila Ágh explores the process of what he calls party "parliamentarization" (or the institutionalization of parliamentary fraktions) in Hungary, and he generalizes from this case about trends in East and Central Europe from the late 1980s onwards. What starts, in the first Hungarian parliament, as a story of "enforced party discipline," involving the adoption of rules to attempt (evidently not entirely successfully) to limit parliamentary indiscipline, culminates in the Second Parliament with what Ágh refers to as "the end of the beginning," with greatly reduced evidence of faction hopping (down from the 20% "political tourism" trends of the First Parliament) and a much more stable and cohesive picture overall.

Chapters 9 and 10 assess the "parliamentarization" process of the European Parliament (EP). Raunio (chap. 9) shows how, despite a range of institutional factors that work against party cohesion, the evidence from examining roll call votes in the EP—which certainly produces significantly lower levels of cohesion than in most West European national legislatures—compares favorably with the record of the U.S. Congress. Bowler and Farrell (chap. 10) assess cohesion levels in the EP from the perspective of theories relating to parliamentary norms, finding pretty sparse evidence of their presence. In their absence (and bearing some similarity to Ágh's discussion of early trends in Hungary), the parliamentary groups in the EP rely on formal rules as a means of maintaining parliamentary discipline.

8

The Parliamentarization of the East Central European Parties: Party Discipline in the Hungarian Parliament, 1990–1996

ATTILA ÁGH

Parliaments are model institutions in the democratic institu-
tion-building process of East Central Europe (ECE), and
they have, among other roles, important elite recruitment and political
learning functions. Parliaments have been the "central sites" and parties
the "major actors" of the democratization process (Ágh 1995a). This
chapter deals with the formation of party discipline in the framework
of the Hungarian "parliamentarization" process. This process has basically been the same in all ECE countries; it has appeared in Hungary in
a most marked way. In Hungary, after the first free (or founding) elections, the First Parliamentary cycle lasted four years: the First Parliament (1990–94) completed its full term, unlike other ECE countries. In
addition, the Second Parliament (1994–98), already in its first two years
(at the time of writing), provides a clear contrast to the First Parliament.
These two very different stages of the party formation process can be
studied in depth. It needs to be pointed out, however, that this chapter
deals only with the problems of party discipline in the case of parliamentary faction behavior; it does not extend its field of inquiry beyond
this. It should be borne in mind that other forms and levels of party
discipline strongly influence the parliamentary behavior of MPs.[1]

It is generally recognized that in ECE—and even more so in the
Balkans or in eastern Europe proper—parties are still weak and fragile.
I think, however, that the (major) ECE parties—when considered as
elements of a party system—have already reached some kind of early
consolidation: in other words, they already represent the relevant social
cleavages with a clear political profile, and they have forged definite connections with their respective European Party Internationals. Their "external" roles are clear and distinct, but their "internal" structures with
regard to organization and program setting are still somewhat weak and
fragile. I have argued elsewhere that the ECE parties are already "at
the end of beginning"; the usual discussions of their general weakness,
lumping them together with the really very weak East European parties,
miss the point (Ágh 1997).

Two factors stand out in this paradoxical development of Hungarian
parliamentary parties. First, the Hungarian party system has proved to
be the most stable and durable in the region: the same six parties have
been elected to Parliament twice, in 1990 and 1994, so one can analyze
the same parties with solid data. Second, as I have mentioned above,
the First Parliament sat for four years; thus, we have an ample time
horizon for the relevant analysis. The Second Parliament (elected in
1994 for four years), as a good contrast to the First Parliament, enables
us to make conclusive remarks on the changes in party discipline since
the initial period of democratic transition.

Party discipline depends on (1) the development stage of the party,
whether it is still in the formation process or already consolidated; (2)
the particular type of party, originating inside or outside the parliament
and varying party families; and (3) the function of the given party in
the political (power) system. According to Katz and Mair (1995, 10),
for instance, the mass party combines the first two of these features,
especially with its organized membership, and they point out that "these
parties naturally were more amenable to the idea of enforced party
cohesion and discipline" than the other parties. Regarding the third
feature, the political or power context, Mair (1994, 10) refers to the
"parliamentary party complex," which is particularly important for the
ECE parties, existing almost exclusively in and through the parliament.
In our conceptual framework, it is also necessary to note the distinction
between the party of government (as "transition actors," see Pridham
1994, 33, or umbrella organizations) and the party in government (as
consolidated parties with a coalition-making capacity). The first term

indicates the creation of a party to govern, which is quite common in young democracies. Such loose umbrella organizations differ considerably from those stable parties that gain election and form a government, going beyond the "polarized pluralism" of the first years to a "moderate pluralism" of the relative consolidation.

Traditionally, political science has distinguished two different forms of the manifestation of party identities. In discussing the transformation of former ruling parties into modern social democratic parties, Michael Waller (1995, 484) picks his words carefully: "A distinction has been made between the identity that a political party has acquired through its historical experiences on the one hand, and on the other, what it stands for in competition for support within a party system at any given time. It is a distinction, in Sartori's words, between an 'historically derived identity' and 'contemporary political appeals.'" This bears a resemblance to the distinction, drawn by the editors of this book (chap. 1), between *coherence* and *discipline,* such that MPs either work together for party goals on their own or are prepared to accept orders of their party leaders. I understand by *coherence* a spontaneous self-identification with that given party, and by *discipline* conscious, institutional, rule-abiding behavior. Hence, coherence may only be a result of a long party-identity formation process, which was obviously not available at the very beginning of the new multiparty systems.

Furthermore, discipline may take two different forms. First, it may be mechanically imposed upon party or parliamentary faction members through drastic means when coherence is low; second, it can be a means of ensuring the efficient working of the institutional mechanism of mature parties with a high degree of party coherence. Simply put, the ECE parties, and above all the Hungarian parties, have progressed a great deal in the 1990s according to these criteria. They have now achieved a rather high coherence and an effective operation of parliamentary mechanisms through efficient party discipline.

The formation of the multiparty system began much earlier in Hungary than in other ECE countries and also reached relative consolidation sooner. Four of the six Hungarian parliamentary parties emerged from social movements in 1987 through 1989, yet as institutionalized parties, all of them were largely organized from above by a small group of leaders until late 1989. Hence, their party identity was decided at the top and brought down to the party activists and members, as was the case with coherence and party discipline. First the leaders were "disciplined" and then the followers, in a still unfinished process of mutual feedback. Therefore, party discipline in Parliament is of central importance not only to the normal workings of parliamentary systems but also to the party formation process itself. This chapter concentrates on the first issue, above all on the relationships between the party elite and the backbenchers. But the second aspect, the party discipline of activists and rank-and-file members, should not be forgotten, since it can have an eroding or reinforcing effect on the parliamentarization of parties, especially in the case of the loose and heterogeneous "party of government."

In the first stage the obscure nature of party identity undermined to a great extent the efforts of the party elites to form coherent parliamentary party factions. The "undisciplined" behavior of members with diverging political tendencies contributed to an increasing factionalism within parties. In fact, in most ECE countries, the term *faction* has been used to describe the organized unit of the parliamentary parties, except for Poland, where such kinds of factions are called "parliamentary clubs" of parties. I follow this tradition here: *parliamentary faction* refers to all MPs of a given party organized in one parliamentary unit, the rights and duties of which have been regulated in detail by the standing orders. In some ways the entire life of the ECE parliaments can be described through the activities of the parliamentary party factions as the real actors in the parliament. In this chapter party coherence and discipline are analyzed only with regard to these actors. *Faction* as a term, however, has a second meaning. It may also refer to an intraparty organization, namely a relatively solid and permanent group inside a party that has a different political profile within the common political horizon and policy universe of the party. In the United States, *faction* is used to describe the subgroups of a party, and the other meaning has been covered by the term *caucus*.

In sum, by *factionalism* or *factionalization* I mean the increasing tendency for intraparty tensions that may produce in an extreme version the disintegration of parliamentary party factions. Indeed, factionalization finally led to the disintegration of "parties of government" in the late 1970s in Spain and in the early 1990s in Poland, Hungary, and Czechoslovakia (on Spain, see Sánchez de Dios, chap. 7 of this volume; on ECE parties, see Lewis 1995; Kopecky 1995; Malová 1994).

This chapter analyzes Hungarian developments in two parts: first, it examines the attendance and voting behavior of parliamentary party factions; second, it explores the drastic changes in the party factions during the First Parliament in contrast to the first half-period of the Second Parliament. In the closing section, I try to generalize from this analysis about trends in the ECE.

Attendance and Voting Behavior in the First Parliament

Hungary has a unicameral parliament with 386 MPs (176 MPs elected from single-member individual districts and 210 MPs from party lists). The following six parties were represented in the First Parliament and are now present in the Second Parliament: Hungarian Socialist Party (HSP), Alliance of Free Democrats (AFD), Hungarian Democratic Forum (HDF), Independent Smallholders Party (ISP), Christian Democratic Peoples Party (CDPP), and Alliance of Young Democrats (AYD, Fidesz). Four parties emerged from social movements and movement parties in 1988 (HSP, AFD, HDF, and Fidesz). The two others are historical parties (ISP and CDPP), and they were formed, or reemerged, later in 1989. In the first, "founding" elections of 1990, these six "early comers" were elected to the parliament, and dozens of others were left out. The distance between the "insiders" in Parliament and the "dropouts" (including the new parties that appeared in Parliament between 1990 and 1994) grew in the second elections. In 1990 the smallest parliamentary party received 6.46% of the popular vote, and the largest nonparliamentary party 3.68%; in 1994 the respective figures were 7.02 and 3.19%. As a consequence the "dropouts" have been marginalized in the overall framework of party life, and it is enough to deal with the six stable parliamentary parties. Yet before going any further with the analysis, it is necessary to say something about the disintegration or erosion process that affected the parties in the First Parliament (see tables 8.1 and 8.2).

Compared to other ECE parties, Hungarian parliamentary parties have shown that they are relatively strong organizations. Nevertheless, their political profiles and social constituencies were rather obscure in 1990 when they entered the parliament. In all ECE countries the first free elections were plebiscites against state socialism, and the political profiles of the parties were unclear, especially with regard to their programs and the principal characteristics of their social support. All parties based their identities on their opposition to the former system; they emphasized virtually the same goals in their programs, and their social

Table 8.1

The Political Map of the Hungarian Parliament, May 2, 1990, and April 7, 1994

	Votes (%)	Seats	Seats (%)	Changes
HDF	24.73	165	42.75	−29
AFD	21.39	94	24.35	−11
ISP(-C)	11.73	44	11.40	−8
HSP	10.89	33	8.55	0
Fidesz	8.95	22	5.70	+4
CDPP	6.46	21	5.44	+2
PHJL	—	12	3.11	+12
ISP-T	—	9	2.33	+9
Independents	—	7	1.81	+21

Notes: PHJL (Party of Hungarian Justice and Life—MIÉP) was the biggest successor party of the HDF and is led by István Csurka. The others were not able to organize their party factions, since they had fewer than 10 MPs, so their members sat with the independents. This was also the case with the faction of the ISP that left the coalition (ISP-T, indicating the name of József Torgyán, the ISP president). Most of the ISP's MPs (36) remained with the coalition (ISP-C) and were able to organize a faction, but the real party, having only 9 MPs, could not. This breakaway faction of 36 MPs disappeared in the second elections, in 1994, so the ISP once again is the party of Torgyán. During the first parliament, 29 MPs departed (9 died and 20 resigned) and were replaced (5 in by-elections in individual constituencies and 24 from the party lists). Altogether 56 people moved inside the parliament by changing factions (6 MPs twice), including 12 MPs who later formed the PHJL faction and the 9 MPs of ISP-T who remained outside their party faction after the split in the ISP. This table shows the aggregate results of both changes, i.e., inside the parliament, as well as the effects of the five by-elections from "outside."

For party acronyms, see chapter appendix.

support was rather diffuse. For example, the two strongest parties in 1990, Hungarian Democratic Forum (HDF) and Alliance of Free Democrats (AFD), were indistinguishable in their social constituencies. Moreover, at that time they had the support of the same social strata, although the competition between them was fierce politically and culturally. Their original party memberships took on a somewhat "random" character, depending upon family and friendly circles and local circumstances, including the leading politicians and MPs of the respective parties. One recurring feature was that some politicians moved several times between different parties by "faction hopping," and this included shifts between the parliamentary factions of the HDF and AFD—despite the fact that these two particular parties were archenemies in the First Parliament. This period of 1988 through 1990 can be characterized as the "original organizational chaos" in party develop-

Table 8.2

The Political Map of the Hungarian Parliament, June 28, 1994, and
July 3, 1996

	Votes (%)	Seats	Seats (%)	Changes
HSP	32.99	209	54.14	0
AFD	19.74	71	18.39	−3
HDF	11.74	38	9.84	−19
ISP	8.82	26	6.73	+1
CDPP	7.03	22	5.69	0
Fidesz	7.02	20	5.18	0
HDPP	—	15	3.88	+15
Independents	—	6	1.55	+6

Notes: Two MPs, counted here in the AFD faction, were elected as candidates of other parties (Agrarian Alliance and Party of Entrepreneurs, respectively), which were in electoral alliance with the AFD. The Hungarian Democratic People's Party (HDPP) is a breakaway faction of the HDF.

For party acronyms, see chapter appendix.

ment. This chaos was significantly reduced in personal and organizational terms in 1990 by the natural selection of the first elections, although it did not disappear. In the abstract sense, this is the starting period of missing party coherence involving the mechanistic imposition of party discipline for the required parliamentary party behavior. The problem is more complex in real life, however, since the ECE parties emerged from particular political subcultures—that is, from friendly circles of the intelligentsia. Therefore, there was some kind of common mentality from the very beginning that created an elementary level of party coherence.[2]

Yet this common mentality, or set of values, was insufficient for a coherent policy-making process in the parliament, where the intellectually minded new politicians had to face concrete decision-making situations instead of the more nebulous ideological debates that they preferred. The uncertainty in the sociopolitical character and the interest representation function of parties was reflected, first, in the relationships that rank-and-file party members in general had with their own parties. Second, this was particularly evident and appeared much more markedly in the parliament with regard to the MPs of the respective party factions. This is illustrated very well in the everyday behavior of MPs in connection with their attendance and voting, and even more so in those instances when they left and/or changed factions in the First Parliament (Szarvas 1995, 207).

There was a certain consolidation of Hungarian parties caused by the "pressure" of the decision-making process in the First Parliament. This partial consolidation (with a higher coherence) was finalized by the second elections of 1994. The HDF and (Alliance of Young Democrats) Fidesz have changed the most, the Hungarian Socialist Party (HSP) and the Christian Democratic Peoples Party (CDPP) the least, but the Independent Smallholders Party (ISP) and AFD have also undergone significant changes. The HDF emerged in the late 1980s as a typical "transition actor," an umbrella organization and movement party (the name "Forum" then became widespread in the region). It evinced some characteristic leftist features in the form of a "third way" populist ideology. However, as a "party of government" it gradually changed into a rightist, national conservative party, and as a result its first president and one of the vice presidents (Zoltán Bíró and Csaba Gy. Kiss, respectively) left the party. Apart from this, power glued the diverging tendencies of the HDF together. During the First Parliamentary cycle, the extreme right initially became organized within the HDF, and after some years of tense conflict, at the end of the First Parliament, it split off. On June 1, 1993, four MPs were expelled from the HDF faction as a final means of a disciplinary action; this triggered, on June 14, the formation of the new extreme nationalist party in the parliament (Party of Hungarian Justice and Life—PHJL) as a new party faction. Thus, it can be said that after this factionalization, the HDF consolidated in its final form as a national-conservative center-right party.

The Fidesz did not change too much as far as the parliamentary faction is concerned, but it changed its political profile a great deal. It appeared on the political scene in the late 1980s as a left-liberal generational party (with a membership age limit of 35 years at that time). At first it displayed a rather radical-anarchistic political style, but by the end of the first parliamentary cycle it had transmogrified into a modernist center-right conservative party. Hence, some of the founders of Fidesz left the party in late 1993 and joined the AFD, but this split did not reach the level of factionalization. Finally, the relationship in the First Parliament between the two "liberal" parties—the AFD and Fidesz—became sour, if not inimical. The AFD moved left and was stabilized as a centrist-leftist, social-liberal party. After a short leadership crisis in 1992, the party has become rather cohesive and well balanced. The ISP took a right-populist turn in early 1992, producing a split in the party, and more recently it has occupied the extreme rightist place in the Hungarian parliament, with a harsh populist-nationalist style.

Table 8.3
Legislation in the First Parliament, May 1990–April 1994

	1990	*1991*	*1992*	*1993*	*1994*	*1990–94*
New laws	29	55	50	61	24	219
Amendments	48	38	42	60	25	213
Resolutions	55	73	92	103	31	354
Opinions	3	3	2	2	0	10
All decisions	135	169	186	226	80	796

The changes in the characters of the parties in this formation process led concomitantly to changes in the loyalties of politicians, and it was noticeable that institutional-political and personnel changes went in parallel. MPs, of course, were not idle and passive during this process of self-determination or self-definition by the parties. When the decisions were made, they were faced with two options: to comply or to leave the party. It was a feature of all Hungarian parliamentary parties that the majority did the first, while the minority chose the second. In this atmosphere of "creative chaos," the inexperienced MPs faced a tremendously heavy legislative burden in the First Parliament. The First Parliament worked as a "law factory" (table 8.3), passing about 100 laws annually (and 100 other decisions). In this respect, the Second Parliament has followed suit, producing even more laws than before, increasing even more the legislative burden on the MPs (see below). "Extraordinary" sessions were eventually held on a regular basis, and these were caused not only by legislative overload but also by disorganized governmental activities in the legislative agenda, as well as by the low level of preparatory work for draft bills. The figures show that in the First Parliament, MPs met for almost 100 days each year and that about 80% of MPs (being committee members) sat an additional day every week. One has to approach the problem of attendance at the plenary and committee sessions, and in voting procedures, from this angle: it shows that the burden of participation was heavy. In general, the attendance in Parliament was rather high in the first part of the parliamentary cycle, but it declined drastically in the second part. It seemed that the First Parliament had almost decided to "dissolve itself" by the low attendance in the last months of its life, this being the result of physical and political fatigue.

Attendance and voting participation in the First Parliament were much higher in the governing parties than in the opposition.[3] As the data suggest, there were two contradictory tendencies in the First Parliament. As we have seen, two parties (HDF and ISP) experienced splits, and the other parties some erosion. Otherwise the process can be described as one of a widening of party centers in voting: that is, an increasing party discipline in voting behavior around the "party center." The HDF, CDPP, and Fidesz had 95% of members voting with the party faction on about 95% of issues. After the split in the ISP, the progovernment ISP faction (ISP-C) also manifested voting discipline. Therefore, the "voting machinery" of the three governing parties (HDF, ISP-C, and CDPP) worked well. On the other side, it seems that the opposition MPs, disappointed by the defeats they had suffered in Parliament, demonstrated their resentment by decreasing even further their attendance and voting participation. The governing coalition (HDF, ISP-C, and CDPP) had a comfortable majority at the beginning of the cycle (59.59%), and although at the end of the cycle its majority had become more critical (50.51%), it was never voted down in the First Parliament (except for interpellations; see below).

The relationship between the governing parties in the coalition was not always harmonious, but they were fused together by power; the oppositional parties (AFD, HSP, and Fidesz) lacked the incentive to vote together, since they were much more fragmented politically in their parliamentary behavior and party discipline. Most of the MPs of the governing coalition, however, were forced into passivity because rank-and-file MPs were not given an opportunity to play important roles and to take part meaningfully in the decision-making process of their party faction. This passivity was not caused simply by the general nature of party operations, as found elsewhere; rather, it stemmed from the special nature of the party formation process, during which the party leaders concentrated all important decisions in their hands and neglected the other faction members. Nevertheless, the MPs of the governing coalition took revenge for their situation as a silent and loyal majority not involved in decision making but disciplined in and through voting procedures. To compensate for the passivity in their voting behavior, they were very undisciplined before the final vote and in the plenary discussions. Strangely enough, the MPs of the governing coalition initiated many private motions, not in consultation with their own government, and raised a huge number of interpellations and parliamentary questions against their own government. For example, a progovernment MP began his interpellation by making excuses: "As a progovernment MP I would have preferred not to be forced to submit this interpellation, but . . . " As a sheer absurdity and showing the tensions within the government, the political state secretaries (deputies of ministers) interpellated each other several times (see Papp 1995, 111).

Interpellations and parliamentary questions, following the continental European tradition, are the major means of legislative control over executive power in ECE, and especially in Hungary. Interpellations have a long tradition in the history of parliaments as a means of ensuring the accountability of ministers and through them the entire executive. The right of interpellation in the Hungarian parliament is not collective but is a right of the individual MPs. The interpellation is, however, always of a political nature: that is, although it concerns a particular policy issue, it still questions the respective minister's personal performance and overall capacity to handle this particular issue. In the Hungarian parliament, interpellations are distinguished from simple parliamentary questions. They are the most direct and vigorous form of parliamentary control because they are followed by the answer of that given minister, then by the rejoinder of the interpellator, and finally by a vote in the plenary session over the minister's answer. Until the 1990 constitutional amendments, Hungarian ministers were individually responsible to the parliament, which meant that a minister would have to resign if the parliament did not approve his or her answer. Under prime ministerial government, this practice has been discontinued, but a negative vote of Parliament after an interpellation is still a big defeat for the whole government and especially for the relevant minister. Parliamentary questions are of less importance politically, since they are not followed by a rejoinder and vote. Altogether, the opposition submitted 467 interpellations in the First Parliament and the ruling coalition 95 interpellations (with 423 versus 221 parliamentary questions). The progovernment interpellators did not accept the minister's answer in 28 cases, and the parliament concurred in 17 of those cases. Such manifest and extremely undisciplined behavior by individual MPs is quite unusual in West European parliaments, and where it occurs it is punished by expelling the MP from the party faction. This did not happen in the first Hungarian parliament to those progovernment MPs who raised an interpellation against their own government or who voted negatively after the debate, indicating big intraparty tensions on some policy issues, above all on the privatization process. In this particularly undisciplined behavior, there was a clear difference between those MPs representing individual districts and those elected on party lists: the former apparently felt they were more independent from their parties and acted accordingly.[4]

We can conclude that the MPs of governing parties in the First Parliament were more disciplined in the act of voting itself than in their general political behavior: that is, they acted under the pressure of different political tensions. As a result of this contradiction, namely the enforced party discipline in voting, the governing parties finally "exploded" in the First Parliament. To put this more accurately, in the First Parliament, among the coalition parties, the HDF and ISP were the first to change beyond recognition, and then the CDPP became marginalized. The ISP experienced a split in February 1991; the rump of the party (ISP-T; the T indicates the name of its president, József Torgyán) formally left the coalition with some of its MPs, but the majority of the MPs (ISP-C) continued to support the coalition, though without being attached to a party. (Incidentally, they established a substitute party in 1993 under the name of Unified Smallholders Party, but this entity vanished in the 1994 elections.) The HDF also went through a series of splits in 1993, before the second elections, with the emergence of the Party of Hungarian Justice and Life (PHJL). Whereas the HDF was a large umbrella organization in the First Parliament, it has become a small center-right party in the Second Parliament. Thus, the strong party discipline that was imposed upon the governing parties resulted in the weakening of the parties themselves because of their lack of organically developed party coherence; nevertheless, at the same time the splits have produced much clearer party profiles and rather mature party coherence. The whole process of "redefinition" of parties can be detected in detail through the very intensive movements among the factions in the First Parliament.

Faction Movements and Changes in the First Parliament

In the parliamentarization process the newly emerging parties faced a paradoxical situation in the First Parliament. First, the parties were initially formed from social movements; thus, strong formal party organization and disciplined political behavior were unfamiliar and uncomfortable to most party members, including the MPs. Second, the dividing lines between the newly emerging parties were neither strictly nor precisely formulated in their political programs. This reflects the fact that the (parliamentary) parties had emerged from different political subcultures; they may have had their own particular political discourses, but they lacked distinct profiles and programs. Therefore, in most cases, parties were internally heterogeneous ("several parties in one"). Third, it is worth noting that party discipline was not a result of internal discussions but was imposed upon the party members from "outside"—that is, from the top, by the new party leaderships, in a rather authoritarian way. Fourth, party discipline itself, either as a principle or as a practice, was an alien and inimical concept for the members of the newly emerging parties. It reminded them of the principles and practices of the former ruling party (Democratic Centralism). It took a long time for the new parties and their members to understand that party discipline—albeit in a radically different form from the form to which they were accustomed—was also very important, even crucial, for democratic parties. One should not forget that most of the MPs in the first ECE parliaments were former members of the ruling party, especially in Hungary, with its long, smooth, and evolutionary transformation. As a recent study reveals, "In each of our countries [the party members] are also overwhelmingly former members of the communist party. In other words, it is largely the same people active in politics now as were active in the communist period" (Wyman et al. 1995, 538–39).

This paradoxical situation produced very intensive, sometimes even chaotic, changes in the parliamentary factions of the First Parliament. As a cumulative effect of the above-mentioned factors, many MPs left their factions and joined another faction or became "independents." The independents, as a separate "party faction" in the First Parliament, showed all the characteristic weaknesses of the new parties concerning party discipline and party identity. The First Parliament started out with 7 independent MPs, but by its end this figure had increased to 28—this despite the fact that in the first weeks of the parliamentary cycle some independents joined parties. Eleven MPs were formally elected as independents, but only seven MPs remained independent when the First Parliament was convened. Later, however, a movement in the other direction became dominant: dozens of MPs left their party factions because of their deep confrontations with the party line, and they ended up joining the independents. In a 386-member parliament there were 56 changes between factions by 50 MPs (six MPs changed twice; one MP even returned to his original faction!). These moves between factions, or faction hopping, meant that altogether the party affiliation of MPs changed by about 20%: that is, virtually one in every five MPs moved between factions in the First Parliament (Szarvas 1995, 208). The "faction" of independents proved to be very heterogeneous. It collected two kinds of MPs: the real independents, having no party connections and affiliations (transitory or permanent), and party members who could not form their own party factions because they did not constitute a large enough group. The standing orders of the First Parliament prescribed a 10-member minimum for party factions. For example, when the ISP split, the 9 remaining MPs of the original party (ISP-T) could not form their own faction, but the breakaway group of 35 (later 36) MPs could. Thus, they were able to maintain the former ISP faction, although this created a constitutional debate, since there was no party behind them.

In fact, this manifest lack of party discipline, which led to "mass migrations" or "political tourism" among the factions, raised some other constitutional issues as well. Toward the end of the First Parliament, there were representatives of about 20 parties, although there were only seven party factions (the original six and the PHJL) and the faction of independents in the parliament. These new parties emerged in the parliament mainly due to the erosion of the other parliamentary parties, starting with the HDF. Yet they were not visible or manifest because they did not represent party factions (having fewer than 10 MPs), so formally they were independents. This dissolution process threatened the workings of parliament and its majority and raised the legal issue of whether parties could be formed inside the parliament or whether it should be laid down legally that only those parties that received popular legitimacy in the elections could be recognized as parliamentary factions. The "20-party parliament," as it eventually became, still worked normally despite the significant reduction of governmental majority (from 59.59% to 50.51%) because some of the deserters still supported the coalition and because the opposition did not want to vote down the government, preferring to wait for the next elections. Altogether, there were 61 cases of party faction-related changes in the First Parliament: in addition to the 56 cases of "faction hopping," in 5 cases, when the MP from the individual district resigned or died, by-elections were held, and this caused a party faction-related change on each occasion (Szarvas 1995, 208).

In the end, all these questions were solved by the fortunes of political life (i.e., by the 1994 elections) and not by theory or legal principles. The newest parties, formed in the First Parliament by the breakaway groups, are not present in the Second Parliament. Consequently, the theoretical debates on the free mandate (for both those from the single-member individual districts and those from party lists) have lost their practical significance to a great extent. The Second Parliament has brought a fundamental turning point in the party formation process, including party discipline. I have described here the parliamentarization of the Hungarian parties as an institutionalization process from the angle of party discipline. It is obvious that the imposed party discipline in the voting procedure, as well as the manifest lack of party discipline in interfactional changes, were only the phenomena of birth pangs of the party formation process. In other words, in an institutional sense, they represent the characteristic contradictions of the reemergence of the multiparty system; they are not the "normal" party change familiar to consolidated democracies. At the same time, however, imposed party discipline was necessary for governability; it provided the opportunity for a special political learning process to be experienced by MPs and indeed for the whole of Hungarian politics. Party identity on one hand and party discipline and party coherence on the other developed in a parallel fashion during the First Parliament. The results of this process have appeared very markedly in the Second Parliament.

Party Discipline in the Second Parliament

In the Second Parliament the same six parties were reelected, but these parties now have much clearer political profiles and identities and have no "random" or "by chance" members. The incumbency retention rate was only 36% after the second elections. This drastic "natural selection," eliminating two-thirds of the MPs of the First Parliament from the Second Parliament, has had a very strong disciplinary effect on the MPs (Ágh and Kurtán 1995, 25). All MPs (new and old) now understand that democratic parties need strong party discipline. Debates currently taking place are only about how to reach democratic decisions efficiently within a framework of strong party discipline. At the very beginning of the Second Parliament, there were no independents. In the 1994 elections, only two MPs were elected as independents. Their parties failed to reach the 5% threshold at the elections, and they were successful in single-member individual districts. One of them joined the AFD faction in full accordance with the regulations, and the other independent MP, for a while, cooperated with the same party faction. After the "disappearance" of these two independent MPs, there have been very few interfaction movements in the first two years of the Second Parliament. Only eight MPs have left their factions—among them, one who was expelled from the ISP faction as a disciplinary measure—and two of these have already joined other parties. The only big move was that the HDF split once again and a new faction of the Hungarian Democratic People's Party (HDPP) emerged with 15 MPs. Altogether, there have only been 23 changes so far (the new 15-member faction and 8 individual moves); this proves that the parliamentary parties are relatively "ready-made" and that the newly elected MPs have understood that interfaction movement, or faction hopping, would mean committing political suicide. The party formation process has reached a new stage in the Second Parliament, where the problems of party discipline can be formulated in a completely different way. Hungarian parties have more or less finished the party formation process, and Hungary now experiences the "normal" tensions and contradictions of party change caused by environmental factors or internal party dynamics.

Of course, the problems of party factionalization and difficulties with party discipline have not entirely disappeared. The HSP, with its landslide victory (54% of seats), has emerged as a much more coherent umbrella organization than the HDF was. But most of the HSP MPs are from individual districts, feeling more independence and local engagement than those from party lists (of the 209 HSP MPs, 159 represent individual districts). There are competing, rival groups in the HSP, reflecting inside the party almost all the contradictions of Hungarian society. But they have learned the lesson from the fate of the HDF and fight only for influencing party decisions, carefully avoiding any manifest factionalization. For some time it was an open question whether this large party faction could be kept together during the whole period of the Second Parliament. The question was first raised over the serious economic austerity measures introduced by the HSP and AFD coalition government on March 12, 1995. There were some angry reactions to these measures by some MPs (those with a trade union background), but unlike the HDF before it, the HSP did not "explode" under the pressure of economic crisis management. This party has always had the greatest party coherence and discipline among the Hungarian parties, with a clear party identity; thus, it has a good survival chance as a governing party without splits and factionalization in the Second Parliament.[5]

In general, the Second Parliament reveals rather mature parties with relatively high coherence and discipline. As in the First Parliament, attendance and voting participation have been higher in the government factions, ensuring the efficient workings of the parliament. Apart from this, the behavior of the progovernment MPs is very different from that

Table 8.4

Legislation in the Second Parliament, July 1994–July 1996

	1994	*1995*	*1996*	*1994–96*
New laws	19	67	37	123
Amendments	31	59	29	119
Resolutions	44	128	68	240
All decisions	94	254	134	482

in the First Parliament: higher party coherence means that the MPs need less "recompense" through other activities before the final vote. The legislative burden has even increased slightly compared to the First Parliament (see table 8.4), but with a more democratic decision-making process in the factions and with an extended committee system, even the backbenchers of the ruling coalitions have not been forced into passivity. Thus, there has been no interpellation and there have been very few parliamentary questions by progovernment MPs; also, there has been little erosion of the progovernment parliamentary factions. Only the AFD faction of the governing coalition has lost three MPs, one of whom was originally an independent, and two MPs left for political reasons. There has been no factionalization so far in the ruling coalition. The progovernment MPs have been voting in a disciplined way, with smaller deviations in the detailed debate on the amendments, but with around 95% support for the ruling coalition, with only some abstentions, in the final votes. Both coherence and discipline have been lower in the four opposition parties because they are small and fragmented, but the erosion of attendance and voting participation has been less than was the case in the opposition of the former parliament. With these mature parties, the party formation process in Hungary has reached a threshold. We find here a situation of "party in government" instead of "party of government"—that is, a moderate pluralism instead of polarized pluralism—since two former enemies (HSP and AFD) have joined to form a coalition government.[6]

Common projects with our ECE research partners have led us to a conclusion that the process of forming party coherence and discipline has been very similar in all ECE countries, and indeed earlier, in the 1970s, in the South European countries as well (see chap. 7 of this volume). The special character of the Hungarian developments is that the parties emerged earlier and the First Parliamentary cycle was longer than elsewhere in the region; this makes the problems of party coherence and discipline more visible and manifest. The other ECE countries have not yet reached the "party in government" stage, but both party coherence and discipline have been rather high in their parliamentary parties. ECE parties already have their own "history" as a base for their organic coherence and are not simply united by "contemporary political appeals," such as the tasks of governing and opposing. Hence, the mechanical party discipline has also evolved into a more conscious kind of self-discipline based on the newly gained organic party coherence.

This analysis of Hungarian party formation has demonstrated that there have been three specific factors of party coherence in the ECE:

1. The social movements as preparties created a feeling of cohesion and a common mentality that was initially disturbed by the party formation process but that has been reinforced since by the common fight against other parties.
2. The heterogeneous character of the new parties was the biggest obstacle to party cohesion, especially in the case of large umbrella organizations like the HDF, but party erosion and splits have paved the way for party homogenization.
3. The political subcultures were the starting points and triggered a process of ideology formation and program setting that has intensified party coherence and made it more conscious and organic.

The change from mechanical to conscious party discipline has had other dominant factors:

1. Different party traditions have mattered a great deal: the leftist tradition has embraced more discipline than the rightist one, but the formation of the party system, in parallel with that of the individual parties, has made some models of political behavior mandatory.
2. The ECE countries have their own traditions of political organization and institutional behavior that date back to the early postwar period or even to the interwar period: party loyalty has been traditionally the highest in Czechoslovakia and lowest in Poland, with Hungary in the middle.
3. Parliamentary regulations (especially the standing orders) and practices have been very instrumental in promoting party disci-

pline through legal and moral norms; accordingly, these rules and expectations have been reformulated several times.[7]

The ECE parties have recently become more organically coherent and consciously disciplined and have reached a new level of party consolidation. As a result, the party formation period has been more or less completed with the parliamentarization of the ECE parties. This may go against the conventional wisdom that all "East European" parties are weak and fragile, but this "Prague-Vladivostok hypothesis" neglects both the increasing regional specificities in the postcommunist world and the tremendous recent developments in the ECE parties. At this point, the first stage of elite recruitment and political learning has come to an end, and the "normal" stage of party change has begun, in which parties react to social demands and international pressures in a quasi-stable institutional environment and in a rather predictable way. We are, indeed, at the end of the beginning in the ECE, but there is still a long way to go until the ECE parties have become mature in their entire organizational structure and not just at the party elite level.

APPENDIX: HUNGARIAN PARLIAMENTARY PARTIES

Hungarian Democratic Forum (HDF)—Magyar Demokrata Fórum (MDF)
Alliance of Free Democrats (AFD)—Szabad Demokraták Szövetsége (SZDSZ)
Independent Smallholders Party (ISP)—Független Kisgazda Párt (FKGP)
Hungarian Socialist Party (HSP)—Magyar Szocialista Párt (MSZP)
Alliance of Young Democrats (Fidesz)—Fiatal Demokraták Szövetsége (Fidesz)
Christian Democratic Peoples Party (CDPP)—Kereszténydemokrata Néppárt (KDNP)

NOTES

1. I am very grateful to Professor Ronald Weber (University of Wisconsin, Milwaukee) for his comments on a draft of this paper. I have discussed the ECE party formation process in several papers: see Ágh (1994b, 1995a,

1995b). For parliamentary developments, see Ágh (1994a, 1996), Ágh and Kurtán (1995), and Ágh and Ilonszki (1996). The data used here are from the book I edited about the First Parliament (Ágh 1994a). Most of these data were complied by my colleagues, Sándor Kurtán and László Szarvas. I make use of Szarvas's (1995, especially 207–8) material on changes in parliamentary factions.

2. In chapter 2 of this volume, Laver and Shepsle refer to parties "emerging from the primeval slime," but they do not specify the situation in regional cases, such as in the ECE. They characterize these ready-made parties as "unitary actors" with "perfect party discipline" such that all members abide by all party decisions.

3. This discussion is based on data showing participation and voting in the Hungarian parliament for each year of the cycle, available in Kurtán, Sándor, and Vass (1995), as well as Ágh and Kurtán 1995)

4. On the full data of factions voting together, see Kurtán et al. 1995, 428–31. The *First Parliament* volume (Ágh and Kurtán 1995) includes chapters on legislative activity in connection with interpellations and questions in the Hungarian parliament, and full data are included therein. The above data are taken from Papp (1995, 111, 126–27).

5. For example, as a protest action to the drastic measures, the leader of the biggest Hungarian trade union confederation (National Alliance of Hungarian Trade Unions), Sándor Nagy, resigned from his two functions in the parliament. In addition, two HSP ministers (ministers of social policy and national security) resigned, but this did not shake the HSP faction.

6. So far, there have been very few personnel changes in the second Hungarian parliament; there have been no by-elections. Only one Fidesz MP has resigned, but his intention was known before the elections, and he has been replaced from the party list. In the second half of the term, MPs will be even more disciplined and avoid conflicts with the party faction because they want to be reelected. Given space, attention could also have been paid here to the parliamentary committees. Committee positions are allocated by the party factions proportionally to their seats. The MPs on these committees behave more as party members than as "individuals," and, particularly since they get extra pay for their committee work, they are interested in keeping their committee positions.

7. Lewis (1995, 107) cites opinions in Poland that factionalization and fragmentation have been part of the Polish tradition of political culture, explaining why they are higher than in other ECE countries. Ania van der Meer-Krok-Paszkowska and Marc van der Muyzenberg (1996, 200) also compare Hungarian and Polish parliamentary behavior and conclude that party discipline by and large is higher in Hungary than in Poland. Zdenka Mansfeldová in a recent paper (1996, 3) written after the end of the 1992–96 cycle of the Czech parliament, refers to the massive fluctuations among the parliamentary

factions, which have exceeded the Polish and Hungarian levels: "More than seventy MPs out of two hundred went over to a different party than they have been elected for during that term. Two MPs changed their party even more than once."

REFERENCES

Ágh, Attila, ed. 1994a. *The Emergence of East Central European Parliaments: The First Steps.* Budapest: Hungarian Centre for Democracy Studies.

———. 1994b. "The Hungarian Party System and Party Theory in the Transition of Central Europe." *Journal of Theoretical Politics* 6(2): 217–38.

———. 1995a. "The Experiences of the First Democratic Parliaments in East Central Europe." *Communist and Post-Communist Studies* 28(2): 203–14.

———. 1995b. "Partial Consolidation of the East-Central European Parties: The Case of the Hungarian Socialist Party." *Party Politics* 1(4): 491–514.

———. 1996. "Democratic Parliamentarism in Hungary: The First Parliament (1990–94) and the Entry of the Second Parliament." In David Olson and Philip Norton, eds., *The New Parliaments of Central and Eastern Europe.* London: Frank Cass.

———. 1997. "The End of the Beginning: The Partial Consolidation of East Central European Parties and Party Systems." In Jan-Erik Lane and Paul Pennings, eds., *Comparing Party System Change.* London: Routledge.

Ágh, Attila, and Gabriella Ilonszki, eds. 1996. *Parliaments and Organised Interests in Central Europe: The Second Steps.* Budapest: Hungarian Center for Democracy Studies.

Ágh, Attila, and Sándor Kurtán, eds. 1995. *Democratization and Europeanization in Hungary: The First Parliament, 1990–1994.* Budapest: Hungarian Center for Democracy Studies.

Katz, Richard, and Peter Mair. 1995. "Changing Models of Party Organization and Party Democracy: The Emergence of the Cartel Party." *Party Politics* 1(1): 5–28.

Kopecky, Petr. 1995. "Factionalism in Parliamentary Parties in the Czech Republic: A Concept and Some Empirical Findings." *Democratization* 2(1): 138–51.

Kurtán, Sándor, Péter Sándor, and László Vass. 1995. *Magyarország Politikai Évkönyve 1994* [Political Yearbook of Hungary 1994]. Budapest: Hungarian Center for Democracy Studies.

Lewis, Paul. 1995. "Poland and Eastern Europe: Perspectives on Party Factions and Factionalism." *Democratization* 2(1): 102–26.

Mair, Peter. 1994. "Party Organizations: From Civil Society to the State." In

Richard Katz and Peter Mair, eds., *How Parties Organize.* Thousand Oaks, CA: Sage.

Malová, Darina. 1994. "The Relationship between the State, Political Parties and Civil Society in Postcommunist Czecho-Slovakia." In Sona Szomolányi and Grigorij Meseznikov, eds., *The Slovak Path of Transition—to Democracy?* Bratislava: Slovak Political Science Association.

Mansfeldová, Zdenka. 1996. "The First Czech Parliament in the View of the Members of Parliament." Paper prepared for the International Conference on "The New Democratic Parliaments: The First Years," June 24–26, 1996, Ljubljana, Slovenia.

Papp, Imre. 1995. "The Stepchild of Parliament (or on Parliamentary Control in Front of the Plenary)." In Attila Ágh and Sándor Kurtán, eds., *Democratization and Europeanization in Hungary: The First Parliament, 1990–1994.* Budapest: Hungarian Center for Democracy Studies.

Pridham, Geoffrey. 1994. "Democratic Transitions in Theory and Practice: Southern European Lessons for Eastern Europe?" In Geoffrey Pridham and Tatu Vanhanen, eds., *Democratization in Eastern Europe.* London: Routledge.

Szarvas, László. 1995. "Parties and Party Factions in the Hungarian Parliament." In Terry Cox and Andy Furlong, eds., *Hungary: The Politics of Transition.* London: Frank Cass.

Van der Meer-Krok-Paszkowska, Ania, and Marc van der Muyzenberg. 1996. "The Role of the Parliamentary Party in the New Democracies: The Case of Hungary and Poland." In Máté Szabó, ed., *The Challenge of Europeanization in the Region: East Central Europe.* Budapest: Hungarian Political Science Association.

Waller, Michael. 1995. "Adaptation of Former Communist Parties of East-Central Europe: A Case of Social-Democratization?" *Party Politics* 1(4): 473–90.

Wyman, Matthew, Stephen White, Bill Miller, and Paul Heywood. 1995. "The Place of 'Party' in Post-Communist Europe." *Party Politics* 1(4): 535–48.

9

The Challenge of Diversity: Party Cohesion in the European Parliament

Tapio Raunio

How cohesive are the transnational political groups in the European Parliament? Is there much variation between the groups? What explains coalition behavior in the chamber? This chapter analyses the voting behavior of the party groups in the European Parliament (EP). The period under analysis is the third directly elected parliament of 1989–94. The sample consists of 159 roll call votes.

This chapter examines the nature of the EP's party system, with particular emphasis on factors that have been argued to undermine party cohesion in the Strasbourg Chamber. We analyze the significance of a consensual mode of decision making within and between the party groups, the acceptability and cost of voting against the group line, and the connection between legislative majority requirements and coalition behavior. The fourth European elections were held in June 1994, and in the final section we discuss the relevance of our findings to the party structure of the 1994–99 EP.

Party Discipline in Strasbourg

When analyzing the level of Europeanization achieved by the transnational party groups in the EP and their respective Europarties, political scientists, without exception, agree that we still have a long way to go before we have true European-wide parties. Palmer (1981, 71) has described political groups as "broad coalitions and alliances of parliamentarians with similar, but not necessarily totally shared philosophies and objectives," while in a more recent account on the European People's Party (EPP), Hanley (1994, 194–95) has applied the term to describe "an organization which unites national parties of similar style into a loose framework for political cooperation within European institutions for the pursuit of broad goals." Regardless of the actual wording, academics and politicians stress both cooperation and coordination as the primary tools for understanding the nature of party discipline within the parliament's party groups.

A number of interrelated factors are said to undermine the cohesion of EP party groups. The first of these is *a lack of meaningful government and opposition roles within the chamber.* The European Union (EU) lacks the kind of legislative-executive relationship characteristic of the individual EU member states. Even though the parliament's power of control vis-à-vis the commission has increased, the latter institution still consists of individuals nominated by their respective member state governments. Thus, with no government to defend or to bring down, the party groups face inevitable difficulties in enforcing voting discipline.

A second factor is *the distance of MEPs from their voters.* Lack of public awareness of the role and work of the parliament has been deplored by members of the European Parliament (MEPs) and others seeking more powers for the EP. The citizens' knowledge of their parliament remains at an alarmingly low level. Media coverage of part-sessions is also sporadic, with most national media interested only in grand or sensational themes. Individual representatives in Strasbourg thus need not take their voters into account when voting on a specific issue, unless, of course, the issue attracts considerable media attention in the MEP's home country. This factor thus gives the members freedom to maneuver when making their voting decisions.

A third factor is *national party delegations undermining consensus within political groups.* Political groups are formations uniting various national parties, and these national party delegations, especially larger ones such as the German Social Democratic Party (SPD) or the British Labour Party, carry much weight within the transnational groups. National party contingents have their own hierarchical structures, and "on important issues, groups will try to negotiate compromises among their national delegations before taking a decision. When groups fail to vote cohesively, it is usually because one or more national delegations have decided to opt out of a group position" (Jacobs, Corbett, and Shackleton 1995, 90). While usually these national party delegations cannot accept the group line because of differing views on the issue decided upon, the reason for voting against the group position is on occasions much more straightforward. Over half, 54.2%, of a sample of MEPs from (former West) Germany identified "national egoism" and not "political-ideological interests" or "group interests" as the main factor accounting for intragroup dissent (Hrbek and Schweitzer 1989, 6).

Furthermore, it has been argued that as the EP's legislative role continues to be strengthened, national parties will start to pay more attention to the behavior of their representatives in the parliament. According to Fitzmaurice (1975, 210), parties will reevaluate the EP as an institution: "Parties are about power and the exercise of power: they react to a new power center by attempting to structure it. . . . Members of the EP would be called to account by their national parties for their votes and actions in the EP. . . . Party discipline would be imposed, but it might well not be the discipline of the present European party groups but of national parties." National parties are arguably in a better position than the political groups to impose voting discipline on their representatives, especially since MEPs need their parties' approval for nomination as candidates on their lists in the next election.

A fourth factor is *voting by nationalities and other cross-group coalitions.* Research on the concept of representation in the EP has shown that MEPs regard themselves as representing multiple interests (Bardi 1989; Bowler and Farrell 1992; Raunio 1996a). While the members' primary allegiance is to their political groups, on occasion national delegations join forces in a vote with significant national implications. A good example was in July 1984, when the parliament rejected the Fontainebleau agreement, which gave the United Kingdom a budget refund. All British representatives, regardless of their party group affiliation, voted against the rejection (Vallance and Davies 1986, 29). Standard accounts of the EP are replete with examples of how nationally important issues unite MEPs on a cross-group basis.

Committees play a significant part in the parliament's internal organization, and individual members display high levels of specialization within the EP's committee structure (Bowler and Farrell 1995). Even though votes in the committees are often uncontested, cross-party alignments can occur at the committee level. The MEPs come together in various intergroups, approximately 50 of which were in existence after the 1989 and 1994 European elections, and of course MEPs maintain other informal contacts with their colleagues in the corridors and restaurants of the parliament. Certain significant topics, such as the Common Agricultural Policy (CAP) and the further deepening of integration, also attract varying levels of support within the political groups, their controversial nature leading to dissent within the party groups when votes are taken.

A fifth factor is *the acceptability and cost of voting against the group line.* When casting their votes, MEPs must consider the cost of voting against the group line. Above, it was argued that since their reselection as candidates in the next elections is dependent on their national parties, MEPs have a career motive for adhering to the party view. Within the parliament, they develop a certain reputation, and if their activities in the chamber, including voting behavior, suffer from inconsistencies, they may not be able to cultivate support among colleagues (Lord 1994). Such MEPs may expect not to be given important posts within the parliament or their groups or to receive assignments or rapporteurships of their own choice.

When asked to rate the "acceptability of forms of behavior," 53% of MEPs considered voting against the group line as "acceptable" or "most acceptable." In a comparison of the answers across the party groups, the highest percentages of members thinking it "unacceptable" to vote against the group line were in the ranks of the Socialist Group and the European Democratic Alliance (EDA) (Bowler and Farrell 1992).

A sixth factor is *the transnationality and fractionalization of the political groups.* According to this widely formulated view, the cohesion of a party group depends on the number of national parties included in the group. The logic is the same as in the Council of Ministers: the more views that need to be accommodated, the more problematic it becomes to find common ground. Many groups, notably the Liberals, are considered to be broad churches, with the member parties spanning a wide ideological spectrum. Indeed, some groups even include more than one party from the same member state.

A seventh factor is *the different cleavages found at the European level.* According to this line of reasoning, the transnational party groups—based on cleavage structures found at the national level—do not reflect the cleavage structure of EU politics (Andeweg 1995). In the context of EU decision making, a substantial proportion of issues, or at least the most important of them, are on the pro/anti-integration dimension. Party groups, and national party delegations within them, are bound to face internal problems when issues concerning the future of European integration are on the agenda.

An eighth and final factor is *the weakness of transnational parties.* At the national level, the behavior of a parliamentary party group is usually subjected to scrutiny by the extraparliamentary organs of that party. No equivalent is found at the European level, where the role of transnational parties has remained limited. While the three main party families, the Social Democrats (Party of the European Socialists [PES]), the Liberals (European Liberal, Democrat, and Reformist Party [ELDR]), and the Conservatives (EPP), have all established their own transnational Europarties, these parties "have been nothing more than clearing houses; providing information, campaign materials, and organizing (poorly attended) conferences and candidate exchanges" (Hix 1995, 535). Weak in terms of resources, with national parties in control over candidates and campaigns, the Europarties have hardly any power or means with which to exert control over "their" MEPs.

To counterbalance these factors, EP parties have created intragroup mechanisms designed to foster group cohesion. A detailed analysis of these factors is beyond the scope of this chapter, but it is worthwhile introducing the importance of intragroup decision making and legislative majorities.[1]

The political groups, at least the larger ones, have their own *whips.* However, the position of the whip should not be overestimated: "In terms of mechanics, the 'Whip' is normally nothing more than a list, prepared by the group secretariats and circulated to members' benches in the hemicycle before voting periods, setting out the recommended group position on each amendment as well as on final resolutions and reports. . . . On most uncontroversial business the group position is determined and indicated by the group's spokesman. . . . More controversial business would normally be taken to a discussion in the group, and a group line decided, frequently by a vote" (Westlake 1994a, 238).

While all groups allow their MEPs room for dissent, some groups invest more resources in building intragroup consensus than others. It is a common custom within all groups that if certain members feel they cannot accept the group line, they are given permission to defy it. Reasons behind these "opt-outs" vary, with MEPs often choosing to vote against the group line because of national political concerns. Especially in larger groups, in such situations it is expected that the MEP will announce his or her intentions before the vote in a group meeting. *Group meetings* provide important forums for consensus building, with extensive negotiations often taking place in search of mutually acceptable compromises. Willingness to build consensus is a crucial factor in explaining group cohesion.

To make the most of its existing powers and to fulfill its institutional role in passing, amending, or rejecting legislation, the EU's decision-making rules require the parliament to muster so-called *legislative majorities*.[2] The codecision, cooperation, assent, and budget procedures require the chamber to achieve absolute majorities; thus, in the 1989–94 EP, the need to reach the threshold figure of 260 became a pressing concern.[3]

Since the ability of the parliament to build these majorities depends on cooperation between the two largest groups, the Socialists and the EPP, the leaders of these two groups soon recognized the necessity of consensual decision making based on extensive negotiations. This approach was formalized after the 1984 European elections at "the meeting of the giants," where, according to Rudi Arndt (1992, 66–67), former chairman of the Socialist Group, the major groups "agreed that there was no point in a mutual flexing of ideological muscles: the only sensible strategy was to achieve appropriate majorities." This approach has not been without its negative consequences. Smaller groups have often felt neglected and pushed aside. Arndt (1992, 67) also admitted this fact, agreeing that "it has meant steamrolling the smaller factions in the group and, of course, the smaller groups who often got very annoyed, because they regarded Parliament as a forum for making known their views, whereas we regarded it as a forum for achieving majorities." Thus, the requirement to achieve legislative majorities has led to what Weiler (1991, 429) has called the "neutralization of ideology," with the result that certain MEPs have become ideologically marginalized within the chamber, a factor contributing to high levels of absenteeism from the hemicycle when votes are taken.

The literature on the EP party system has so far been skeptical about the ability of party groups to achieve and maintain cohesion. While I certainly agree that the EP party groups are definitely more vulnerable to internal dissent than parliamentary parties in EU member state legislatures, more empirical research is needed to falsify or support the arguments put forward.

Voting in the European Parliament

According to the ninth edition of the parliament's *Rules of Procedure* (European Parliament 1994), "The right to vote is a personal right.

Members shall cast their votes individually and in person" (Rule 117), and "Normally Parliament shall vote by show of hands. If the President decides that the result is doubtful, a fresh vote shall be taken using the electronic voting system and, if the latter is not working, by sitting and standing" (Rule 118). Voting by secret ballot is primarily used in the case of appointments to Parliament's top hierarchical positions. Rule 119 states that "the vote shall be taken by roll-call if so requested in writing by at least twenty-nine Members or a political group before voting has begun. . . . In calculating whether a motion has been adopted or rejected account shall be taken only of votes cast for and against. . . . Voting shall be recorded in the minutes of proceedings of the sitting by political group in the alphabetical order of Members' names." Roll call voting used to be done by word of mouth, but since the installation of electronic voting machines, representatives have been able to cast their "Yes," "No," or "I abstain" votes by using their voting cards. If MEPs feel that their position on the matter needs to be clarified, they "may give an oral explanation on the final vote for not longer than one minute or give a written explanation of no more than 200 words, which shall be included in the verbatim report of proceedings" (Rule 122).

Roll call voting is mainly requested by the political groups for the following reasons: it enables groups to make their positions known to the wider audience; it can be used by groups to highlight the opposing view adopted by other groups; and it helps the groups in checking how their own MEPs voted (Jacobs et al. 1995, 160).

Poor and erratic attendance is a problem frequently associated with national legislatures, and the EP is definitely no exception. Attendance in the chamber during voting periods tends to vary depending on the significance of the issue voted upon. When legislative measures requiring absolute majorities are on the agenda, MEPs take their seats in the hemicycle. In fact, these votes are grouped together at noon on Wednesdays to increase the probability that the required number of members is present in the chamber when votes are taken.[4]

The Sample

Parliament's voting records are published in the C-Series of the *Official Journal of the European Communities*. The temporal scope of this research is the third term of the directly elected parliament, excluding, however, the plenary sessions held in the final months preceding the

June 1994 European elections. The sample includes 159 votes. The following quantitative criteria were used in selecting votes for further analysis.

1. At least a quorum, one-third of the elected MEPs, were required to have taken part in the vote (173/518).
2. The indices of agreement and voting likeness were calculated only when at least a quarter of the members of the group voted.
3. Not only final votes but also votes on individual paragraphs and amendments are included in the analysis. Of the 159 votes, 62 are votes on paragraphs or amendments. The reason for including votes on amendments in the sample is that often votes on specific amendments are more significant and contested than the final votes. Indeed, while the index of agreement (IA) for the EP as a whole on all votes is .513, on votes on amendments it is only .354.
4. No minimum level of conflict was required in this study.

Voting behavior analysis presents obviously only one possible solution to studying party cohesion and the dimensionality of cleavages and alignments in legislatures.[5] Roll call analysis needs to be supplemented by other methods before anything close to a comprehensive picture of the nature of political groups will emerge. However, it can be argued that roll call analysis is a particularly worthwhile exercise in the context of the EP. Considering that before most reports and resolutions are put to vote, lengthy negotiations have often taken place within and between the groups, lack of unitary voting behavior by groups can be interpreted as definitive evidence of intragroup conflict on the matter.

Party Cohesion in the 1989–94 Parliament

An IA is used to examine the cohesion of the political groups. "The index is a measure of the relation that exists between the three modalities of votes—in favor, against and abstention—cast by the members of a group; more exactly, it is the percentage measure of the relation between (a) the difference between the highest numbering modality and the sum of the other two modalities in a vote by the MEPs of a group, and (b) the total number of votes cast by the group" (Attinà 1990, 564). It can be expressed as follows:

$$IA = \frac{(\text{highest modality} - \text{sum of the other two modalities})}{\text{total number of votes}} \times 100$$

The index reaches the value 1.00 when all the deputies belonging to a group vote in the same way. Between .999 and .001, agreement decreases, but more than half of the voters express the same voting modality. "At 0 we have a split in half of the votes in two modalities or, with three modalities, one of these is exactly equal to the sum of the other two. When the index has a negative value, the votes break down into three modalities, and even the highest number of votes in one modality is less than half of the total group vote" (Attinà 1990, 564). To calculate the IAs for the EP and its party groups, the sum of the IAs of individual votes was divided by the number of votes.

A methodological problem concerns those MEPs who abstain. According to the parliament's *Rules of Procedure* (European Parliament 1994), only votes cast for or against are taken into account. From this point of view, it would make sense to consider abstentions as neutral positions. However, here abstentions (if the minority position within the group) are regarded as failure to accept the official group line. By abstaining, representatives do not actively support the position of their groups; thus, they increase the voting power of their opposition.

Hypothesis 1: There is a direct relationship between party group cohesion and party group heterogeneity.

National political parties have their roots in their respective political systems, and the behavior and ideology of these delegations are expected to reflect their experiences in the context of national politics. The degree of party group transnationality (the number of member states sending representatives to the group) and fractionalization (the number of party delegations in a group) is thus expected to have an effect on the cohesion of the groups. The more heterogeneous the group, the less cohesive it is, and vice versa.

The larger groups have much higher degrees of transnationality and fractionalization than the smaller political groups (table 9.1). The only exception is the Rainbow Group. The group functioned as a loose coalition, bringing together various regionalist and other smaller parties, including four Danish antimarketeers. The very low values of the European Democratic Group (EDG) result from the fact that 32 out of the group's 34 MEPs represented the British Conservatives. Four out of 10 political groups—EDG, Group of the United European Left (EUL),

Table 9.1

Political Groups' Transnationality and Fractionalization after the 1989 Elections and Their Cohesion in the 1989–1994 EP

Groups	Seats	National Delegations	IT[a]	Party Delegations	IF[b]	IA[c]
PES	180	12	.852	16	.858	.786
EPP	121	12	.841	16	.873	.882
ELDR	49	10	.851	20	.917	.857
EDG	34	2	.111	2	.111	.922
V	29	7	.790	12	.837	.875
EUL	28	4	.360	4	.360	.923
EDA	22	4	.566	4	.566	.645
ER	17	3	.526	3	.526	.889
LU	14	4	.653	5	.673	.938
RB	13	8	.824	9	.840	.695

Note: PES = Party of the European Socialists; EPP = European People's Party; ELDR = European Liberal, Democrat, and Reformist Party; V = The Greens; EUL = Group of the United European Left; EDA = European Democratic Alliance; ER = Technical Group of the European Right; LU = Left Unity; RB = Rainbow Group. The sizes of the groups underwent much variation during the 1989–94 legislative term. Two groups disappeared altogether, the EDG joining the EPP in May 1992, and the EUL joining the Socialists in January 1993.
[a]The index of transnationality (IT) is based on Rae's index of fractionalization. The formula for its calculation is

$$ IT = 1 - \left(\sum_{i=1}^{n} SC^2 \right), $$

where SC is the respective share of MEPs from the various countries within a group and n is the number of countries involved. The greater the index value, the higher the degree of transnationality of a political group. It should be noted, however, that the maximum value (1) is a hypothetical one. Since the number of units is an integral part of the index, the given number of member states limits the degree of transnationality that a group within the EP can come up to (Niedermayer 1983, 241). In the 1989–94 Community of 12 member states, a political group with member country delegations of exactly equal size from each member state would have had the index value of .917.
[b]The index of fractionalization (IF) is computed in the same way as the transnationality index, with only the number of national party delegations replacing the number of member state delegations.
[c]IA = index of agreement.

EDA, and the European Right (ER)—have coalescing transnationality and fractionalization indices: none of these groups included more than one party delegation per member state. On the other hand, 6 of the 10 national delegations to the Liberals' group have MEPs representing two or more parties, and the Italian MEPs in the Greens group represent four different parties.[6]

Political groups with high degrees of transnationality and fractionalization—Socialists, EPP, Liberals, and the Rainbow Group—were expected to be less cohesive than the more homogeneous groups. The IAs of the Socialists and the Rainbow Group are indeed low, with the former remaining clearly behind EPP, the other large group in the parliament. The low IA of the Rainbow Group comes as no surprise. The group's ideologically very diverse composition was not conducive to successful coordination of points of view. Furthermore, the Rainbow Group was largely a product of the EP's internal rules. Since, in the 1989–94 parliament, 23 members from one member state, 18 from two member states, and only 12 from three or more member states were needed to form a group, the national party delegations in question decided to join a group to increase their influence in the chamber and to gain the material benefits that group status entails. The low IA of the EDA group is also as expected. It is interesting to note that Socialists and the EDA both have low levels of party cohesion, even though their members regard voting against group line as unacceptable (see above).

The high cohesion of the EDG, the ER, EUL, and the Left Unity (LU) result from these groups' rather homogeneous character. The EDG, which dissolved in the spring of 1992, consisted almost exclusively of British Conservatives; the influence of Jean-Marie Le Pen's Front National only increased within the ER after the departure of half of the German contingent within the group; and the two communist groups, EUL and LU, were dominated by Italian (PDS—Partito Democratico della Sinistra) and French (PCF—Parti Communiste Français) communists respectively. The relatively high cohesion of the Greens is a somewhat unexpected result, considering the differences in the ideological profiles between the parties in the group.

The EPP and the Liberals are two groups with high degrees of transnationality and fractionalization that have been able to achieve intragroup consensus during voting periods. These two party families have been at the heart of the European integration process from its very beginning, and both party groups like to stress in their programs and electoral manifestos their commitment to achieving closer economic and political union. The EPP has indeed attained rather similar levels of cohesion throughout the directly elected parliament. The Liberals' performance has been more inconsistent: having been the second most cohesive party group in the 1979–84 EP, the group has been much more prone to internal conflict in the second and fourth parliaments (Attinà 1990).

Thus, the findings do not confirm hypothesis 1: there is no direct relationship between party group heterogeneity and party group cohesion. Group cohesion cannot be analyzed by counting the number of national parties represented in a group.

A comparison of EP parties with parliamentary parties in national legislatures shows that party groups in Strasbourg are still less cohesive than parties in selected western European legislatures. Interestingly, the two parties in the U.S. Congress are behind the EP parties in terms of cohesion. Since the American federal system of governance resembles the emerging European version of federation, it can be argued that the Congress provides a better benchmark for comparison than EU member state legislatures (see Raunio 1996b).

Distances between the Groups: EP Party System, 1989–1994

Despite the inevitable differences in the ideological outlook of the national parties forming party groups in the parliament, the EP party system is based on the traditional left-right dimension. While political groups overlap ideologically in some cases, the cohesion of the groups indicates that most national parties have had surprisingly little problem in finding a suitable political home in the Strasbourg Chamber. Various analyses on the left-right placement of parties—based on MEPs' own coalition preferences, voting behavior, national coalition behavior, surveys of party activists, and expert statements—have produced similar enough results to enable us to locate the party groups from the left to right.[7]

In the 1989–94 EP, parties of the left were, from the extreme to the center, LU, EUL, the Greens, and the Socialists. And the parties of the right were, from the center to the far right, the Liberals, the EPP, the EDG, EDA, and the ER. The Rainbow Group cannot be placed on the axis due to the group's internal diversity. Overlapping is particularly evident between the Liberals and the EPP, with the internal diversity of the ELDR making it virtually impossible to locate the group firmly on either side of the EPP. Rice's (1928) Index of Voting Likeness (IVL) is used to measure the degree of voting similarity between the political groups:

$$IVL = 100 - (A - B),$$

where A = percentage of party group A voting pro on resolution X, B = percentage of party group B voting pro on resolution X, and (A − B) = absolute value of A − B. The IVL ranges between 0 (maximum disagreement) and 100 (maximum voting similarity). Average IVLs are calculated by summing up the IVLs on individual votes and then dividing the sum by the number of votes (Hurwitz 1983, 205).

Hypothesis 2: The voting similarity of the EP political groups reflects their positions on the left-right dimension.

The left-right division is not the only existing one in the Strasbourg assembly. Among other possible cleavages are northern versus southern member states, federalists versus anti-integrationists, and the agricultural lobby versus those against high levels of CAP spending. However, it is expected that even though—or because—coalitions in the EP are often ad hoc and very issue specific, the left-right division is the dominant one in the parliament.

Hypothesis 3: The ideologically extremist groups do not form coalitions with other parties within the chamber.

Writing right after the 1989 European elections, Bogdanor (1989, 213) argued that the EP party system is characterized by "an immobile centre and two incompatible extremes," with the center parties (Socialists, EPP, Liberals) all committed to further integration and leaving no room for effective opposition. The ER was excluded from intraparliamentary appointments, and the other groups refused to work with its far-right members. At the left end of the axis, LU is regarded as hostile to the current form of European integration, and that is also the position of the Greens. It is thus expected that these three groups will be ideologically distant both from each other and from the other groups.

Table 9.2 proves the existence of a left-right dimension in the chamber. The political groups on the left—the Socialists, EUL and LU, and the Greens—have higher IVLs among them than with the groups to the right of the center—EPP, Liberals, EDG, and EDA—and vice versa. The Socialists are shown to be in the center of the axis, almost equally far from six of the groups. The only group relatively close to them is EUL, and the two indeed merged in January 1993. LU is behaviorally closest to the Greens and the EUL but remains far apart from the

Table 9.2

Political Groups' Voting Similarity in the 1989–1994 EP

	PES	EPP	ELDR	EDG	V	EUL	EDA	ER	LU	RB
PES	—	66.0	65.0	65.3	56.7	81.8	63.1	47.6	65.7	65.8
EPP	66.0	—	78.8	94.0	48.0	59.7	72.6	47.2	39.0	58.9
ELDR	65.0	78.8	—	90.3	52.6	60.1	64.0	46.1	38.9	70.3
EDG	65.3	94.0	90.3	—	43.4	55.2	72.7	43.3	32.8	55.2
V	56.7	48.0	52.6	43.4	—	66.5	49.6	53.4	75.3	72.2
EUL	81.8	59.7	60.1	55.2	66.5	—	46.1	44.9	74.3	64.4
EDA	63.1	72.6	64.0	72.7	49.6	46.1	—	58.8	37.0	57.1
ER	47.6	47.2	46.1	43.3	53.4	44.9	58.8	—	52.2	53.8
LU	65.7	39.0	38.9	32.8	75.3	74.3	37.0	52.2	—	64.5
RB	65.8	58.9	70.3	55.2	72.2	64.4	57.1	53.8	64.5	—

Note: For key to party acronyms, see note to table 9.1.

center-right groups. Voting behavior analysis also confirms the Greens' leftist position on the axis, but the group was nevertheless fairly isolated in the chamber.

On the right there is a bloc of three groups with close voting proximity: the EPP, the Liberals, and the EDG. The EDG joined the EPP in May 1992, and the high degree of voting similarity between the two groups confirms the logic of their merger. The EDA stands clearly to the right of the EPP and the Liberals. The ER is behaviorally very distant from the other groups, and the group no longer exists in the fourth parliament. The Rainbow Group behaves as expected, its voting behavior reflecting the group's diverse membership. However, it is interesting to note that of the five groups closest to the Rainbow Group, four are positioned left of center.

Hypothesis 2 is thus confirmed: party groups' voting behavior reflects their corresponding positions on the left-right dimension. Moreover, comparing the findings with earlier research on the parliament, it appears that the EP party system is fairly stable. Even though the number of political groups has varied between 1979 and 1994, their positions on the left-right axis have remained the same.

Hypothesis 3 is also confirmed: the three party groups expected not to form coalitions with other groups in the chamber—the ER, LU, and the Greens—were all ideologically distant from the political center. All three Martin reports, for example, were adopted by overwhelming majorities, with only the ER and LU groups opposing the resolutions.[8] The Greens and the LU were also closest to each other in their voting behavior, a finding reflecting both groups' ideological opposition to the integration process.

Conclusion

The fourth European elections, held in June 1994, led to further changes in the EP party system, with three completely new political groups emerging: Europe of the Nations (EN), an anti-Maastricht group built around representatives of the French l'Autre Europe party and the Danish antimarketeers; Forza Europa (FE), a mononational group of MEPs from Berlusconi's Forza Italia; and European Radical Alliance (ERA), led by Bernard Tapie's Energie Radicale. The ER and Rainbow Group no longer exist in the chamber, with the former failing to work out an arrangement between the Italian National Alliance (NA) and the French Front National that would have enabled them to form a group. Now the far-right MEPs sit as nonattached members. FE and EDA joined forces in the summer of 1995, and the new group, Union for Europe (UPE), is the third largest group in the parliament.

The larger groups continue to dominate the organization of the parliament. With cooperation between the Socialists and the EPP necessary for building required legislative majorities, the political center has an incentive to vote together on most issues falling under the various legislative procedures. The political opposition in the chamber now mainly comes from members of LU, the Greens, EN, and the far-right nonattached MEPs—that is, the predominantly antifederalist bloc. Thus, the situation remains much the same as after 1989: the fragmentation of opposition has only consolidated the dominance of the political center. Voting power analysis of the directly elected EP has shown that the influence of the smaller groups diminishes as majority rules become more stringent (Wiberg and Raunio 1997). The smaller groups are also more vulnerable to electoral misfortunes and to defections to rival groups during the legislative term (Bardi 1996).

Political groups have reached much higher levels of unity than initially expected. There is, however, much variation between the groups. Voting behavior analysis has shown that party cohesion in the EP is not dependent on the transnationality and fractionalization of the groups. Either the national party delegations have little difficulty in accepting the group positions, or the weak links between MEPs and their national parties have left representatives room for maneuvering in the parliament. Voting data from the 1994–99 parliament shows that party cohesion remains relatively high in the fourth parliament (Hix and Lord 1997).

The left-right dimension dominates in the EP, but on certain subject matters MEPs form coalitions on a cross-group basis. However, these alignments are not durable; thus, they serve only to strengthen the value of the left-right axis in explaining the coalition behavior of the party groups. According to Collie (1984, 22–23), "There is some point at which coalitions are so highly issue-specific that policy dimensions have no value," and research that I undertook on votes on foreign policy matters in the EP produced similar results (Raunio 1997). Considering that the EP is still an institution in search of a clear constitutional mandate, the behavior of MEPs remains largely conditioned by the majority requirements, an explanatory variable at least as significant as the subject matter itself.

NOTES

1. The internal organization of the EP parties remains an underresearched topic. For information on the internal structures and working methods of the political groups, see Hix and Lord (1997) and Raunio (1996b).

2. For a list of the required parliamentary majorities, see Westlake (1994b, 261–63).

3. In the case of the assent procedure, the Maastricht Treaty removed the absolute majority requirement except in two cases: accession of new member states to the EU and uniform procedure for European elections. Apart from these two cases, a simple majority of those voting is enough.

4. Absenteeism not only gives the parliament a bad image in the eyes of the electorate but also is an indicator of group indiscipline, since groups often invest many resources in mobilizing their members to be present in the chamber when votes are taken. See the data in Bay Brzinski (1995).

5. For earlier research on MEPs' voting behavior, see Attinà (1990, 1992b), Bay Brzinski (1995), Hurwitz (1983, 1987), Quanjel and Wolters (1992), and Zellentin (1967). The work of Fulvio Attinà is particularly worthy of attention. Attinà measures the cohesion of the political groups in the first (1979–84) and second (1984–89) terms of the elected EP and investigates how issue areas and majority requirements affect group cohesion. The volume by Hix and Lord (1997) contains voting data from the early 1994–99 legislature. An alternative approach is to concentrate on certain significant "key" votes. Studies on the nomination of Jacques Santer as the commission president have revealed the way in which domestic party political considerations undermine the cohesion of EP parties. See Hix and Lord (1996) and Johansson (1997).

6. These facts need to be treated with some caution. For example, the party affiliation of the French members within the Liberals group is somewhat unclear. Different sources—including party documents provided by the ELDR headquarters—report different party affiliations.

7. See, e.g., Attinà (1992a, 1994), Niedermayer (1983), Quanjel and Wolters (1992), and Rattinger (1982).

8. The Martin reports, named after their rapporteur David Martin, stated the EP's position with regard to the Intergovernmental Conference on Political Union of 1991 (Vanhoonacker 1992, 216–18). Similarly, in the vote on the Maastricht Treaty in April 1992, the opposition came from the Greens, the ER, LU, and the Rainbow Group (Mengelberg 1994).

REFERENCES

Andeweg, Rudy. 1995. "The Reshaping of National Party Systems." *West European Politics* 18(3): 58–78.

Arndt, Rudi. 1992. "The Political Groups in the European Parliament." In *The European Community in the Historical Context of its Parliament,* Proceedings of the 40th Anniversary Symposium, Strasbourg. Strasbourg: European Parliament.

Attinà, Fulvio. 1990. "The Voting Behavior of the European Parliament Members and the Problem of the Europarties." *European Journal of Political Research* 18: 557–79.

———. 1992a. "Parties, Party Systems and Democracy in the European Union." *International Spectator* 27(3): 67–86.

———. 1992b. *Il sistema politico della Comunita Europea.* Milano: Giuffre.

———. 1994. "Political Parties, Federalism and the European Union." In Franz Knipping, ed., *Federal Conceptions in EU Member States: Traditions and Perspectives.* Baden-Baden: Nomos.

Bardi, Luciano. 1989. *Il parlamento della Comunita Europea. Legittimita e riforma.* Bologna: Il Mulino.

———. 1996. "Transnational Trends in European Parties and the 1994 European Elections of the European Parliament." *Party Politics* 2: 99–113.

Bay Brzinski, Joanne. 1995. "Political Group Cohesion in the European Parliament, 1989–1994." In Carolyn Rhodes and Sonia Mazey, eds., *The State of the European Union.* Vol. 3: *Building a European Polity?* Boulder, CO: Lynne Rienner.

Bogdanor, Vernon. 1989. "Direct Elections, Representative Democracy and European Integration." *Electoral Studies* 8: 205–16.

Bowler, Shaun, and David Farrell. 1992. *MEPs, Voters and Interest Groups: Representation at the European Level.* Final Report to the Commission of the European Community, Directorate General for Information, Communication, Culture.

———. 1995. "The Organizing of the European Parliament: Committees, Specialization and Coordination." *British Journal of Political Science* 25: 219–43.

Collie, Melissa P. 1984. "Voting Behavior in Legislatures." *Legislative Studies Quarterly* 9: 3–50.

European Parliament. 1994. *Rules of Procedure.* 9th ed. Strasbourg: European Parliament.

Fitzmaurice, John. 1975. *The Party Groups in the European Parliament.* Farnborough, UK: Saxon House.

Hanley, David. 1994. "The European People's Party: Towards a New Party Form?" In David Hanley, ed., *Christian Democracy in Europe: A Comparative Perspective.* London: Pinter.

Hix, Simon. 1995. "Parties at the European Level and the Legitimacy of EU Socio-Economic Policy." *Journal of Common Market Studies* 33: 527–54.

Hix, Simon, and Christopher Lord. 1996. "The Making of a President: The European Parliament and the Confirmation of Jacques Santer as President of the Commission." *Government and Opposition* 31: 62–76.

———. 1997. *Political Parties in the European Union.* New York: Macmillan.

Hrbek, Rudolf, and Carl-Christoph Schweitzer. 1989. "Die deutschen Europa-Parlamentarier." *Aus Politik und Zeitgeschichte* B3/89: 3–18.

Hurwitz, Leon. 1983. "Partisan Ideology or National Interest? An Analysis of the Members of the European Parliament." In Leon Hurwitz, ed., *The Harmonization of European Public Policy: Regional Responses to Transnational Challenges.* Westport, CT: Greenwood Press.

———. 1987. *The European Community and the Management of International Cooperation.* Westport, CT: Greenwood Press.

Jacobs, Francis, Richard Corbett, and Michael Shackleton. 1995. *The European Parliament.* 3rd ed. London: Cartermill.

Johansson, Karl Magnus. 1997. "Party Group Dynamics in the European Parliament." In Ernst Kuper and Uwe Jun, eds., *National Interest and Integrative Politics in Transnational Assemblies.* London: Frank Cass.

Lord, Christopher. 1994. "Party Groups in the European Parliament: Rethinking the Role of Transnational Parties in the Democratization of the European Union." Paper to the European Consortium of Political Research, April, Madrid Joint Sessions.

Mengelberg, Sabine. 1994. "The European Parliament and the Ratification of the Maastricht Treaty." In Finn Laursen and Sophie Vanhoonacker, eds., *The Ratification of the Maastricht Treaty: Issues, Debates and Future Implications.* Maastricht: European Institute of Public Administration.

Niedermayer, Oskar. 1983. *Europäische Parteien? Zur grenzüberschreitenden Interaktion politischer Parteien im Rahmen der Europäischen Gemeinschaft.* Frankfurt: Campus.

Official Journal of the European Communities, C-series, 1989–94.

Palmer, Michael. 1981. *The European Parliament: What It Is, What It Does, How It Works.* New York: Pergamon Press.

Quanjel, Marcel, and Menno Wolters. 1992. "Het Europees Parlement." In Menno Wolters, ed., *Democratie en beleid in de Europese Gemeeschap.* Alphen aan den Rijn: Samson H. D. Tjeenk Willink.

Rattinger, Hans. 1982. "Abstimmungsmacht, politische Distanzen und Abstimmungskoalitionen zwischen den Fraktionen im Europäischen Parlament." *Zeitschrift für Soziologie* 11: 133–49.

Raunio, Tapio. 1996a. "Parliamentary Questions in the European Parliament: Representation, Information, and Control." *Journal of Legislative Studies* 2: 356–82.

———. 1996b. *Party Group Behavior in the European Parliament: An Analysis of Transnational Political Groups in the 1989–94 Parliament.* Acta Universitatis Tamperensis, Vammalan Kirjapaino, Vammala, Finland.

———. 1997. "Cleavages and Alignments in the European Parliament: MEP Voting Behavior, 1989–1994." In David S. Bell and Christopher Lord, eds., *Transnational Party Politics in the European Union.* Aldershot, UK: Dartmouth.

Rice, S. A. 1928. *Quantitative Methods in Politics.* New York: Knopf.

Vallance, Elizabeth, and Elizabeth Davies. 1986. *Women of Europe: Women MEPs and Equality Policy.* Cambridge: Cambridge University Press.

Vanhoonacker, Sophie. 1992. "The European Parliament and European Political Union." In Finn Laursen and Sophie Vanhoonacker, eds., *The Intergovernmental Conference on Political Union: Institutional Reforms, New Policies and International Identity of the European Community.* Dordrecht: Martinus Nijhoff.

Weiler, J. H. H. 1991. "Problems of Legitimacy in Post 1992 Europe." *Aussenwirtschaft* 46: 411–37.

Westlake, Martin. 1994a. *Britain's Emerging Euro-Elite? The British in the Directly-Elected European Parliament, 1979–1992.* Aldershot, UK: Dartmouth.

———. 1994b. *A Modern Guide to the European Parliament.* London: Pinter.

Wiberg, Matti, and Tapio Raunio. 1997. "Controlling Voting Outcomes: Voting Power in the European Parliament, 1979–1995." In Ernst Kuper and Uwe Jun, eds., *National Interest and Integrative Politics in Transnational Assemblies.* London: Frank Cass.

Zellentin, Gerda. 1967. "Form and Function of the Opposition in the European Communities." *Government and Opposition* 2: 416–35.

10

Parties and Party Discipline within the European Parliament: A Norms-Based Approach

SHAUN BOWLER AND
DAVID M. FARRELL

The European Parliament as a Legislature

The building and maintenance of coherent voting blocs is a central component of any legislative body. Within European parliaments, the need to maintain an executive in office provides a powerful incentive for members to act in unison, either for or against the executive. The central control of electoral resources such as money, party label, or list of members provides yet other incentives to keep members in line. Within the European Parliament (EP), however, most of these kinds of resources are not available to members of the central party groups. Nomination and election are in the hands of national bodies, while the absence of an executive means a lack of one of the major incentives to collective action. This suggests that party discipline is hardly likely to be prevalent, particularly within an institution that is often plagued by absenteeism (Jacobs, Corbett, and Shackleton 1995).

Yet party discipline within the EP is an interesting area for examination, for there are reasons to expect that the EP as an institution can benefit from having its members act in concert. Formal work, for example, has recently shown that the EP does have the potential to exercise influence within the European Union (EU), provided that its members can act in concert. If its members can act in this way, then the EP can be seen as a "conditional agenda setter" (Tsebelis 1994) with the scope to impose its views on EU policy settlements. And in other areas too, such as the writing of reports, the codecision procedure, and the ratification of the commission president, there is scope for MEPs to exercise an influence on EU affairs (e.g., Hix and Lord 1997). While it is clear that even when we take these factors into account, no one is likely to claim the EP as one of the more powerful legislatures in the world, it is also clear that the EU is far from being the simple "talking shop" of the 1970s. And once space is opened up through constitutional developments such as the codecision procedure, there are obvious incentives for rival groups to mobilize in order to stamp their point of view on the eventual outcome.

This makes the EP an especially intriguing legislative institution from the point of view of party discipline and coherence. On the one hand, it would seem that the EP can exercise influence, provided that it can muster the will to use it. On the other hand, the usual range of incentives and inducements open to party leaders to help shape action *en bloc* seem to be lacking—although this is not to say that the party group leaders are not trying to exercise control over the EP as a legislature.

Even a rather cursory look at the institution shows that there are attempts to place parties at the center of the EP. We can show this quite readily by comparing the internal structure of the EP with national-level legislatures. Table 10.1 provides a number of points of comparison between the EP and member states' parliaments (not including the three new members), relating to committee structure, role of party groups, and so on—areas that have been identified by previous studies as important components of legislative structure. On the basis of these comparisons, we can make three broad points in increasing order of importance.

First, we should note that the fairly elaborate development of the internal organization of the EP—which is entirely under the control of the MEPs themselves—helps to underscore the general point that this institution is more than just a "talking shop." There would seem to be little need for MEPs to go to such lengths to develop such a detailed structure if they were not interested in building a serious legislative institution.

Second, of all the possible parliamentary forms upon which to model

Table 10.1

Comparison of the Internal Structure of the EP with National Legislatures of the 12 EU Member States in the Early 1990s

	EP	B	Dk	F	G	GR	I	It	L	N	P	S	UK
Presiding body													
Collective body/bureau	x	x	x	x	x	x		x				x	
Party groups													
represented	x		x	x	x			x	x				
Decides order of													
business	x	x	x		x			x				x	
Committees													
No quorum needed for													
meeting	x		x	x						x		x	
Quorum needed for													
vote	x			x	x				x		x	x	
Chair formally chosen													
by committee	x	x			x	x	x		x	x	x	x	x
Appointment via party													
group	x	x		x	x	x	x	x	x	x	x	x	x
Party-proportional													
membership	x	x	x	x	x				x	x	x		
Party-proporptional													
chairs	x	x	x		x				x		x	?	
No restriction on													
multiple membership	x	x	x		x		x		x	x		x	x

Sources: EP Rules of Procedure, 5th ed., 1989; Strøm (1984); Jacobs et al. (1995); *Parliaments of the World,* IPU, 1986.

Note: EP = European Parliament; B = Belgium; Dk = Denmark; F = France; G = Germany; GR = Greece; I = Ireland; It = Italy; L = Luxembourg; N = Netherlands; P = Portugal; S = Spain; UK = United Kingdom.

itself, the EP looks more like Germany's Bundestag than like any other national parliament. If we simply add up the points of comparison, we note that the EP has more elements in common with the Bundestag than with any other legislature. Of particular note is the quite sharp distinction between the way the EP is structured internally and the internal organization of majoritarian legislatures in the United Kingdom, Ireland, and France. The EP, in fact, seems to bear the hallmarks of an institution attempting to build consensus among its members, a point we return to below.

Third, and most important, we note that the internal structure of the EP gives a great deal of prominence to party groups. The internal operation of the EP is controlled by the Conference of Presidents, in which party groups are represented. Furthermore, committee places and presidencies (chairs) are given over to party groups in proportion to their strength in the chamber. Given that the formal structures of the EP provide such scope for party group influence, this presents an opportunity for members of party groups to exercise considerable influence, providing they act as a group.

Thus, the party groups can be seen as central players within the EP and its organization (Bardi 1996; Bowler and Farrell 1995; Jacobs et al. 1995). Yet part of their influence depends upon the willingness of members to submit to their constraints. One way in which we can begin to tap this willingness is by examining the attitudes of MEPs themselves. How members view the acceptability (or otherwise) of going against the group in some form or other will tell us about some of the limits to that influence. In other words, one avenue of approach to the issue of party discipline within the EP is to look at norms among MEPs. (The other avenue of approach—examining roll call votes—is dealt with by Raunio in chap. 9 of this volume.)

Norms within Legislatures

"Norms" or "folkways" within legislatures were one of the earliest subjects of interest for behavioral studies of legislatures. They are regarded as important aspects of the social organization within parliaments. While there may exist written rules of procedure, much of the way in which the chamber operates may be determined by unwritten rules. This fact has shaped much of the literature on legislatures, especially in a comparative setting. According to Williams (1968, 204), "Norms are rules of conduct . . . standards by reference to which behavior is judged and approved or disapproved." Norms govern the behavior of individuals either as a principle of individual action or as a property of a social system (Coleman 1990; Turner 1989). Norms provide some degree of predictability about an individual's likely behavior, both to outside observers and to others engaged in social activities with that individual. The closely related idea of a "role" is defined as "a set of expectations held for a position by its incumbent and by the incumbents of related positions" (Kornberg 1967, 8).

The common element in these ideas of norms and roles is that, to the extent that either are present, they imply that members of a given social setting have stable and convergent expectations regarding the behavior of other actors. More technical game-theoretic treatments of norms suggest that they may be regarded as predictable behavior (evolutionary stable strategies) in a repeated setting (e.g., Ordeshook 1992, 181). A less technical study of the U.S. Senate notes: "For norms or folkways to be operative, the expectations about behavior must be fairly widely shared" (Rohde, Ornstein, and Peabody 1985, 149). Searing's work (1991, 1241) addresses this question by stating that "informal rules are critical to an organization, for it is not possible to operate without them. Every organization, therefore develops and maintains a structure of informal rules. And the principal components of these informal rules are norms and roles."

To some extent, the U.S. literature tends to see norms as important from the point of view of the individual member rather than the institution (system) as a whole (Fenno 1973, 1978; Foley 1980; Matthews 1973; Rohde et al. 1985; Sinclair 1989). But there is a body of literature that also argues that norms are important from the point of view of the overall institution. Norms may "contribute to the transformation of an assortment of individual politicians into members of an institution collectively engaging in a set of common activities" (Loewenberg and Mans 1988, 155).

The focus on what norms do for individual legislators (rather than the system) allows the literature as a whole to provide an explanation for changes in norms. This is an important step, since norms are, by definition, self-replicating, so that some motor for change is required. An emphasis upon the utility of norms to individual members does provide some mechanism that may account for change; if prevailing norms frustrate the wishes of enough individual members, then norms will change (e.g., Sinclair 1989, 106). But the emphasis, perhaps inevitably, in discussions of norms is upon stability of opinions, a stability that repetition, communication, and enforcement play key roles in maintaining (Asher 1973).

What kind of norms does the literature suggest as relevant within the EP? Loewenberg and Mans (1988, 162) make a useful distinction between two types of norms. First, there are "norms of parliamentary courtesy," which show an "underlying collegial sensitivity of MPs towards each other." These courtesy norms are likely to be the easiest to spot. As Loewenberg and Mans note (1988, 166), norms "in parliamentary bodies may help members with differing political beliefs and values to work with one another." At a basic minimum, therefore, we should expect to see simple norms of courtesy.

A second and more telling set of norms relates to the way in which decisions are made. In particular, given their importance within the chamber, we can examine attitudes toward party groups and party group discipline. Loewenberg and Mans (1988, 162) refer to these as norms of "parliamentary party loyalty": "Since parties are so important in organizing the work of these legislatures and because parties often make demands on the loyalties of members, it is not surprising that a set of norm perceptions defines the acceptable and unacceptable behavior linking parliamentarians and their parties."

But some features of the EP give us reasons to suspect that some norms may not develop at all among MEPs. Recalling Asher's identification of repetition and communication as important means for establishing norms, we may note that the unusual degree of diversity within the EP would seem to work against communicating norms, while the relatively high turnover rate might suggest that repetition is undermined. The EP is a relatively young institution with a diverse membership and a very high turnover rate: for instance, around 46% of the 1989–94 MEPs were elected in 1989. The MEPs speak 12 official languages, come from 15 different states, and are currently formed into eight different ideological groups.[1]

This suggests yet another reason for studying the EP from the point of view of norm-based behavior, namely that while the literature to date indicates that norms are vital to the study of legislative institutions, a few simple facts about the EP suggest that it provides very poor soil in which norm-based behavior may root itself. Given this, and despite the importance accorded to norms for the functioning of legislatures in general, perhaps we shall see no unwritten norms within the EP.

But how do we recognize a norm when we see one? In this chapter we follow the standard practice within legislative studies of tapping opinions and expectations of the legislators themselves. But what kind of distribution is consistent with the presence of norms? While flat or U-shaped distributions of opinion may be read as a sign of no norms being present and a point distribution (unanimity) as a strong sign of commonly held beliefs and expectations, there is clearly scope for an infinite range of distributions within these end points.

The lack of a clear yardstick is somewhat puzzling given the very considerable attention that social science as a whole has paid to norm-based behavior. One question here is whether norms may be said to be linear with respect to individual opinions: whether they can be said to apply to a greater or lesser degree. The discussion in the first part of this chapter followed the general social science treatment of norms in suggesting that they are not linear or continuous. Norms are more usually said to operate like a switch: they are either present or absent, on or off, and thus are more properly characterized as nonlinear and discontinuous with regard to opinion.

While it may well be in keeping with general conceptions of norms to discuss them as holding true only after a certain proportion of the membership goes along with them, this simply begs the question of how we establish that proportion. Clearly, a majority will have to go along: the idea of thresholds strongly suggests that we look to supermajorities, but there is virtually no indication of what that figure should be.

Of course, there is no reason to believe that all norms require the same supermajority. Some norms may be easily toppled, but others may be more robust. We are left, then, with no pat answer to the question of how we recognize a norm when we see one. Our answer here is somewhat arbitrary but, we suggest, at least workable. The requirement of a supermajority would suggest that something over two-thirds agreement would provide a necessary but not sufficient condition for the presence of norms, two-thirds being a standard benchmark for voting supermajorities.

Norms within the EP

The empirical basis for this study consists of data gathered from a mail survey of MEPs conducted between May and December 1990.[2] Our survey asked a series of 12 questions relating to the acceptability (or otherwise) of various types of behavior that previous research on legislatures had identified as being especially relevant to parliamentary behavior (Loewenberg and Mans 1988). Our expectation here is that if norms are present, we should see fairly widespread agreement among MEPs that certain types of behavior are generally held to be acceptable (or unacceptable). The MEPs were given a 5-point scale, ranging from *most acceptable* (scored 1) to *most unacceptable* (scored 5). They were asked to indicate their position on the scale.

Following Loewenberg and Mans's approach, we factor-analyzed the responses to these questions, and results from this analysis are displayed in table 10.2. The factor analysis highlights two dimensions of opinion. On the first dimension, the party loyalty norms load highly; on the second dimension, we see the more general courtesy, or civilized behavior, norms. This analysis thus suggests that the two sets of norms are distinct

Table 10.2
Different Levels of Norms among MEPs: Factor Analysis

	Factor I Party Norms	Factor II Civilized Behavior Norms
Publicly speak against the position of group leaders	.75	−.05
Vote against the group line	.74	−.13
Introduce a motion without party group advice	.55	−.09
Be absent from Parliament to prevent a quorum	.49	.39
In principle reject unanimous decisions	.36	.42
Publicly question a colleague's sincerity	.34	.40
Give priority to special interests	.31	.29
Disclose to the press a decision taken in private	.31	.05
Never take a position	−0.09	.77
Always stay away from conflict	−0.09	.76
Always give priority to one's own electoral considerations	−.11	.59
Demand that decisions be reached by simple majority	−.14	−.08
% of total variance explained	18.197	17.890

Source: 1990 Survey of MEPs.

from each other, as indeed was also the case in Loewenberg and Mans's (1988) study of three national legislatures. And in fact, these results are remarkably similar to those obtained in Loewenberg and Mans's original work. Attitudes toward party seem to be a distinct set of attitudes among MEPs.

More revealing, however, are some of the simple descriptive data that underlie the factor analysis. Table 10.3 shows the basic trends, combining the "acceptable" and "most acceptable" categories and the "unacceptable" and "most unacceptable" categories respectively. Numbers of responses vary slightly, but generally there are around 180 valid responses for each question. On several of the issues we see a high degree of consensus. For example, over 80% of respondents think it unacceptable to disclose to the press decisions taken in private, to never take a position and to "always stay away from conflict." Slightly lower, but still notable, trends are seen on other issues: for instance, whether to publicly question a colleague's sincerity, whether to give priority to one's own electoral considerations, and whether in principle to reject unanimous decisions. On a number of these issues, then, we do see the kind of

Table 10.3
Acceptability of Forms of Behavior in the EP

Form of Behavior	Unacceptable or Most Unacceptable (%)	Acceptable or Most Acceptable (%)
Never take a position	89	0
Always stay away from conflict	83	6
Publicly question a colleague's sincerity	68	17
Always give priority to one's own electoral considerations	75	17
Disclose to the press a decision taken in private	84	13
Be absent from Parliament to prevent a quorum	62	21
In principle reject unanimous decisions	78	9
Demand that decisions be reached by simple majority	18	57
Give priority to special interests	46	37
Publicly speak against the position of group leaders	56	30
Introduce a motion without party group advice	36	55
Vote against the group line	38	53

Source: 1990 Survey of MEPs.

clustering of opinion that would suggest that MEPs share a broadly similar set of expectations concerning what constitutes appropriate behavior. For the most part, these represent the norms of courtesy referred to above.

But this is not the whole story by any means. Opinion is far more divided upon the remaining issues, more important for our current concerns. While it is comparatively easy for MEPs to appear to be above the fray by denying baser motives of reelection, a much tougher test comes in deciding attitudes toward party groups. Opinion is divided on the issue of whether to give priority to special interests. And on the three questions concerning party group discipline (introducing motions without group advice, voting against the group, and speaking against group leaders), opinion is much more noticeably divided, so much so that we may reasonably argue that there is no consensus of expectations—there are no norms operating here.

Even so, some subgroups of stable opinions may exist within the overall body of MEPs. Following the lead of earlier literature, it seems sensible to propose that those MEPs who have been in the chamber

Table 10.4

Opinions of MEPs toward Party Discipline

	Introduce a Motion without Group Advice	Publicly Speak Out against the Position of Group Leaders	Vote against the Group Line
Constant	−2.2	−0.26	1.41
Rainbow	−2.01*	−0.7	1.52
	(1.1)	(1.2)	(1.1)
Communists	1.1	−0.55	1.59**
	(.81)	(.89)	(.8)
European People's	0.13	0.08	0.09
Party	(.25)	(.28)	(.25)
Liberals, Democrats,	−0.61**	−0.13	−0.27
Reformists	(.29)	(.31)	(.29)
Socialists	0.06	−0.26	0.44**
	(.21)	(.23)	(.21)
Entry	0.05**	0.039+	0.013
	(.02)	(.02)	(.02)
Role	0.06	0.09**	0.04
	(.04)	(.05)	(.04)
Past position	−0.10	0.50*	0.45*
	(.25)	(.27)	(.24)
Leader	0.02	0.14	−0.23
	(.23)	(.25)	(.22)
R^2	0.11	.07	0.09
N	173	169	169

Source: 1990 survey of MEPs.

$**p \leq 0.05$; $*p \leq 0.10$; $+p \leq 0.10$ (one-tailed).

longer should exhibit somewhat different views than those who have only recently arrived. We might also suggest that those MEPs in leadership positions within the chamber (i.e., those who are committee presidents or vice presidents or who occupy a similar position within the party groups) should be more in favor of group discipline than ordinary members. Finally, we ought to note that MEPs do have a variety of roles from which they may choose by virtue of the unusual position of the EP as an international institution. MEPs can see themselves as representing ordinary citizens and/or as representing a party—either a national-level party or a European party group (for more details on the range of choices, see Bowler and Farrell 1993). It seems reasonable to suppose that those MEPs who already see themselves as being representatives of their party groups should be especially keen to toe the group line. Table 10.4 presents some simple regression analysis aimed at flushing out some of the possibilities for the existence of distinct sub-groups of opinion within the chamber.

These regressions take as their dependent variable the 5-point response to the three questions most connected to the issue of party discipline (where 5 = *most unacceptable*). Independent variables examine the main party groups (Communists, European People's Party, Liberals, Democrats and Reformists, Socialist Group, Rainbow Group), and the variable "leader" is a dummy (scored 1 if the respondent occupies a leadership position as defined in the text above and 0 otherwise). "Past position" is similarly scored, where 1 indicates that the respondent held such a position in a previous EP. "Entry" is simply the year of entry of each MEP into the EP (the larger the number, the more recent the entrant). The EP has been directly elected since 1979, and it existed as an appointed assembly well before then. It may be objected that this is hardly a long time in terms of parliamentary traditions, but it is a period of time that roughly corresponds to that of the Bundestag at the point at which Loewenberg (1967) wrote his seminal study of that institution. "Role" is the variable that taps whether respondents see themselves as a representative of a party group (a 5-point scale, ranging from 5 = *applicable* to 1 = *not applicable*).

A number of comments are in order here. First, the leftist groups are generally more willing to go along with the party group than other groups, a finding broadly in keeping with the roll call analysis of Attinà (1990; though see the discussion in chap. 9 of this volume). Second, past experience of the chamber does have an impact in helping to reinforce a predisposition toward group loyalty, but only insofar as the MEP has previous experience of a leadership position. Coupled with this seems to be the arrival of a relatively new group of rank-and-file entrants who are predisposed toward group loyalty. But these admittedly slender findings can, perhaps, be understood better in a broader interpretation of norms within the EP.

Discipline, Unwritten Rules, and Written Rules within the EP

In an international body such as the EP, is it unusual to find evidence of nationally based differences of opinion? Perhaps not. Indeed, it may be more surprising to find that, given the levels of diversity and turnover in membership noted above, there are in fact a set of expectations on broad patterns of parliamentary behavior shared by the majority of MEPs. But on what we might term the tougher issues of party group loyalty, there do not appear to be any shared set of expectations. We should also remind ourselves that any agreement we do see is drawn in fairly broad brushstrokes. On this basis it seems sensible to conclude that norms are not as well developed in the EP as in other legislatures. This raises the question: Is it worth making this point?

Our answer, not surprisingly, is yes—for two reasons. First, it means that in the EP we have found an example of a legislature that seems to function without norms, which should lead to some modification of the view of the central importance of norms to parliaments. Whether the EP functions well or poorly in consequence is not the issue (though the evidence does appear to suggest the former; see Bowler and Farrell 1995; chap. 9 of this volume); the fact that it functions at all is surprising in light of past literature on this topic. Moreover, we have no real way of knowing how norms will develop in the EP, which leads us to draw what are, perhaps, more surprising conclusions. While the standard account of the development of norms stresses the socialization of new members by the old, it is also entirely possible that existing "norms" may be upset by new subgroups. The diversity of opinion within the EP seems so great that it is far from obvious which opinion could conceivably form the basis for a future widely adopted norm. The subgroups we have found, then, may or may not be the focal point for the development of norms; we have no way of knowing which of them will be.

We suggest that this kind of inconclusiveness with regard to informal rules of behavior helps prompt the development of formal rules and ones that help provide a consensual approach to decision making more generally. In other words, the comparisons found in table 10.1 can, perhaps, be understood as being far from accidental. The very diversity of the EP might mean that norm-based behavior is not likely to be a tenable basis for organization. This, in turn, means that formal rules of procedure make a great deal of sense for a body that has so many linguistic and cultural diversities and hence a greater likelihood of misunderstanding of informal rules. Lijphart (1984) notes that one of the consequences of diversity at a societal level is a reliance upon written rules. We might further note that such diversity also presents problems in terms of the evolution of norms. The types of communication that precede norms are clearly hampered by multiple languages. Indeed, as

EP Rule 102 makes plain, there are likely to be occasions in which "there are discrepancies between different language versions" even of written documents (European Parliament, 1994). In such cases the president of the EP can decide which version is regarded as being adopted.

As the EP has grown in both size and importance, so have the rules. The 1972 edition listed 54 rules, whereas the 1994 edition listed 166. Of course, many of these new rules reflect changes in the European Community's (and now Union's) legal and constitutional structure and the development of the EP's powers, such as over council legislation. These rules may also be used as a negotiating tool with the other institutions as the EP seeks to interpret institutional change to its best advantage. Nevertheless, a major part of the rules of procedure consists of attempts to govern the behavior of members within the chamber. For example, Rule 127.3 limits speaking time on points of order to one minute (down from five minutes under Rule 31.5 in the 1973 version). As a more telling indication of what can happen when norms of behavior may not agree, we note rule No. 111, which allows the president to suspend the sitting of the parliament in the face of disturbances obstructing the business of the House.

In general it may be that the conditions within the EP do not provide a fertile ground for social governance by unwritten rules. Rather, the EP is a setting where written rules supplant, even if they do not replace, unwritten ones. Thus, our general conclusion is that the experience of the EP suggests that we should moderate the importance that we accord norms within a legislative setting and, in turn, attach greater importance to written rules of procedure. Clearly, this conclusion could be proven wrong in future research; indeed, within this chapter we have provided the means for us to be proven wrong. It has been our intention to establish a rough benchmark against which to check the future development of norms within the EP. To the extent that norms do develop, we have presented evidence that relates to an early (and hence crucial) period. If we are wrong in emphasizing the role of formal rules, the future will see the eventual disappearance of subgroups of opinion and of disagreements; consensus will be more tightly drawn. If, however, we are correct, we should see continued instability and only vague agreements among MEPs on the issues we have discussed. Any future convergence of expectations among members is likely to reflect the effects of amendments to the written procedures. It is the institutional structure that will provide the grounds for stable expectations and hence norms.

NOTES

This is a substantially revised version of a paper that first appeared as a *European Policy Research Unit [EPRU] Paper* 4/93, Manchester University, Department of Government. We gratefully acknowledge the financial support of the Commission of the European Union (DGX).

1. At the time in which the survey used in this chapter was conducted, there were nine EU member countries and 518 MEPs, arranged into 11 different party groups.

2. This had a response rate of 37.6%. The national breakdowns are: France, 17 (out of 81 MEPs); Germany, 31/81; Belgium, 10/24; Denmark, 6/16; Portugal, 9/24; Spain, 16/60; Netherlands, 13/25; Luxembourg, 2/6; United Kingdom, 60/81; Ireland, 10/15; Italy, 15/81; Greece, 6/24. For more details, see Bowler and Farrell (1993).

REFERENCES

Asher, H. 1973. "The Learning of Legislative Norms." *American Political Science Review* 67: 499–513.

Attinà, F. 1990. "The Voting Behaviour of the European Parliament Members and the Problem of Europarties." *European Journal of Political Research* 18: 557–79.

Bardi, Luciano. 1996. "Transnational Trends in European Parties and the 1994 European Elections of the European Parliament." *Party Politics* 2: 99–113.

Bowler, Shaun, and David Farrell. 1993. "Legislator Shirking and Voter Monitoring: Impacts of European Parliament Electoral Systems upon Legislator-Voter Relationships." *Journal of Common Market Studies* 31: 45–69.

———. 1995. "The Organizing of the European Parliament: Committees, Specialization and Coordination." *British Journal of Political Science* 25: 219–43.

Coleman, J. 1990. "The Emergence of Norms." In M. Hechter, K.-D. Opp, and R. Wippler, eds., *Social Institutions: Their Emergence, Maintenance and Effects.* New York: de Gruyter.

European Parliament. 1989. *Rules of Procedure.* 5th ed. Strasbourg: European Parliament.

———. 1994. *Rules of Procedure.* 9th ed. Strasbourg: European Parliament.

Fenno, R. 1973. *Congressmen in Committees.* Boston: Little, Brown.

———. 1978. *Home Style.* Boston: Little, Brown.

Foley, M. 1980. *The New Senate.* New Haven, CT: Yale University Press.

Hix, Simon, and Christopher Lord. 1997. *Political Parties in the European Union.* New York: Macmillan.

Jacobs, Francis, Richard Corbett, and Michael Shackleton. 1995. *The European Parliament.* 3rd ed. London: Cartermill.

Kornberg, A. 1967. *Canadian Legislative Behavior.* New York: Holt, Rinehart, & Winston.

Lijphart, A. 1984. *Democracies.* New Haven, CT: Yale University Press.

Loewenberg, Gerhard. 1967. *Parliament in the German Political System.* Ithaca, NY: Cornell University Press.

Loewenberg, G., and T. Mans. 1988. "Individual and Structural Influence on the Perception of Legislative Norms in Three European Parliaments." *American Journal of Political Science* 32: 155–77.

Matthews, D. 1973. *U.S. Senators and Their World.* New York: Norton.

Ordeshook, P. 1992. *A Political Theory Primer.* London: Routledge.

Parliaments of the World: C Comparative Reference Compendium. 2d ed. 1986. Hants: Gower.

Rohde, D., Norman Ornstein, and Robert Peabody. 1985. "Political Change and Legislative Norms in the U.S. Senate 1957–1974." In Glenn Parker, ed., *Studies of Congress.* Washington, DC: Congressional Quarterly Press.

Searing, D. 1991. "Roles, Rules and Rationality in the New Institutionalism." *American Political Science Review* 85: 1240–60.

Sinclair, B. 1989. *The Transformation of the U.S. Senate.* Baltimore: Johns Hopkins University Press.

Strøm, K. 1984. "Minority Governments in Parliamentary Democracies: The Rationality of Nonwinning Cabinet Solutions." *Comparative Political Studies* 17: 199–228.

Tsebelis, George. 1994. "The Power of the European Parliament as a Conditional Agenda Setter." *American Political Science Review* 88: 128–42.

Turner, J. 1989. "A Theory of Microdynamics Advances." *Group Processes* 6: 1–26.

Williams, R. 1968. "The Concept of Norms." In D. Sills, ed., *International Encyclopedia of the Social Sciences.* Vol. 10. New York: Macmillan.

PART V

Parliamentary Discipline and Coalition Governments

Not only are party cohesion and discipline important for the smooth running of parliaments, they are also crucial to the formation and survival of governments. Given that in this volume we have for the most part been dealing with parliamentary systems, where governments (usually coalitions) are formed by and from the ranks of the parliament and (with few exceptions, such as Switzerland) are reliant on the continuing support of Parliament to remain in office, it makes sense to round off this book with some consideration of the relationship between parliamentary discipline and coalition government stability.

The two chapters in this part deal with this subject from different perspectives. Carol Mershon's chapter starts with a puzzle: how to explain prereform Italy, characterized as it was by the coexistence of instability with stability. The former refers to the regular changes of government, the latter to the fact of low turnover in government and in particular the unremitting dominance of the Christian Democrats. Through a detailed analysis of the Italian case, buttressed with material on four other cases (Netherlands, Finland, Norway, and Ireland), Mershon points to the particular spatial (the nature of the party system and the policy space of voter preferences) and institutional (e.g., preferential voting, secret voting in Parliament, the committee structure) conditions that, she argues, affect the costs associated with making and breaking coalition governments. In a nutshell, she suggests that the prereform Italian coalitions "were not easily sustained, since breakups caused little damage."

While Mershon is concerned with assessing the institutional and party/voter–environmental factors influencing coalition stability, Paul Mitchell focuses more on the internal dynamics of debate within coalitions. In contrast to Laver and Shepsle's "portfolio allocation approach," which is based on office-seeking motivations (see chap. 2), Mitchell's analysis is centered on the policy pursuits of the different actors at two principal levels. First, at the interparty level, Mitchell stresses the importance of the coalition policy document forged between the parties on forming government, arguing that, particularly with regard to the smaller party(ies), this operates as a "treaty" to protect their interests—as, for instance, in the case of those ministries controlled by the larger party where there is a danger of policies not being implemented quite as the junior partner might want. Second, at the intraparty level, Mitchell's study of the Irish case shows that the ability of a party to bargain over policy with other parties can be significantly constrained by the nature of intraparty politics; this suggests that "intraparty politics play a greater role during the life of a government than assumed by traditional coalition theories that concentrate on a period [i.e., during government formation] when unitary behavior is most imperative."

11

The Costs of Coalition: A Five-Nation Comparison

CAROL MERSHON

The record of Italian governments displays a pattern that is deeply perplexing. As figure 11.1 shows, from 1946 to 1992, cabinets in Italy both changed and remained the same. The Christian Democratic Party (DC) always held governing power. But almost no government stayed in office for more than a few years, and many governments collapsed after only a few months. Italy exhibited the lowest turnover rate of any parliamentary democracy (Strøm 1990b, 128),[1] yet it had, except for the defunct French Fourth Republic, the most short-lived governments (King et al. 1990, 867).

How can instability coexist with stability in this way? How can governments break up at such low cost and with so little effect on alternation? These are the key questions that animate this chapter's comparison of Italy and four other parliamentary democracies.

In pursuing these questions, I am guided by the game-theoretic literature on coalitional behavior. My question about (in)stability reflects a central result in this literature: that voting games in multidimensional policy space under simple majority rule are subject to endless cycles among alternative decisions (e.g., McKelvey 1976, 1979; Schofield 1983). I move beyond extant research to deal with an anomaly that to date has not been adequately explored: the combination of decisional stability and instability found in Italy.

My question about costs, too, is rooted in the body of work on coalitions. An implicit but widely shared assumption of coalition theorists is that government coalitions, once installed, can withstand much internal tension because their members want to avoid the costs associated

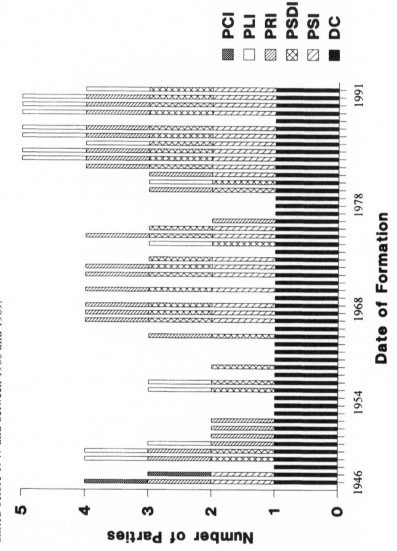

Figure 11.1 The Composition of Italian Governments, 1946–1992. Governments are ordered chronologically on the horizontal axis, with tick marks representing separate cabinets. For simplicity, this figure always depicts the Socialists (PSI) and Social Democrats (PSDI) as separate parties, even though they were united before 1947 and between 1966 and 1969.

with destroying a coalition. As figure 11.1 suggests, however, such costs seem to be very limited in Italy. Why?

The answer offered here is that politicians' purposive actions can reduce the costs of coalition. I argue that the costs of making, breaking, and maintaining coalitions depend on political institutions and on the array of parties and voters in policy space. Institutional and spatial conditions structure politicians' opportunities and attempts to lower costs. Under some conditions, as I demonstrate, coalitions are cheap and politicians can easily make coalitions even cheaper.

Such conditions, I contend, are not unique to Italy. Figure 11.2 illustrates the broad correlation between cabinet duration and alternation in office.[2] Governments in Italy, the French Fourth Republic, Israel, and Portugal (and to a degree Finland and Belgium) last a short while and are subject to limited turnover. Ireland, Iceland, and Norway (and to some extent Canada and the United Kingdom) evince long duration and high alternation. In Sweden, Spain, Denmark, and the Netherlands, cabinets attain an average duration resembling that of the second group but experience fairly restricted turnover. Italy is an extreme case, then, and looks anomalous in light of coalition theories. But it is not sui generis. Italy's extremity points up that a key, common assumption among coalition analysts—the notion that coalitions are costly to build and break—fails to hold under certain conditions. I reason that in Italy (and France, Israel, Portugal, Finland, and Belgium), institutional and spatial conditions curb the costs of coalition and induce politicians to try to lower costs further.

The first section of the chapter assesses the treatment of costs in the literature on coalition bargaining. The second section distinguishes several kinds of costs attached to coalitions and advances an explanation for variations in those costs across party systems. The third part evaluates the explanation in light of evidence from five parliamentary democracies. The conclusion sketches additional applications of the argument.

Costs in Coalition Theories

In what follows, I outline predictions from four schools of research on coalitions. I discuss how each school portrays the costs of coalition and how each prediction fits the record of coalition governments (for a fuller treatment, see Mershon 1996, n.d.). The extensive cross-national

Figure 11.2   Cabinet Duration and Alternation in Office in 15 Parliamentary Democracies

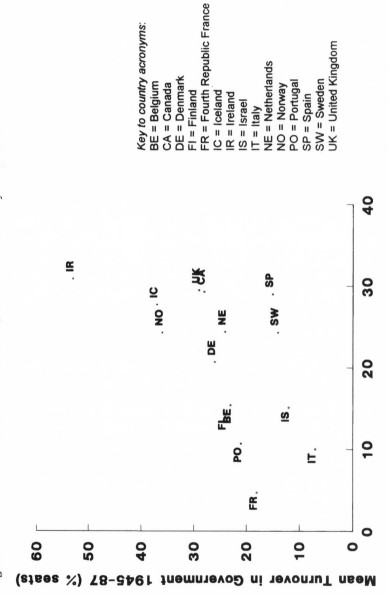

Key to country acronyms:
BE = Belgium
CA = Canada
DE = Denmark
FI = Finland
FR = Fourth Republic France
IC = Iceland
IR = Ireland
IS = Israel
IT = Italy
NE = Netherlands
NO = Norway
PO = Portugal
SP = Spain
SW = Sweden
UK = United Kingdom

aggregate evidence already accumulated enables me to devote intensive attention to Italy, an outlier in study after study.

Consider first the seminal prediction in the office-driven school. Riker (1962) predicts the formation of minimal-winning coalitions, which would lose their parliamentary majority if any member party were to withdraw from them. This model highlights the costs of enlarging coalitions and operationalizes costs in foregone cabinet portfolios. The minimal-winning prediction is usually inaccurate in Italy (e.g., Franklin and Mackie 1984, 686). Almost all of Italy's governments have been either minority cabinets (less than winning) or surplus coalitions (more than minimal). Only one Italian government—of 52 total from 1946 to 1992—unambiguously qualifies as a minimal-winning coalition, and even that cabinet contradicts the logic of minimal-winning theory.[3]

Next consider institution-free models of multidimensional policy space, which predict that a party will control policy and will govern if it occupies the core—a policy position that cannot be overturned, given the overall configuration of actors' sizes and positions (e.g., McKelvey and Schofield 1987; Schofield 1986, 1993). For a core party, allies represent no gain in policy, which the core party already dictates. A core party is thus likely to form a minority cabinet. This school expects lasting governments only in the presence of a stable core (Schofield, Grofman, and Feld 1988, 206). In Italy, the two-dimensional array of parties' sizes and positions qualifies the DC as a core party from 1946 to 1992 (Laver and Schofield 1990, 136, drawing on Budge, Robertson, and Hearl 1987). The prediction is thus that the DC should always govern, and this has indeed been true. But it would be inexplicable within this reasoning if two fragmented systems with strong core parties (such as Italy and the Netherlands) featured governments with substantially different average durations, which is in fact the case. Why do Italian governments display shorter tenures (King et al. 1990, 867) and yet also lower turnover in office (Strøm 1990b, 128) than do Dutch governments? If the balance of costs and benefits brings core parties to form minority governments, why are minority cabinets much less common in the Netherlands than in Italy?

A third school examines how institutions restrict the alternatives open to politicians and thus shape the coalitions they build. Laver and Shepsle (1990, 1994, 1996; chap. 2 of this volume) have developed the most ambitious institution-focused model to date. They isolate two types of portfolio allocations—one held by a single party, termed a "strong" party, and the other constituting a coalition—that cannot be overturned. Where a strong party exists, it should govern and is able to govern even as a one-party minority. A "dimension-by-dimension median" (DDM) cabinet always exists for any set of dimensions, but it cannot beat all alternative cabinets. Whether the DDM cabinet is staffed by one (strong) party or by a coalition, it is expected to govern—even as a minority—as long as it is majority-preferred to all alternative cabinets. This model generally fares well in identifying incumbents (Laver and Shepsle 1996, chaps. 8–9). Nonetheless, since postwar Italy lacks a majority-preferred DDM and lacks a strong party, Laver and Shepsle predict "that government formation would be chaotic [in Italy], as any cabinet that might form can be beaten by some other" (personal communication). This model accounts for the short duration of Italian governments but does not illuminate the constant presence of the Christian Democrats in power. If "cabinet cycles" obtain in Italy (Laver and Shepsle, personal communication), how can the DC keep entering office over and over again?

A large body of research on coalition composition and durability incorporates ideas from the game-theoretic literature but does not use formal deductive methodology (e.g., Dodd 1976; Lijphart 1984). One prominent contributor is Strøm (1990b), who contends that minority cabinets tend to result where policy benefits from governing are low (where strong parliamentary committees give opposition parties the opportunity to influence policy) and, above all, where electoral costs are high (where elections are competitive and decisive, so that incumbency carries a penalty and bargaining power hinges on electoral verdicts). Strøm (1990b, 151) expects minorities to govern with "intermediate frequency" in Italy, since electoral costs and policy benefits from governing there are low. As he documents, however, the percentage of minority cabinets in Italy stands "well above the mean" for the 15 countries he examines (132). Why? Strøm cites electoral costs, even though they are relatively low. Just how Italian politicians weigh the costs of coalition in bargaining over governments remains unresolved.

In sum, anomalies appear when predictions from extant coalition theories are matched against Italian governments. A recurring theme in discussion of the anomalies is how actors think about the costs and benefits of sealing, keeping, and severing alliances. The alternative framework I propose addresses what reduces the costs of coalition and shows how governments can undergo constant change and yet remain much the same.

Explaining Cost Reduction in Coalition Bargaining

The essence of my argument is that political actors do not just see prices; they attempt to set prices attached to coalition bargaining. I assume that actors pursue gains, that they project beyond the short term, and that, if they anticipate losses, they do what they can to cut their losses. Actors will not always avoid what they identify as a costly course of action but will at times follow that course and try to lower its costs. I assume that actors face uncertainty and imperfect information. I further assume that all actors care to some extent about office, policy, and votes (Strøm 1990a). The relative priority given these objectives varies, but no political actor is utterly unmoved by the prospect of holding office, just as none is completely oblivious to policy or electoral concerns.

The game of bargaining over governments is also a game of maneuvering around or modifying the costs that coalitions entail. Political actors incur costs when they build a coalition. They must award ministerial portfolios to other parties, as stressed in office-driven theory. They must compromise on policy in order to come up with the government's program, as spatial theory highlights for parties outside the core. Partners in a new cabinet look ahead to the electoral benefits or burdens that governing will bring (Strøm 1990b). As Axelrod (1970) reasons, potential allies spend time and effort in negotiating to overcome differences. Similarly, it is costly to sustain a coalition. And governing parties meet costs when a coalition breaks apart. Actors engaged in a coalition risk or incur office, policy, electoral, and bargaining costs at distinct stages in the coalition's history.

I contend that political actors do not simply encounter prices but attempt to manage them. When building a coalition, actors can increase the number of portfolios; they can limit public information about policy compromises so as to ease agreement inside the coalition; and they can delegitimate opponents so as to escape voters' blame. To diminish bargaining costs, actors can devise rules to guide bargaining. Once installed, a coalition is sustained at relatively low cost if allies expand spoils and emphasize special-interest legislation. Along similar lines, actors can take steps to curtail risks when a coalition breaks up. Throughout the history of a coalition, actors can lower their costs by choosing to manipulate various levers, such as office benefits, information, and rules.

Is this sort of choice equally open and viable in all political settings?

I think not. Building on existing themes in the literature (Laver and Schofield 1990; Strøm 1990a), I argue that the sizes and positions of *parties in policy space,* the distribution of *voters' preferences in policy space,* and *political institutions* (in particular, electoral laws, legislative rules, and links between the executive and the legislature) affect how costly it is to break, make, and maintain coalitions and affect which cost-reduction strategies actors are likely to see as available and potentially successful. Spatial and institutional conditions are hypothesized to influence costs directly. For instance, when a government falls, a party occupying the core of policy space faces a relatively low risk of not regaining office. The anonymity afforded legislators by a secret ballot means that they can sabotage a government with little fear of losing office, antagonizing voters, or complicating bargaining. Spatial and institutional conditions are also hypothesized to influence costs indirectly by structuring the opportunities that actors have to try to lower costs. To illustrate: office benefits are more easily increased if a core party controls government for some length of time.

Procedures and Measures in Empirical Analysis

Before evaluating this argument, three issues of research design and methods deserve discussion. The first involves my two-pronged approach: I undertake broad cross-national comparisons and in-depth study of Italy. A multicountry comparison has the obvious advantage of providing substantial variation in configurations of parties and voters in policy space. I examine three multipolar party systems, two with strong core parties (Italy and the Netherlands) and one without (Finland), and two unipolar systems (Ireland and Norway).[4] These nations also present a wide range of electoral and parliamentary institutions, as shown below, and they evince differing patterns of cabinet duration and alternation in office, as seen in figure 11.2. All the same, cross-national empirical research on coalitions necessarily relies on fairly large leaps in inference about the causal mechanisms linking one aggregate indicator to another.

Detailed examination of Italy redresses this problem. Intensive study of one country allows the analyst to move closer to decision-making processes, to sift more finely through varied sources of evidence, and to pursue traces of politicians' reasoning and calculations in ways not possible when the field of observation spans many national settings. Because the Italian record poses a stiff challenge to coalition theories, and because scientific understanding advances by assimilating anomalies into a general framework, the empirical analysis of coalition politics in this case holds special theoretical promise. Yet it is worth repeating that Italy is extreme but not unique. Several other countries feature short-lived cabinets and limited alternation. I posit that some of the spatial and institutional conditions present in Italy also appear in those cases (and are rare or absent in still other cases, such as Ireland) and that some strategies deployed in Italy should appear in those cases as well.

Second, to perform the analysis, I need to measure when governments begin and end. I count a new government with each change of party composition, parliamentary election, by-election altering a government's majority or minority status, change of prime minister, and accepted cabinet resignation.[5]

Finally, a test of the argument offered here plainly entails measuring the costs of coalition. To tap office costs, I count the number of ministers and junior ministers per party in a cabinet and take averages across cabinets; figure the percentage share of all ministerial and junior ministerial posts that each party controls; and compute the ratio between that share and the party's share of all seats in the lower house held by a government. I measure electoral costs and benefits as mean changes in parties' shares of the vote between pairs of consecutive elections to the lower house of Parliament. Policy payoffs are indexed by participation in government, which gives parties special instruments of influence on policy. To calculate the office, electoral, and policy costs of coalition breakups, I code information on which parties were (and were not) responsible for cabinet collapses.[6] Bargaining costs are captured by the time elapsed between the fall of one government and the rise of its successor. Further details on these measures appear in the analysis that follows.

Assessing the Costs of Coalition in Five Parliamentary Systems

I compare costs and strategies across parties, across time, and across countries to weigh the impact of spatial and institutional conditions on the costs of assembling and dismantling coalitions. If spatial conditions matter, then different parties within one country should incur different costs and should diverge in their pursuit of cost-reduction strategies. If spatial or institutional conditions change over time, then the costs and strategies characteristic of different parties should also undergo some shift. I expect to find distinctions in the record of costs incurred and strategies implemented across different kinds of party systems—for example, those with and without core parties. Distinctions should also appear across countries with contrasting electoral and parliamentary institutions. Given this logic, a useful first step in the empirical investigation is to sketch political institutions and configurations of policy space in the five countries under study.

Electoral and Parliamentary Institutions

Whereas Ireland uses a single transferable vote (STV) version of proportional representation (PR), the other four countries feature some form of party-list PR. Beyond this basic categorization, the electoral systems differ in the degree of proportionality attained (given district size, method of seat allocation, and so forth) and the role of personalized voting. As table 11.1 displays, proportionality in translations of vote shares into seat shares reaches moderate levels in Ireland and Norway, high levels in Finland and Italy, and very high levels in the Netherlands. Each of the four list PR systems includes some provision for intraparty preference voting (Katz 1986, 88–91). Under STV, to the extent that a party puts up more candidates than it can elect, "Voters determine which particular candidates will be elected by determining the order in which they reach the quota" (91). As exhibited in table 11.1, preference voting has a weak impact on candidates' election (or defeat) in the Netherlands and Norway and a stronger impact in Finland, Ireland, and Italy. Indeed, it is often claimed that preference voting has encouraged factionalism in Italian parties (e.g., Zuckerman 1979). Amid mounting criticism of this effect, a 1991 referendum restricted preference voting in Italy. Table 11.1 registers this change and the dates of other major electoral reforms.[7]

According to a constitutional lawyer who has twice headed the premier's office in Italy, "No government is weaker in parliament than the Italian" (quoted in Spotts and Wieser 1986, 111). Taken together, three rules summarized in table 11.1 bear out this judgment, at least for the five countries examined here. In particular, governments are obliged to pass votes of investiture only in Italy and Ireland. Government control of the parliament's plenary agenda is most tenuous in Italy and the Netherlands. Only in the Italian chamber (until 1988) were secret ballots

Table 11.1

Institutional and Spatial Conditions in Five Democracies

	Finland	*Ireland*	*Italy*	*Netherlands*	*Norway*
Electoral Institutions					
Proportionality[a]	High	Moderate	High	Very high	Moderate
Preference voting[b]	3	2	3	1	1
Dates of major changes[c]	None	None	1948, 1956 1991, 1993	1956	1953 1989
Parliamentary Institutions					
Vote of investiture	No	Yes	Yes	No	No
Govt. control over agenda[d]	3	7	2	1	4
Secret ballot	Possible	No	Required[e]	No	Possible
Committee strength[f]	3	1	4	2	5
Policy Space					
Number of dimensions	1	2	2	2	1
Effective *N* parties	5.2	2.7	3.4	4.6	3.2
Core party	KP median	No core	DC strong core	KVP/CDA strong core	DNA median 1945–61

Sources: Döring (1995); Herman (1976); Katz (1986); Laver and Schofield (1990); Lijphart (1994); Nohlen (1984); Schofield (1993); Strøm (1990b).

Note: KP = Center Party; DC = Christian Democrats; KVP = Catholic People's Party; CDA = Christian Democratic Appeal; DNA = Norwegian Labor Party.

[a]Values on the least-squares index of *dis*proportionality (Lijphart 1994) are coded as follows: under 2 = very high proportionality; from 2 to 3 = high proportionality; from 3 to 6 = moderate.
[b]Index combines cross-national rankings on the minimum number of voters needed to modify the party-defined order of candidates (Katz 1986, 94) and the percentage of intraparty defeats attributable to the preference vote (98). A value of 3 identifies the highest impact on candidates' election/defeat.
[c]A 20% criterion marks "major" changes in district size, thresholds, and assembly size.
[d]Index shows increasing control over plenary agenda. I reserve Döring's (1995) coding, so that a value of 7 means that the government alone sets the agenda.
[e]Chamber final votes until 1988.
[f]Strøm's (1990b) index shows increasing strength, with the greatest strength assigned a score of 5.

required on final votes. Out of these five democracies, only Italy lands on the side of legislative assertiveness for all three rules.

Two additional sets of parliamentary institutions deserve mention, committees and supramajoritarian rules. Among these countries, as table 11.1 reports, the parliamentary committee system is least developed in Ireland and most developed and decentralized in Norway. A strong committee structure such as that found in Norway and Italy affords the opposition influence over policy, as already observed, and thus favors minority government (Strøm 1990b). Supramajoritarian rules instead give politicians incentives to seek surplus coalitions. Such rules are used often in Finland, where since 1919 a two-thirds majority has been required for approval of the budget, bills affecting taxation for over one year, price freezes, and income policies (Arter 1987, 43). From 1919 to 1992, furthermore, one-third of Finnish MPs could postpone most kinds of legislation for one to two years (Anckar 1992, 161–62; Nousiainen 1994, 97–98).

It should also be noted that directly elected presidents are found in Finland and Ireland. Finnish presidents are more powerful than their Irish counterparts but less powerful than presidents in the French Fifth Republic (Arter 1987; Lijphart 1984). Most analysts agree that Finland is at bottom a parliamentary system, unlike the Fifth Republic (e.g., Anckar 1992).

Parties and Voters in Policy Space

The effective number of parties and the number of dimensions in policy space establish Finland, Italy, and the Netherlands as "multipolar" party systems and Ireland and Norway as "unipolar" systems (Laver and Schofield 1990; Schofield 1993).[8] As the labels suggest, parties in multipolar systems face competitors in several directions, whereas a single party attracts and orients competition in a unipolar system. Multipolar systems have a relatively high effective number of parties and are often two-dimensional, as is the case in Italy and the Netherlands. Where the effective number of parties is quite high, as in Finland, multipolar competition can occur along one dimension. As noted above and in table 11.1, the DC in Italy qualified as a core party from 1946 to 1992. The 1976 elections made the Socialist Party (PSI) pivotal, for it became the essential ally in any DC-based coalition capable of commanding a majority while excluding the Communist Party (Pasquino 1981). The DC's sizable losses in the 1992 elections ended its core status as a party, and in 1992 the PSI ceased to be pivotal as well. In the Netherlands the Catholic People's Party (KVP) or its heir, the Christian Democratic Appeal (CDA, which joined the KVP and two Protestant parties in 1977), has occupied the core of the policy space for most of the postwar period. The Center Party (KP, called the Agrarian Union before 1965) has usually been the median party in Finland. In the Norwegian unipolar system, which is organized by the left-right dimension, the Labor Party (A) was located at the median from 1945 to 1961 and again in 1973 and 1977. Otherwise, a center-right party has taken the median position (Strøm and Leipart 1993, 879). The Irish two-dimensional system has lacked a core party and thus Fianna Fáil one-party governments have alternated with Fine Gael-Labour coalitions (but see Mair 1987).

The property of voters' preferences of greatest interest here is the degree to which a national electorate is segmented or subdivided into blocs, with each bloc steadfastly backing "its" party and securely insulated from the appeals of rival parties. Parties that can draw on such reservoirs of support should meet relatively low electoral costs of coalition. A salient theme in studies of Dutch and Italian electoral politics is that religious and class identities have indeed segmented the electorate and anchored particular sets of voters to particular parties (e.g., Daalder 1966; Galli and Prandi 1970). Thus, a well-known typology of Italian electoral behavior (Parisi and Pasquino 1979) distinguishes a vote of belonging, affirming an enduring allegiance to either the Catholic or the Communist subculture; a vote of opinion, motivated by a broad interest in policy; and a vote of exchange, awarded in return for patronage goods. Mannheimer and Sani (1987, 93) use a 1985 survey to estimate that subcultural voters constitute 60% of the DC electorate and 67% of the Italian Communist Party (PCI) electorate. It is accepted wisdom that socioeconomic change has recently eroded the subcultural vote and augmented the opinion vote in Italy.[9]

The same measures tapping subcultural belonging have not been used outside Italy. Yet scholars agree that in the Netherlands the Catholic, Protestant, Socialist, and Liberal "pillars," which stood firm in the 1950s, "have now largely crumbled" under the impact of secularization, economic growth, and mass education (Daalder 1987, 223). Class identities long attached Finnish industrial workers to the Social Democrats and Communists, and farmers to the Agrarians. In the 1950s industrial and rural working-class Norwegians solidly voted for the Labor Party, while middle-class voters supported center-right parties. By the 1970s, however, the class lines that had once partitioned the Finnish and Norwegian electorates began to blur (Arter 1987; Borre 1984). Electoral politics in Ireland has traditionally been viewed as a candidate-focused "politics without social bases" (Whyte 1974). Although a vigorous debate has recently developed to challenge that characterization (Laver 1992; Mair 1987, 1992; Marsh 1992), scholars concur that Ireland joins the prevailing European trend "toward the fragmentation and 'particularization' of political preferences" (Gallagher, Laver, and Mair 1995, 226).

In an ongoing large-scale research project (Mershon n.d.), I examine

Table 11.2

Office Payoffs (Ministers and Undersecretaries) by Type of Government, Italy 1946–1992

Office Payoffs	One-Party Governments (N = 16)	All Coalitions (N = 36)	Coalitions Including PSI (N = 22)	1976–92 Coalitions Including PSI (N = 11)
	Mean Share of All Cabinet Posts Held by DC[a]			
Ministers	94.4%	61.0%	55.3%	52.1%
Undersecretaries	99.1%	64.2%	55.3%	54.2%
	Mean Ratios[b] of Cabinet Post Shares to Government Seat Shares[c] for DC			
Ministers	.94	.82	.83	.78
Undersecretaries	.99	.85	.83	.81
	Mean No. of Posts Held by DC			
Ministers	20	15	15	15
Undersecretaries	36	29	29	33

Sources: Calculations based on portfolio data in Petracca (1980) and *Corriere della Sera,* various issues, and on seat data in Mershon (1996, Appendix B).

Note: DC = Christian Democrats; PSI = Socialist Party.

[a]Entries are mean percentage shares for all governments of the type listed at the head of each column.

[b]Entries are mean ratios for all governments of the type listed at the head of each column.

[c]Government seat share is defined as a party's percentage share of the seats in the chamber that are controlled by all governing parties.

how spatial and institutional conditions shape the costs of coalition in the countries chosen here and in five others as well. The more limited analysis in this paper starts with office costs.

The Office Costs of Building Coalitions and Strategies for Managing Office Costs

Table 11.2 measures the office price that Italy's DC paid when it governed with coalition partners. The top two rows of the table report the mean percentage of portfolios held by the DC in different types of governments from 1946 to 1992. As the first column indicates, in one-party governments the DC occasionally awarded a few posts to independent experts. In coalitions (shown in the second column), the DC sacrificed this near-monopoly on cabinet slots. The third and fourth columns disclose that the DC relinquished a greater percentage of offices when the coalition embraced the medium-sized Socialist Party (PSI), and still more in the 1976–92 coalitions, when the PSI made a pivotal contribution to the government's majority.

The middle two rows of table 11.2 establish that the division of portfolios between the DC and its allies illustrates a well-known finding from cross-national portfolio studies: the largest party in a coalition obtains a share of senior cabinet posts that is somewhat smaller than that party's share of the parliamentary seats controlled by the government (Browne and Franklin 1973; Laver and Schofield 1990). The disadvantage that the DC met is only slightly less pronounced for shares of undersecretary posts. Intervals of one-party government thus compensated the DC for disproportionate shares of portfolios surrendered to allies at other times (see Marradi 1982).

The last two rows of table 11.2 spotlight average numbers of offices. In these terms, the DC spent less to construct coalitions than might be expected—and much less than pure office-driven theory would predict. On average, it cost Italy's core party *nothing* in number of cabinet slots to include the PSI in a coalition, even when the PSI was pivotal. Indeed, DC undersecretaries were *more* numerous in coalitions containing a pivotal PSI than in other types of coalitions.

As figure 11.3 reveals, portfolio inflation was the cost-management strategy producing these outcomes. Offices—especially undersecretaryships—were like balloons, inflated when needs arose. The number of allies changed, but the number of Christian Democrats in government remained remarkably stable.

The distinction between ministers and undersecretaries is worth weighing. As coalitions expanded from two parties to three, four, and then five parties, the number of ministers was pumped up steadily, but the number of undersecretaries rather unevenly. The largest boosts in undersecretaries separated two- from three-party coalitions and four- from five-party coalitions. Why? None of Italy's two-party coalitions included the PSI and all five-party coalitions governed when the PSI was pivotal. The competition for office between the DC and the PSI led to mutual accommodation and thus drove portfolio inflation.

As figure 11.4 plots, the steepest increases in ministerial and undersecretary posts occurred when the PSI reentered government after a sojourn in the opposition (the early 1960s, when center-left coalitions were prepared and implemented, and the early 1980s, when five-party coalitions were instituted).[10] Those hikes enabled the DC to protect or even add to its portfolios. Why have undersecretaryships been more elastic balloons than senior cabinet posts? Undersecretaries are arguably less

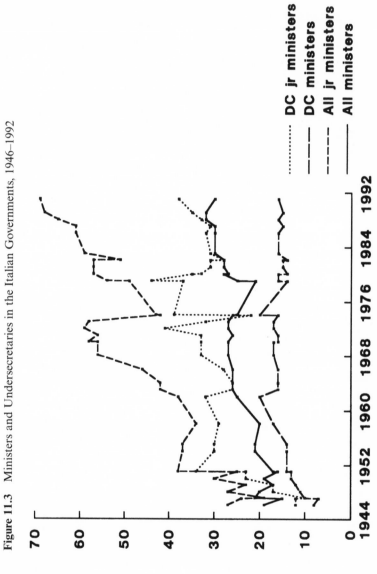

Figure 11.3 Ministers and Undersecretaries in the Italian Governments, 1946–1992

.... DC jr ministers
— — — DC ministers
– – – – All jr ministers
———— All ministers

70
60
50
40
30
20
10
0

1944 1952 1960 1968 1976 1984 1992

Year of Coalition Formation

Figure 11.4 Office Payoffs, by Number of Parties in Italian Government, 1946–1992 (Means)

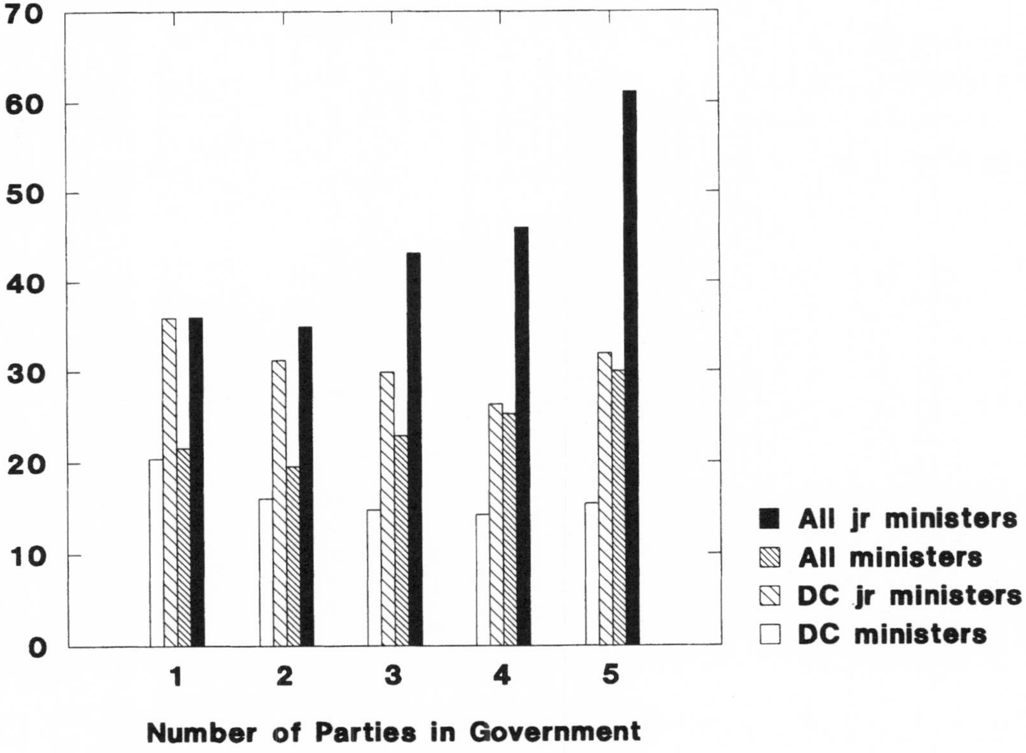

visible to voters and imply a less permanent, more flexible commitment of resources. Moreover, in a long-standing "informal division of ministerial labour, [an undersecretary] is left free to distribute the patronage of the ministry in his constituency" (Allum 1973, 90). The secret ballot made it "necessary . . . to satisfy the greatest possible number of deputies," and coalition builders used undersecretary posts as a convenient currency with which to gratify deputies and buy loyalty (Dogan 1984, 164). Since parliamentary rules require that members of government—both ministers and undersecretaries—step down from parliamentary committees (Nocifero and Valdini 1992), an increase in cabinet posts has the advantage of enlarging access to committee positions for parliamentarians without cabinet responsibilities. Given committee powers in the Italian parliament, members of multiple committees are well equipped to pipe narrow benefits to clienteles.

The evidence is persuasive that spatial and institutional conditions have influenced the office costs of building Italian coalitions. Do analogous effects appear in the Netherlands, the case that most closely resembles Italy in spatial terms? Figure 11.5A, like figure 11.4, displays average numbers of officeholders in the core party and in the entire government for coalitions joining different numbers of allies.[11] Figure 11.5A cannot fully duplicate the comparisons in figure 11.4, for the Dutch Christian Democrats (KVP/CDA) never governed alone between 1946 and 1987. Figure 11.5A does show that as coalitions stretched from two to five parties, governmental offices overall tended to rise and the number of KVP/CDA ministers and junior ministers declined only slightly.

Yet glances at the vertical scales of figures 11.4 and 11.5A are enough to establish that Dutch portfolio inflation is a pale copy of the Italian phenomenon. Why? Since Dutch governments do not confront votes of investiture, and since secret ballots are the exception rather than the rule in the Dutch parliament, the builders of Dutch cabinets lack the incentives that their Italian counterparts face to use office as "glue" to bind assertive parliamentarians to governments. Disincentives operate as well. Additions of cabinet posts can trigger resignations in Dutch parliamentary parties, for in the Netherlands (and Norway) ministers cannot hold seats in Parliament; the same is true for Dutch junior ministers since 1948 (Andeweg and Bakema 1994; Gladdish 1991; Strøm 1994). Finally, unlike the Italian DC, the KVP/CDA lost its core status a few times—while retaining office—before the early 1990s (see note 11).

The Finnish Agrarian/Center Party (KP) briefly lost core status in the early postwar period, unlike the Italian DC and the Dutch KVP/

Figure 11.5 Office Payoffs, by Party Number of Parties in Dutch (A) and Finnish (B) Government, 1946–87 (Means)

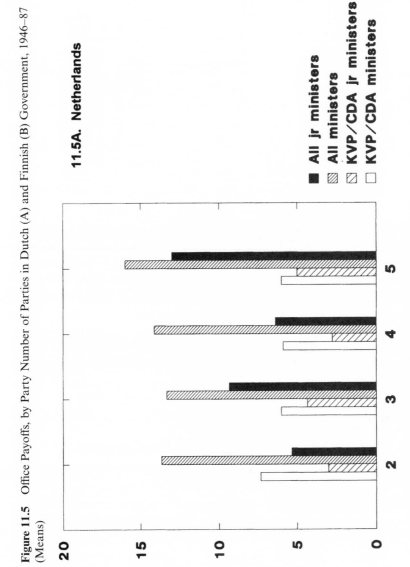

11.5A. Netherlands

■ All jr ministers
▨ All ministers
▧ KVP/CDA jr ministers
☐ KVP/CDA ministers

Number of Parties in Dutch Government

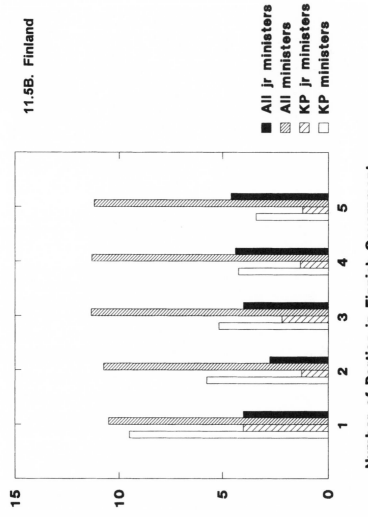

11.5B. Finland

All jr ministers
All ministers
KP jr ministers
KP ministers

Number of Parties in Finnish Government

CDA.[12] Moreover, the KP has not achieved the uninterrupted incumbency that sets apart the DC and the KVP/CDA. Although "green-red" coalitions dominated by the KP and Social Democrats (SSDP) have been rather common, the SSDP has occasionally governed without the KP (even in 1972, when the KP was the median party; Laver and Schofield 1990, 117). Seven nonpartisan cabinets have formed, which in part testifies to the prerogatives of the Finnish president (Arter 1987).

Given these contrasts between Italy and the Netherlands, on the one hand, and Finland, on the other, some differences in outcomes should emerge. And some do. Figure 11.5B depicts only those governments between 1946 and 1987 that contained the KP.[13] It reveals that the number of ministers and junior ministers remained roughly the same, on average, across the KP's one-party governments and coalitions—even for coalitions spanning five parties. The Center Party paid an obvious office price for assembling coalitions. All the same, it responded to institutional incentives to coalesce: the Finnish parliament follows supramajoritarian rules. Those rules also raise obstacles to manipulating offices, for "a change in law is required to establish a new ministry" in Finland (Nousiainen 1994, 89).

Consider now Norway and Ireland, which introduce greater spatial variations. The comparisons just executed for Finland—of the KP's one-party governments and coalitions—cannot be duplicated for Norway, for the Labor Party (A) has always governed alone. In Ireland, Fianna Fáil (FF) maintained a commitment to one-party government throughout the four decades studied here.[14] Labor was Norway's median party from 1945 to 1961 and in 1973 and 1977, as observed above. If the Irish party system were unidimensional, FF would generally qualify as the median party on the left-right spectrum, but Irish politics is probably best characterized as two-dimensional.

As figures 11.6A and 11.6B chart, the one-party governments staffed by Labor and FF between 1946 and 1987 looked rather similar. Furthermore, for both Norway and Ireland, fluctuations in the totals of ministerial and junior ministerial posts did not prevent parties from relinquishing offices as governments embraced additional allies. In particular, even though the Center Party (SP) was Norway's median party in 1981 and 1985, both the smallish SP and in Ireland the bigger Fine Gael (FG) paid an office price when they governed with more parties rather than fewer. The similarities should not be overstressed: when the SP governed as a median party, it received weighted shares of cabinet posts (the well-known measures reported for Italy in table 11.2) that

Figure 11.6 Office Payoffs, by Number of Parties in Norwegian (A) and Irish (B) Governments, 1946–1987 (Means)

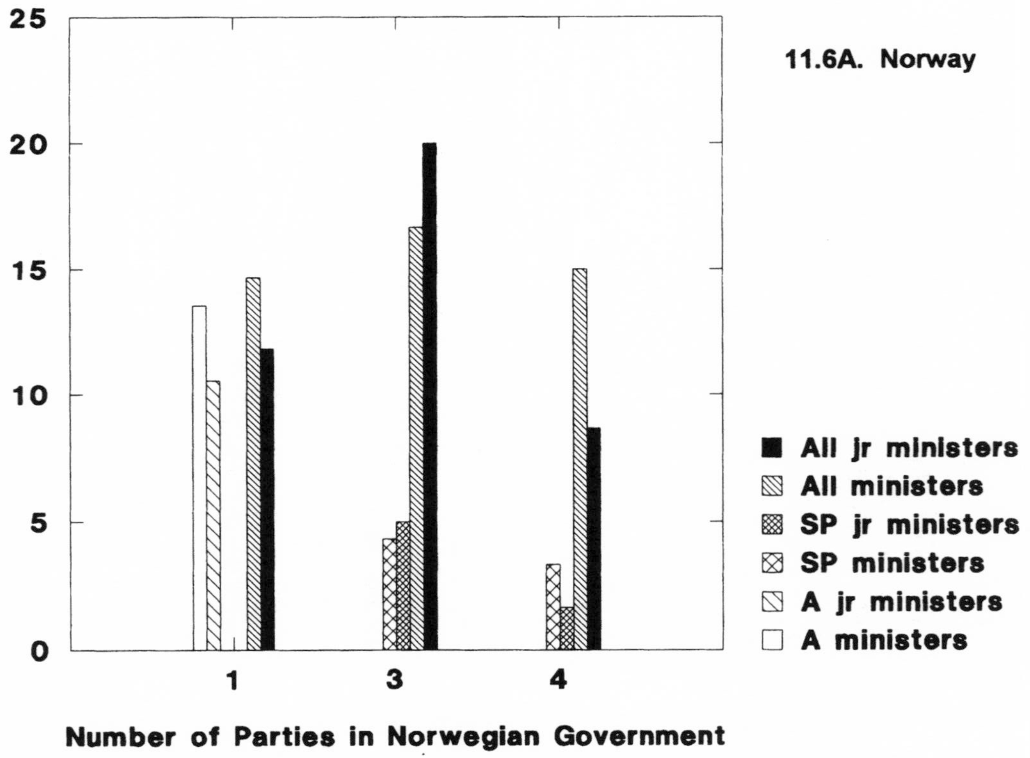
25
20
15
10
5
0
1
3
4
Number of Parties in Norwegian Government
11.6A. Norway
All jr ministers
All ministers
SP jr ministers
SP ministers
A jr ministers
A ministers

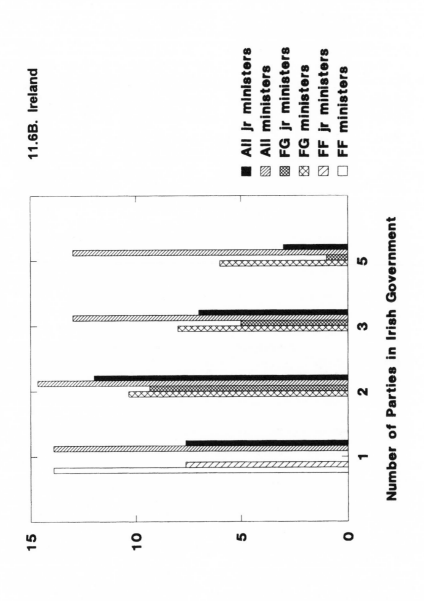

11.6B. Ireland

All Jr ministers
All ministers
FG jr ministers
FG ministers
FF jr ministers
FF ministers

Number of Parties in Irish Government

were relatively high—relative to the SP's weighted shares at other times and relative to Fine Gael. Yet despite spatial differences, similarities do exist. They may be explained by institutional constraints. In Norway, as stated earlier, ministerial office is incompatible with membership in Parliament. The 1937 Irish constitution specifies that the number of ministers should range from 7 to 15 (Farrell 1994).

Given Italy's spatial and institutional conditions, Italian politicians have been able and willing to manipulate offices so as to offset the office costs of building coalitions. An echo of this pattern appears in the Netherlands, where the party system roughly resembles the Italian. That the echo is faint becomes comprehensible when institutions and finer spatial distinctions are taken into account. Beyond those two fairly similar cases, as differences in party systems become more pronounced—that is, as attention shifts to Finland and then to Norway and Ireland—more pronounced differences in outcomes emerge. Variations in institutions also contribute to variations in the office costs incurred in the construction of governments. Analysis of the costs of dismantling governments begins with Italy.

The Office and Policy Costs of Ending Governments and Strategies for Managing Costs

As typically measured, the office price of ending governments is negligible in Italy. As table 11.3 exhibits, all five governing parties in Italy received a weighted share of senior cabinet posts that stayed roughly steady, on average, whether or not they had overthrown the preceding government. The same statement holds true for weighted shares of undersecretary posts. Not a single pair of ratios in the top two rows of table 11.3 is significantly different. This finding runs counter to conventional assumptions about the office costs of breakups. It becomes even more remarkable when average numbers are considered. The total of cabinet posts varied little according to whether or not the Social Democrats (PSDI), Republicans (PRI), and Liberals (PLI) had pulled down the prior government. But an Italian government's ministers and undersecretaries, on average, were significantly *more* numerous after the Socialists had sabotaged, as compared to sustained, its predecessor. With the PSI's percentage of offices unaltered and the number of all offices up, more Socialists filled cabinet slots. Office *benefits* went to the PSI after it had eliminated a government, above all when the PSI was pivotal. Along similar lines, but only from 1976 to 1992, a constant

Table 11.3

Office Payoffs, by Party and Responsibility for Government Collapse, Italy 1946–1992

| | *Was Party Responsible for Collapse at Time* t − *1?* | | | | | | | | | |
| | DC | | PSI | | PSDI | | PRI | | PLI | |
Offices at t	No	Yes	No	Yes	No	Yes	No	Yes	No	Yes
	Ratios of Cabinet Post Shares to Government Seat Shares[a] (Means)									
Party ministers	0.89	0.83	1.30	1.23	1.84	1.84	3.00	2.25	2.09	2.12
Party undersecretaries	0.91	0.89	1.39	1.34	1.70	1.53	1.85	1.55	2.16	1.85
N cabinets	(21)	(30)	(3)	(18)	(21)	(8)	(17)	(8)	(12)	(4)
	No. of Posts (Means)									
All ministers	23	24	21	25**	24	23	23	25	24	24
All undersecretaries	42	45	35	49**	44	44	41	48	44	44
N cabinets	(21)	(30)	(20)	(31)	(33)	(18)	(35)	(16)	(43)	(8)
	No. of Posts 1976–92 (Means)									
All ministers	26	30*	NA	27	27	30	28	26	27	28
All undersecretaries	53	62*	NA	56	55	61	55	56	55	59
N cabinets	(5)	(11)	(0)	(16)	(14)	(2)	(11)	(5)	(11)	(3)

Sources: Calculations based on portfolio data in Petracca (1980) and *Corriere della Sera,* various issues, seat data in Mershon (1996, Appendix B), and coding of information in *Keesing's Contemporary Archives.*

Notes: DC = Christian Democrats; PSI = Socialist Party; PSDI = Social Democrats; PRI = Republicans; PLI = Liberals.

Means are computed, party by party, for two groups of cabinets: those whose predecessor was a cabinet the party helped to topple, and those whose predecessor fell for reasons other than the party's withdrawal of support. *T*-tests compare the means of the two groups (i.e., for each party, entries in the "yes" and "no" columns). Numbers of applicable cabinets are in parentheses. NA = not applicable.

[a]Government seat share = a party's share of the chamber seats controlled by all governing parties.

*p < .05 (separate-variances *t*-test); **p < .001 (separate-variances *t*-test).

share and a significantly larger total of offices meant that more Christian Democrats attained cabinet positions after the DC had toppled a government. In this sense, too, the competition between the DC and PSI drove portfolio inflation.

Membership in government offers parties special opportunities to influence policy. Hence, table 11.4 examines policy benefits at risk by designating the governing status of parties behind government falls in Italy. It shows the policy payoffs by reporting how often parties that bring about one government's demise participate in the next government and produce a change in incumbent parties.[15] Table 11.4A illustrates the DC's unerring ability to regain office after an exit. Yet three similarities across Italian governing parties are noteworthy. First, as detailed in table 11.4B, they tended to overturn cabinets only when assigned

Table 11.4

Party Status in Government and Coalition Formula, and Government Composition, at and after Government Collapses, by Party Responsible for Government Collapse, Italy, 1946–1992

	Party Responsible for Collapse At Time t − 1?				
	DC	PSI	PSDI	PRI	PLI
	All Collapses 1946–92				
A. Status in government at $t-1$					
In government	100.0%	62.5%	66.7%	25.0%	25.0%
Out of government	0	37.5	33.3	75.0	75.0
B. Status in coalition formula at $t-1$					
In coalition formula	100.0%	84.4%	100.0%	87.5%	87.5%
Out of coalition formula	0	15.6	0	12.5	12.5
C. Status in government at t					
In government	100.0%	59.4%	50.0%	50.0%	50.0%
Out of government	0	40.6	50.0	50.0	50.0
D. Government composition at t					
Parties change after fall	58.1%	68.8%	72.2%	56.3%	50.0%
Parties same as before fall	41.9	31.2	27.8	44.7	50.0
N collapses	(31)	(32)	(18)	(16)	(8)
	Coalition Collapses 1946–92				
E. Status in government at t					
In government	100.0%	68.2%	45.5%	55.6%	66.7%
Out of government	0	31.8	54.5	44.4	33.3
F. Government composition at t					
Parties change after fall	50.0%	68.2%	72.7%	66.7%	66.7%
Parties same as before fall	50.0	31.8	27.3	33.3	33.3
N coalition collapses	(18)	(22)	(11)	(9)	(3)
	All Collapses 1976–92				
G. Status in government at t					
In government	100.0%	75.0%	100.0%	80.0%	100.0%
Out of government	0	25.0	0	20.0	0
H. Government composition at t					
Parties change after fall	54.5%	62.5%	50.0%	60.0%	66.7%
Parties same as before fall	45.5	37.5	50.0	40.0	33.3
N collapses 1976–92	(11)	(16)	(2)	(5)	(3)

Sources: Calculations based on coding of information in *Keesing's Contemporary Archives;* and on government status data in Mershon (1996, Appendix A).

Notes: See table 11.3 for party acronyms.

Entries are the percentage of cases in which a party (or government) had the designated status. A "coalition formula" refers to a relatively durable coalition design (e.g., the centrist formula, composed of the DC, PSDI, PRI, and PLI, lasted from 1947 to 1963); a party included in a formula need not serve in *every* cabinet ruling under the formula (e.g., the PLI served in 5 of the 17 cabinets formed under centrism). Parties are coded as included in coalition formulas during the following periods: DC 1946–92; PSI 1946–47, 1963–76, 1979–92; PSDI 1947–76, 1979–92; PRI 1947–76, 1979–92; PLI 1947–63, 1979–92.

long-term governing roles in one of Italy's coalition formulas—one of the lasting designs for government composition that have helped to define political eras in Italy (Mershon 1994). This pattern applied even to the leftmost PSI, excluded from the centrist formula, and the rightmost PLI, excluded from center-left coalitions. The security and stability of coalition formulas freed component parties to destabilize cabinets. Second, parties responsible for cabinet collapses rather often ruled in successor governments, especially after 1976, when the PSI was pivotal. Finally, parties responsible for breakups more often than not triggered a change in government composition. By this criterion, the policy consequences of rupturing coalitions or one-party cabinets, before or after the PSI became pivotal, are roughly alike.

From 1976 to 1992, the PSI decided governments' fate with astonishing frequency. At the same time, the contest between the DC and the pivotal PSI altered the ties between the executive and the legislature. Cabinets met increased difficulties in relying on parliamentary majorities. For instance, the first Italian government with a Socialist premier— Craxi I, a surplus coalition—saw defectors reduce its support to a minority 163 times (Di Scala 1988). As a result of such challenges, executive decrees became much more common after 1976 (Della Sala 1987; Nocifero and Valdini 1992). These changes generated reactions in turn. Legislation in August 1988 limited the conditions under which executive decrees could be issued, and in October 1988 the chamber radically circumscribed use of the secret ballot (Barrera 1989). Further institutional reforms are discussed below.

In Italy spatial conditions have a clear impact on the office and policy costs of destroying governments. What effects can be discerned in the Netherlands, Finland, Norway, and Ireland? Table 11.5 lists for these countries the same sorts of measures of office payoffs that appear in table 11.3: weighted shares and total numbers of cabinet posts. On average, for almost all parties, between 1946 and 1987 weighted shares dipped slightly and—in contrast to the findings for the DC and PSI— total offices stayed roughly constant after the party had contributed to a government's fall. In these systems, then, almost all parties suffered a small penalty in office terms after having upset a cabinet. These statements hold true even for the Dutch KVP/CDA and the Finnish KP, for those core parties have faced the institutional disincentives and obstacles to adding offices identified above. Only four of the differences within pairs arrayed in table 11.5 attain statistical significance; close scrutiny reveals that the substantive significance of those findings is

Table 11.5

Office Payoffs, by Party and Responsibility for Government Collapse, 1946–1987: Netherlands, Finland, Norway, Ireland

Netherlands

Offices at t	Was Party Responsible for Collapse at Time t − 1?							
	KVP/CDA		PvdA		CHU		VVD	
	No	Yes	No	Yes	No	Yes	No	Yes
Ratios of Cabinet Post Shares to Government Seat Shares[a] (Means)								
Party ministers	0.94	0.91	0.93	0.88	1.05	1.18	1.04	0.63
Party junior ministers	0.95	0.93	1.12	0.35	1.05	0	0.71	0
N cabinets	(12)	(6)	(6)	(1)	(9)	(1)	(9)	(1)
No. of Posts (Means)								
All ministers	15	14	14	13	15	12	15	13
All junior ministers	10	9	10	6	10	6	10	6*
N cabinets	(12)	(6)	(15)	(3)	(15)	(3)	(14)	(4)

Finland

Offices at t	KP		SSD		SKDL		SFP		LKP	
	No	Yes	No	Yes	No	Yes	No	Yes	No	Yes
Ratios of Cabinet Post Shares to Government Seat Shares[a] (Means)										
Party ministers	0.95	0.91	0.90	0.94	0.81	0.61	1.25	NA	1.79	NA
Party junior ministers	0.99	0.76	1.16	0.62	0.67	1.23	0.69	NA	0	NA
No. of cabinets	(19)	(8)	(15)	(5)	(5)	(2)	(21)	(16)		
No. of Posts (Means)										
All ministers	11	11	11	11	11	12	11	11	11	11
All junior ministers	4	4	4	4	4	4	4	3	4	4
N cabinets	(25)	(12)	(22)	(15)	(28)	(9)	(34)	(3)	(34)	(3)

Norway

Offices at t	A		H		V		KRF		SP	
	No	Yes	No	Yes	No	Yes	No	Yes	No	Yes
Ratios of Cabinet Post Shares to Government Seat Shares[a] (Means)										
Party ministers	1.00	1.00	0.98	0.88	1.08	1.06	1.09	1.08	1.03	1.22
Party junior ministers	1.00	1.00	1.00	1.03	0.76	0.59	1.34	1.05	0.93	1.20
N cabinets	(9)	(4)	(4)	(2)	(3)	(1)	(4)	(2)	(4)	(2)
No. of Posts (Means)										
All ministers	16	14	15	16	15	15	15	16	15	17
All junior ministers	14	9	13	15	13	13	13	15	13	15
N cabinets	(16)	(4)	(17)	(3)	(18)	(2)	(17)	(3)	(18)	(2)

limited. As the top rows of the table indicate, the Dutch Liberals (VVD) sacrificed offices after having undermined the executive, but that finding hinges on one case of responsibility for a fall. The office benefits extracted from government falls by Fine Gael and Labour in Ireland, depicted in the bottom rows, are more apparent than real.[16]

Table 11.6 records the policy consequences of breaking up governments. As was the case for Italy, the parties responsible for cabinet col-

Table 11.5

Office Payoffs, by Party and Responsibility for Government Collapse, 1946–1987: Netherlands, Finland, Norway, Ireland *continued*

Ireland	FG		Labour		FF	
	Ratios of Cabinet Post Shares to Government Seat Shares[a] (Means)					
Party ministers	0.91	0.89	1.20	1.42	1.00	1.00
Party junior ministers	1.06	0.97	0.56	1.11	1.00	1.00
N cabinets	(1)	(3)	(1)	(3)	(5)	(6)
	No. of Posts (Means)					
All ministers	14	15*	14	15*	14	14
All junior ministers	8	11	7	13*	10	7
N cabinets	(11)	(4)	(11)	(4)	(7)	(8)

Sources: Calculations based on portfolio data and seat data in Mershon (n.d.), and on coding of information in *Keesing's Contemporary Archives* and other sources.

Note: Means are computed for two groups of cabinets: those whose predecessor was a cabinet the party helped to topple; and those whose predecessor fell for reasons other than the party's withdrawal of support. *T* tests compare the means of the two groups (i.e., for each party, entries in the "yes" and "no" columns). Numbers of applicable cabinets are in parentheses. NA = not applicable.
KVP = Catholic People's Party; CDA = Christian Democratic Appeal; PvdA = Labor Party; VVD = People's Party for Freedom and Democracy; KP = Center Party; SSD = Social Democrats; SKDL = Finnish People's Democratic League; SFP = Swedish People's Party; LKP = Liberal People's Party; A = Labour; H = Conservatives; V = Liberals; KRF = Christian People's Party; SP = Center Party; FG = Fine Gael; FF = Fianna Fáil.
[a]Government seat share = a party's share of lower house seats controlled by all governing parties.
*$p < .05$ (separate variances *t* test).

lapses in the Netherlands, Finland, Norway, and Ireland tended to produce shifts in government composition. The most striking contrast between Italy and these four countries is that parties here toppled governments less often. To be sure, in a sense this is obvious: Italy has had more governments. Even in relative terms, though, the contrast holds up. The DC and PSI moved to terminate, respectively, 60% and 62% of the 52 governments that ruled Italy from 1946 to 1992. The Christian Democrats (KVP/CDA) overthrew governments most often among Dutch parties and were responsible for the fall of only 32% of Dutch cabinets from 1946 to 1987. To cite other examples, the Finnish Social Democrats (SSD) were responsible for the fall of 38% of Finnish governments, and the Norwegian Labor (A) and Conservative (H) parties were responsible for the fall of 19% of Norwegian governments.[17] Why were Italian parties—and above all the DC and PSI—so ready to destroy cabinets? Electoral costs should also be considered.

Table 11.6

Party Status in Government and Government Composition, after Government Collapses, by Party Responsible for Government Collapse, 1946–1987: Netherlands, Finland, Norway, Ireland

	Party Responsible for Collapse At Time t − 1				
Netherlands	KVP/CDA	PvdA	CHU	VVD	
A. Status in government at t					
In government	100.0%	33.3%	33.3%	25.0%	
Out of government	0	66.7%	66.7%	75.0%	
B. Government composition at *t*					
Parties change after fall	83.3%	100.0%	66.7%	75.0%	
Parties same as before fall	16.7%	0%	33.3%	25.0%	
N collapses	(6)	(3)	(3)	(4)	
Finland	KP	SSD	SKDL	SFP	LKP
C. Status in government at *t*					
In government	58.3%	33.3%	22.2%	0	0
Out of government	41.7%	66.7%	78.8%	100.0%	100.0%
D. Government composition at *t*					
Parties change after fall	83.3%	86.7%	78.8%	100.0%	100.0%
Parties same as before fall	16.7%	13.3%	22.2%	0	0
N collapses	(12)	(15)	(9)	(3)	(3)
Norway	A	H	V	KRF	SP
E. Status in government at *t*					
In government	100.0%	75.0%	50.0%	66.7%	100.0%
Out of government	0	25.0%	50.0%	33.3%	0
F. Government composition at *t*					
Governing parties change	50.0%	100.0%	100.0%	100.0%	100.0%
Parties same as before fall	50.0%	0	0	0	0
N collapses	(4)	(4)	(2)	(3)	(2)
Ireland	FG	Labour	FF		
G. Status in government at *t*					
In government	75.0%	75.0%	75.0%		
Out of government	25.0%	25.0%	25.0%		
H. Government composition at *t*					
Governing parties change	100.0%	100.0%	75.0%		
Parties same as before fall	0	0	25.0%		
N collapses	(4)	(4)	(8)		

Source: Calculations based on coding of information in *Keesing's Contemporary Archives* and other sources and on government status data in Mershon (n.d.).

Notes: Entries are the percentage of cases in which a party (or government) had the designated status. See table 11.5 for party acronyms.

The Electoral Costs of Ending Governments

My concern is to ascertain how a party fares at the polls after it has contributed to the fall of most governments formed in the span between two elections. Of course, factors other than a party's role in provoking or preventing cabinet dissolutions—such as levels of inflation and unemployment—can bring voters to penalize or reward incumbent parties (e.g., Eulau and Lewis-Beck 1985; Powell and Whitten 1993). I simply wish to observe whether parties that have caused cabinet failures encounter electoral punishment.

Until 1992, the Christian Democrats and Socialists in Italy benefited electorally from knocking down governments. Yet as table 11.7 shows, distinctions separate the DC and PSI in this regard. The top row of the table discloses that the DC gained at the polls when it helped upset most cabinets governing between two successive elections (advancing 0.3%, on average), whereas the PSI contained its electoral losses when it toppled governments (slipping only 0.03%, on average). The bottom row of table 11.7 isolates the years when the PSI held pivotal status. From 1976 to 1992, the PSI won votes despite, or due to, its responsibility for terminating every government launched after 1974. The DC, in contrast, suffered for its role in government falls since 1976.

The electoral payoffs for demolishing Italian governments have reflected spatial conditions and the segmentation of the electorate. For decades the DC undid governments with impunity, since loyal subcultural voters long dominated the DC electorate, and exchange voters long expected a continuing flow of spoils from the large, centrally located DC.[18] Cabinet dissolutions cost the DC votes after 1976 because subcultural voting waned, opinion voting increased, the pivotal PSI put up stiffer competition for spoils, and ideological justifications for delegitimating opponents had less force. After 1976, furthermore, responsibility for breakups became more of an electoral liability for the PSDI and PRI and more of an electoral advantage for the PSI. Some voters seem to have defected in response to perceived disruptions of policy (opinion voters prevalent within the PRI electorate), others in response to potential complications in patronage (the PSDI's exchange voters). Still other voters rewarded the pivotal PSI for its capacity to influence policy and tap spoils, a capacity exhibited and exploited in government falls (see Mannheimer and Sani 1987, 167–82). The rightmost PLI was exposed to relatively severe electoral punishment for dismantling cabinets, which helps explain why it risked punishment relatively rarely. On the whole,

Table 11.7

Electoral Gain or Loss, by Party and Responsibility for Government Collapse, Italy, 1948–1992

Dominant Role in Collapses between Elections	DC	PSI	PSDI	PRI	PLI
Responsible	+0.30 (N = 10)	−0.03 (N = 8)	−0.50 (N = 4)	−0.10 (N = 4)	−0.80 (N = 1)
Not responsible	−8.40 (N = 1)	−1.73 (N = 3)	−0.40 (N = 7)	+0.06 (N = 7)	−0.32 (N = 10)
Responsible, 1976–92	−2.25 (N = 4)	+1.00 (N = 4)	−1.10 (N = 1)	−0.75 (N = 2)	−0.80 (N = 1)

Source: Calculations based on coding of information in *Keesing's Contemporary Archives*, and on electoral data in Mershon (1996, Appendix B).

Note: See table 11.3 for party acronyms.

Entries are mean changes in parties' percentage share of the vote between pairs of consecutive elections to the Chambers of Deputies. Numbers of applicable inter-electoral periods are in parentheses. The baseline year is 1946 for all parties except the PSDI, which first contested elections in 1948. Dominant role is coded as whatever role (responsible or not responsible for collapse) was most frequent between two successive elections.

though, these differences across Italian parties were small. No party courted electoral disaster when it extinguished a government.

In ongoing research, I extend the study of electoral costs to the Netherlands, Finland, Norway, and Ireland and investigate bargaining costs as well. For now, I make additional comparisons across time in Italy.

System Change in Italy

The April 1992 parliamentary elections marked a profound shift in spatial and institutional conditions in Italy. The Lombard/Northern League and the Rete (anti-Mafia Network) recast dimensions of party competition and campaigned against corruption. The DC's support dipped below 30%, which meant that the DC no longer qualified as a core party (Schofield 1993). The 1992 elections were the first national elections held after the secret ballot was restricted in Parliament, the single-preference vote was introduced, and the PCI was converted into the Democratic Party of the Left (PDS). According to my argument, some change in the costs of coalition and cost reduction strategies should have ensued.

The first postelection coalition joined the same four parties that governed on election eve. But the allies were led by Italy's second Socialist premier, their coalition had minimal winning size, and they divided among them a total of 60 portfolios. The preelection coalition contained 99 portfolios overall. The second postelection government was headed by Italy's first nonparty premier, Carlo Azeglio Ciampi, who almost succeeded in allying with the PDS, Greens, and PRI; last-minute disagreements left him with a four-party minimal-winning coalition, a new edition of its predecessor that allocated an unprecedented share of portfolios (12 out of 62) to nonparty experts.[19] In August 1993, pressured by referendum results and Ciampi's exhortations, Parliament passed new electoral laws, which combine plurality and proportional rules for Chamber of Deputies and Senate elections and impose a 4% threshold for representation in the chamber.

Held under the new laws, the March 1994 elections produced even more sweeping change: the end of 50 years of uninterrupted DC incumbency. Public outrage at widespread corruption inflicted devastating losses on the Popular Party (as the DC renamed itself in January 1994) and the PSI. Undone by corruption, the PLI and PSDI did not even contest the elections. In May, media magnate Silvio Berlusconi became premier. His government embraced Forza Italia, the movement he founded in early 1994; the Northern League; the National Alliance, the renamed MSI; and the Centrist Union (UDC) and the Christian Democratic Center (CCD, a right-wing splinter from the DC), which were Forza Italia's electoral allies in some constituencies. The coalition contained 64 portfolios and by one standard had minimal-winning size.[20] Berlusconi resigned in December 1994 when the Northern League withdrew. In January 1995 economist Lamberto Dini became Italy's second nonparty premier, guiding a cabinet made up of 55 ministers and undersecretaries. For the first time in postwar Italy, not a single member of Parliament was included in the executive. The Dini government passed its votes of investiture thanks to support from the PDS.

From 1946 to 1992 in Italy, the office costs of building cabinets, even surplus coalitions, were low. Some parties under some conditions achieved office benefits from undoing governments. Breakups tended to bring influence over policy. Most Italian voters appeared to be "indulgent [and] . . . rapidly forgetful" about cabinet collapses (according to an ex-deputy quoted in *Corriere della Sera,* June 28, 1986). In such a system, as Christian Democrat Giulio Andreotti once summarized in a noted saying, "Power wears out those without it" and power reinforces the powerful. That Italy no longer exists. And the roots of the transformation lie in the two classes of explanatory factors highlighted here.

Conclusion

In postwar Italy until 1992, transitory cabinets were staffed by permanent incumbents. These empirical outcomes make Italy an extreme but not a unique case among parliamentary democracies. The outcomes pose vexing questions when viewed in the light of game-theoretic predictions. What explains the combination of instability and stability? How can governments break up at such low cost?

The framework that I develop solves this puzzle. The evidence indicates that particular spatial and institutional conditions in Italy lowered the costs associated with breaking and building coalitions and favored strategies that further lowered those costs. Italy's coalitions were not easily sustained, since breakups caused little damage. When policy space and institutions were redefined in the early 1990s, costs and outcomes in Italian coalition politics were transformed.

Even among multipolar party systems, Italy's governments display the shortest average duration and the lowest turnover rate. The country that most nearly resembles Italy in spatial terms, the Netherlands, presents relatively long-lived governments and fairly ample turnover. Dutch institutions, working through their influence on the costs of coalition, account for the difference in outcomes. Cabinet duration in Finland approximates that in Italy, but alternation in Finland is somewhat greater. One reason is that Finnish parties have paid a stiffer price for government breakups, as table 11.6 shows. Not only for Italy but also for the Netherlands, Finland, Norway, and Ireland, the findings suggest that spatial and institutional environments shape the costs of coalition that politicians face and structure politicians' efforts to deflate those costs.

I need to do more to explore the posited linkages among spatial and institutional conditions, costs incurred, and records of duration and turnover. I am engaged in weighing electoral costs outside Italy and comparing bargaining costs across countries. Additional intertemporal comparisons within countries (e.g., comparison of costs in Norway before and after 1961) will yield further assessments of the impact of changes in spatial and institutional conditions. A larger set of countries will encompass greater spatial and institutional variation. The study of Belgium and Denmark holds special interest, since both countries saw vast changes in their party systems in the early 1970s (which, for Belgium, contributed to a lengthy process of institutional reform).

The preliminary results support the framework advanced here. To judge from the evidence now available, this explanation accounts for Italy's extremes and for the degrees of stability found in other parliamentary democracies.

NOTES

I thank Janet Adamski, Kerstin Hamann, and Sally Roever for research assistance and David Farrell, Bingham Powell, Herman Schwartz, John Sprague, and seminar participants at Washington University for helpful comments. I am also grateful for the suggestions offered by fellow participants in the workshop "Party Discipline and the Organization of Parliaments," Joint Sessions of the European Consortium for Political Research, Bordeaux, April 27 to May 2, 1995. This chapter presents preliminary findings from my 10-nation study, a book manuscript entitled *The Costs of Coalition* (Mershon n.d.). The evidence from Italy discussed in the chapter is also treated in Mershon 1996.

1. Strøm (1990b, 125) defines the turnover or alternation rate as "the proportion of legislative seats held by parties changing status between government and opposition," averaged across a country's governments.

2. My thanks to Kaare Strøm for providing me with these data on the measure of alternation (or rate of turnover). The Pearson correlation between alternation and duration is 0.575.

3. The three-party cabinet built by Amintore Fanfani in 1962 controlled 51% of the seats in the Chamber of Deputies, whereas three other coalitions held exactly half. The Socialists (PSI) abstained on Fanfani's investiture, extending support that a pure search for power would render superfluous. The architects of the Fanfani coalition saw it as a second-best solution, designed to pave the way for the larger, long-term alliance they preferred, an alliance embracing the PSI.

4. Below, I elaborate on this classification, which is drawn from Laver and Schofield (1990). I am investigating additional country cases in ongoing research.

5. These criteria replicate those used by Strøm (1990b) and others who have borrowed Strøm's data (King et al. 1990). I differ from Laver and Schofield (1990), who use only the first two criteria. By each set of criteria, Italy has the most short-lived governments of any extant parliamentary democracy.

6. This identification relies primarily on *Keesing's Contemporary Archives,* a source often used in coalition studies (e.g., Dodd 1976; Strøm 1990b). Designation of responsibility for a cabinet's fall was usually straightforward. For example, in October 1954, the two largest parties in the Finnish government, the Agrarians (KP) and Social Democrats (SSDP), publicized their differences over economic policy. The KP pushed for prices for farm products higher than those proposed in Prime Minister Torngren's anti-inflation package, whereas the SSDP urged lower food prices. Torngren then submitted his resignation. Responsibility for his government's collapse lay with the KP and SSDP.

7. Following Lijphart (1994), I use a 20% criterion for identifying "major" changes in district size, thresholds, and assembly size.

8. The "effective number" of parties, a well-known index, takes into account not only the number but also the relative strength of parties (Lijphart 1994). Content analyses of parties' election manifestos furnish data on dimensions and party positions in Europe (Budge et al. 1987; Laver and Budge 1992). This paragraph's discussion of median and core parties (which paves the way for cross-party comparisons below) relies primarily on Schofield's publications (Laver and Schofield 1990; Schofield 1987, 1993), with supplementary sources as noted in the text.

9. Mannheimer and Sani's composite measures for subcultural belonging include reports of behavior (e.g., attendance at mass) and attitudinal items (sympathy toward the Church). Other data for Italy suggest that exchange voters form sizable proportions of the DC and PSDI electorates, that opinion voters predominate in the PLI and PRI electorates, and that the PSI draws opinion and exchange voters (e.g., Cazzola 1985; Katz 1985).

10. See Mershon 1994 on center-left (DC-PSI-PSDI-PRI) coalitions, typi-

cal from 1963 to 1976, and five-party coalitions (DC-PSI-PSDI-PRI-PLI), which prevailed from 1979 to 1992.

11. Figure 11.5A excludes the few governments formed when the KVP/CDA did not occupy the core of Dutch policy space: den Uyl (installed in 1973 after the November 1972 elections), van Agt I (1977), and Lubbers I (1982) and II (1986). The CDA's severe losses in the 1994 elections surely disqualified it as the core, as discussed in Mershon (n.d., chaps. 7–8).

12. The KP did not control the median legislator in the parliaments elected in 1958 and 1966. This judgment is based on seat data and a comparison of Laver and Schofield (1990, 117–18), Mylly and Berry (1984), and Soikkanen (1981).

13. To be specific, figure 11.5B excludes the seven nonpartisan cabinets just noted and excludes three party-based governments: Fagerholm I (formed in 1948), Paasio II (1972), and Holkeri I (1987). In all postwar Finnish governments, at least a few important ministries are assigned two ministers, with one of the two "formally considered as the [single] head of the entire ministerial unit" (Nousiainen 1988, 214). Analysts differ as to whether the so-called "second ministers" (those *not* identified as heads) are to be viewed as junior ministers (Arter 1987) or as full ministers (Nousiainen 1988). Figure 11.5B portrays them as junior ministers. No matter how the definitional question is settled, the bottom line stays the same: the KP sacrifices posts when it builds coalitions.

14. Fianna Fáil initiated its first coalition in July 1989, as discussed in Mershon (n.d., chaps. 7–8).

15. These measures have shortcomings. For instance, two DC-only cabinets may have distinct policy colorations, and not all governing parties influence policy to the same extent. Yet parties in government clearly have the potential to shape policy, as the measures capture (Strøm 1990b). In ongoing research, I am probing alternative indices of the policy costs and benefits of governing.

16. As in the case of the VVD, the catch is small *N*. FG and Labour ruled four times during the period covered in table 11.5. The entries in the "no" column for FG and Labour reflect their participation in one cabinet, Costello II, which was also Ireland's only three-party coalition. Naturally, the third ally in Costello II (Clann na Talmhan, literally "People of the Land") obtained some offices. And comparing the division of posts in Ireland's one three-party coalition and three FG-Labour coalitions is equivalent to comparing FG and Labour as incumbents when they held, as opposed to lacked, responsibility for the preceding government's fall.

17. But FF has brought half of Irish governments to a premature end, reflecting the frequency with which FF one-party majority governments have exercised the prerogative to call early elections.

18. The DC's drop when not responsible for cabinet collapses rests on one

datum alone: the difference between 1948, when voters rallied around the DC at the onset of the Cold War, and 1953, when controversy over a newly approved majoritarian electoral law (soon rescinded) repulsed some voters.

19. Even though a PRI senator was undersecretary to Ciampi, the PRI did not consider itself a member of the coalition and abstained on the cabinet's vote of investiture (*Corriere della Sera,* April 29 to May 13, 1993).

20. The Berlusconi government qualifies as minimal winning if electoral alliances (the Freedom Alliance and the Good Government Alliance) are counted as its component units. If parliamentary parties are counted as the units comprising the coalition, it has surplus status and a superfluous member in the CCD.

REFERENCES

Allum, P. A. 1973. *Italy: Republic without Government?* New York: Norton.

Anckar, Dag. 1992. "Finland: Dualism and Consensual Rule." In Erik Damgaard, ed., *Parliamentary Change in the Nordic Countries.* Oslo: Scandinavian University Press.

Andeweg, Rudy, and Wilma Bakema. 1994. "The Netherlands: Ministers and Cabinet Policy." In Michael Laver and Kenneth A. Shepsle, eds., *Cabinet Ministers and Parliamentary Government.* Cambridge: Cambridge University Press.

Arter, David. 1987. *Politics and Policy-Making in Finland.* New York: St. Martin's Press.

Axelrod, Robert. 1970. *Conflict of Interest: A Theory of Divergent Goals with Applications to Politics.* Chicago: Markham.

Barrera, Pietro. 1989. "La prima riforma istituzionale: La nuova disciplina dell'attività di governo." In Raimondo Catanzaro and Raffaella Y. Nanetti, eds., *Politica in Italia: I fatti dell'anno e le interpretazioni, Edizione 89.* Bologna: Il Mulino.

Borre, Ole. 1984. "Critical Electoral Change in Scandinavia." In Russell J. Dalton, Scott C. Flanagan, and Paul Allen Beck, eds., *Electoral Change in Advanced Industrial Democracies.* Princeton, NJ: Princeton University Press.

Browne, Eric C., and Mark Franklin. 1973. "Coalition Payoffs in European Parliamentary Democracies." *American Political Science Review* 67: 453–64.

Budge, Ian, David Robertson, and Derek Hearl, eds. 1987. *Ideology, Strategy and Party Change: Spatial Analyses of Post-War Election Programmes in 19 Democracies.* Cambridge: Cambridge University Press.

Cazzola, Franco. 1985. "Struttura e potere del Partito socialista italiano." In Gianfranco Pasquino, ed., *Il sistema politico italiano.* Bari: Laterza.

Daalder, Hans. 1966. "The Netherlands: Opposition in a Segmented Society." In Robert A. Dahl, ed., *Political Oppositions in Western Democracies.* New Haven, CT: Yale University Press.

———. 1987. "The Dutch Party System: From Segmentation to Polarization—and Then?" In Hans Daalder, ed., *Party Systems in Denmark, Austria, Switzerland, the Netherlands and Belgium.* New York: St. Martin's Press.

Della Sala, Vincent. 1987. "Governare per decreto: Il governo Craxi e l'uso dei decreti-legge." In Piergiorgio Corbetta and Robert Leonardi, eds., *Politica in Italia: I fatti dell'anno e le interpretazioni, Edizione 87.* Bologna: Il Mulino.

Di Scala, and M. Spencer. 1988. *Renewing Italian Socialism: Nenni to Craxi.* London: Oxford University Press.

Dodd, Lawrence C. 1976. *Coalitions in Parliamentary Government.* Princeton, NJ: Princeton University Press.

Dogan, Mattei. 1984. "Come si diventa ministro in Italia: Le regole non scritte del gioco politico." In P. Farneti, ed., *Il sistema politico italiano tra crisi e innovazione.* Milan: Franco Angeli.

Döring, Herbert, ed. 1995. *Parliaments and Majority Rule in Western Europe.* New York: St. Martin's Press.

Eulau, Heinz, and Michael S. Lewis-Beck, eds. 1985. *Economic Conditions and Electoral Outcomes: The United States and Western Europe.* New York: Agathon Press.

Farrell, Brian. 1994. "The Political Role of Cabinet Ministers in Ireland." In Michael Laver and Kenneth A. Shepsle, eds., *Cabinet Ministers and Parliamentary Government.* Cambridge: Cambridge University Press.

Franklin, Mark N., and Thomas T. Mackie. 1984. "Reassessing the Importance of Size and Ideology for the Formation of Governing Coalitions in Parliamentary Democracies." *American Journal of Political Science* 28: 672–91.

Gallagher, Michael, Michael Laver, and Peter Mair. 1995. *Representative Government in Modern Europe.* 2d ed. New York: McGraw-Hill.

Galli, Giorgio, and Alfonso Prandi. 1970. *Patterns of Political Participation in Italy.* New Haven, CT: Yale University Press.

Gladdish, Ken. 1991. *Governing from the Centre: Politics and Policy-Making in the Netherlands.* London: Hurst.

Herman, Valentine. 1976. *Parliaments of the World: A Reference Compendium.* Berlin: De Gruyter.

Katz, Richard S. 1985. "Preference Voting in Italy: Votes of Opinion, Belonging, or Exchange." *Comparative Political Studies* 18: 229–49.

———. 1986. "Intraparty Preference Voting." In Bernard Grofman and Arend Lijphart, eds., *Electoral Laws and Their Political Consequences.* New York: Agathon Press.

Keesing's Contemporary Archives. 1945–. Bristol: Longman.

King, Gary, James E. Alt, Nancy Elizabeth Burns, and Michael Laver. 1990. "A Unified Model of Cabinet Dissolution in Parliamentary Democracies." *American Journal of Political Science* 34: 846–71.

Laver, Michael. 1992. "Are Irish Parties Peculiar?" In John H. Goldthorpe and Christopher T. Whelan, eds., *The Development of Industrial Society in Ireland.* London: Oxford University Press.

Laver, Michael, and Ian Budge, eds. 1992. *Party Policy and Government Coalitions.* New York: St. Martin's Press.

Laver, Michael, and Norman Schofield. 1990. *Multiparty Government: The Politics of Coalition in Europe.* London: Oxford University Press.

Laver, Michael, and Kenneth Shepsle. 1990. "Coalitions and Cabinet Governments." *American Political Science Review* 84: 873–90.

———. 1994. *Cabinet Ministers and Parliamentary Government.* Cambridge: Cambridge University Press.

———. 1996. *Making and Breaking Governments: Cabinets and Legislatures in Parliamentary Democracies.* Cambridge: Cambridge University Press.

Lijphart, Arend. 1984. *Democracies: Patterns of Majoritarian and Consensus Government in Twenty-One Countries.* New Haven, CT: Yale University Press.

———. 1994. *Electoral Systems and Party Systems: A Study of Twenty-Seven Democracies 1945–1990.* London: Oxford University Press.

Mair, Peter. 1987. *The Changing Irish Party System: Organization, Ideology, and Electoral Competition.* London: Pinter.

———. 1992. "Explaining the Absence of Class Politics in Ireland." In John H. Goldthorpe and Christopher T. Whelan, eds., *The Development of Industrial Society in Ireland.* London: Oxford University Press.

Mannheimer, Renato, and Giacomo Sani. 1987. *Il mercato elettorale: Identikit dell'elettore italiano.* Bologna: Il Mulino.

Marradi, Alberto. 1982. "From 'Centrism' to Crisis of the Center-Left Coalitions." In Eric C. Browne and John Dreijmanis, eds., *Government Coalitions in Western Democracies.* London: Longman.

Marsh, Michael. 1992. "Ireland." In Mark N. Franklin, Thomas T. Mackie, and Henry Valen, eds., *Electoral Change: Responses to Evolving Social and Attitudinal Structures in Western Countries.* Cambridge: Cambridge University Press.

McKelvey, Richard D. 1976. "Intransitivities in Multidimensional Voting Models and Some Implications for Agenda Control." *Journal of Economic Theory* 12: 472–82.

———. 1979. "General Conditions for Global Intransitivities in Formal Voting Models." *Econometrica* 47: 1085–1111.

McKelvey, Richard D., and Norman Schofield. 1987. "Generalized Symmetry Conditions at a Core Point." *Econometrica* 55: 923–33.

Mershon, Carol. 1994. "Expectations and Informal Rules in Coalition Formation." *Comparative Political Studies* 27: 40–79.

———. 1996. "The Costs of Coalition: Coalition Theories and Italian Governments." *American Political Science Review* 1996: 534–54.

———. n.d. *The Costs of Coalition.* University of Virginia. Typescript.

Mylly, Juhani, and R. Michael Berry. 1984. *Political Parties in Finland: Essays in History and Politics.* Turku: University of Turku.

Nocifero, Nicolò, and Sergio Valdini. 1992. *Il palazzo di vetro: Il lavoro dei deputati italiani nella decima legislatura.* Florence: Vallecchi.

Nohlen, Dieter. 1984. "Choices and Changes in Electoral Systems." In Arend Lijphart and Bernard Grofman, eds., *Choosing an Electoral System.* New York: Praeger.

Nousiainen, Jaakko. 1988. "Finland." In Jean Blondel and Ferdinand Müller-Rommel, eds., *Cabinets in Western Europe.* New York: St. Martin's Press.

———. 1994. "Finland: Ministerial Autonomy, Constitutional Collectivism, and Party Oligarchy." In Michael Laver and Kenneth A. Shepsle, eds., *Cabinet Ministers and Parliamentary Government.* Cambridge: Cambridge University Press.

Parisi, Arturo, and Gianfranco Pasquino. 1979. "Changes in Italian Electoral Behavior: The Relationships between Parties and Voters." *West European Politics* 2: 6–30.

Pasquino, Gianfranco. 1981. "The Italian Socialist Party: Electoral Stagnation and Political Indispensability." In Howard R. Penniman, ed., *Italy at the Polls, 1979: A Study of the Parliamentary Elections.* Washington, DC: American Enterprise Institute.

Petracca, Orazio M. 1980. *Storia della prima repubblica.* Milan: Mondo Economico.

Powell, G. Bingham, Jr., and Guy D. Whitten. 1993. "A Cross-National Analysis of Economic Voting: Taking Account of the Political Context." *American Journal of Political Science* 37: 391–414.

Riker, William H. 1962. *The Theory of Political Coalitions.* New Haven, CT: Yale University Press.

Schofield, Norman. 1983. "Generic Instability of Majority Rule." *Review of Economic Studies* 50: 696–705.

———. 1986. "Existence of a 'Structurally Stable' Equilibrium for a Noncollegial Voting Rule." *Public Choice* 51: 267–84.

———. 1987. "Coalitions in West European Democracies: 1945–1987." *European Journal of Political Economy* 3: 555–91.

———. 1993. "Political Competition and Multiparty Coalition Governments." *European Journal of Political Research* 23: 1–33.

Schofield, Norman, Bernard Grofman, and Scott L. Feld. 1988. "The Core and the Stability of Group Choice in Spatial Voting Games." *American Political Science Review* 82: 195–211.

Soikkanen, Timo. 1981. *The Structure and Development of the Political Party Spectrum in Finland.* Helsinki: Ministry for Foreign Affairs.

Spotts, Frederic, and Theodor Wieser. 1986. *Italy: A Difficult Democracy.* Cambridge: Cambridge University Press.

Strøm, Kaare. 1990a. "A Behavioral Theory of Competitive Political Parties." *American Journal of Political Science* 34: 565–98.

———. 1990b. *Minority Government and Majority Rule.* Cambridge: Cambridge University Press.

———. 1994. "The Political Role of Norwegian Cabinet Ministers." In Michael Laver and Kenneth A. Shepsle, eds., *Cabinet Ministers and Parliamentary Government.* Cambridge: Cambridge University Press.

Strøm, Kaare, and Jorn Leipart. 1993. "Policy, Institutions, and Coalition Avoidance: Norwegian Governments, 1945–1990." *American Political Science Review* 87: 870–87.

Whyte, J. H. 1974. "Ireland: Politics without Social Bases." In Richard Rose, ed., *Electoral Behavior.* New York: Free Press.

Zuckerman, Alan. 1979. *The Politics of Faction.* New Haven, CT: Yale University Press.

12

Coalition Discipline, Enforcement Mechanisms, and Intraparty Politics

PAUL MITCHELL

Much of what happens in party competition is driven by policy pursuit. This supposition does not require lengthy speculation concerning whether politicians are sincerely committed to public policy.[1] The crucial assumption is that since voters are motivated by policy concerns,[2] parties interested in their future electoral prospects will *at least pretend* to be interested in policy. Put another way, while politicians may harbor all manner of private desires, policy pursuit is the acceptable language of competition, at least on the public stage. Parties fear that they will suffer tangible reputational costs if they are not seen to be exerting every effort to implement the key policy promises that they advertised to their activists and electorate.

Consequently, parties do in practice bargain vigorously over policy commitments, and many of the key events that destabilize coalition governments are policy conflicts. While the precise relationship between "performance" in government and electoral prospects has proved difficult for academics to establish (Fiorina 1981; Lewis-Beck 1986, 1988; Powell and Whitten 1993), political parties clearly believe that their electoral futures significantly depend upon perceptions of their policy performance in government and expend enormous effort and resources to this end.

Recently, some studies of coalition politics have extended the traditional focus on government formation and dissolution to examine the actual "life" of real coalition governments in power (Mitchell 1996;

Timmermans 1996). Central to these studies is the proposition that the life of a government should be interpreted as an ongoing bargaining process in which there is much still to be played for. In other words, the "spoils" of office are not all distributed at the point of government formation, as tends to be assumed by most traditional coalition theories. In particular, the government's policy program is not in any sense simply "implemented" by virtue of the portfolio allocation and the drafting of the coalition policy document. Likewise, while coalition attributes and the initial division of portfolios are clearly important, governments do not automatically continue as a result of formation conditions any more than political parties survive simply because they were present during a country's democratization. Given that governments are confronted with all manner of disturbances, they survive only if key participants choose to work to maintain them.

Parties in office pursue their goals, competing to have their policies adopted as a means of satisfying their members and improving their electoral prospects. However, once parties form a government, they are confronted by a wide range of potentially destabilizing events that threaten their continued tenure in government, their favorite policies, and their electoral expectations. The destabilizing event could be an "external" shock or an integral component of the bargaining process inside cabinet coalitions, such as an attempt by one coalition party to defect from policy concessions made as part of the coalition formation process.

Parties attempt to reduce uncertainty by resorting to a range of enforcement devices. Prominent among these is the negotiation of the government program. European coalition cabinets increasingly resort to lengthy and detailed government policy programs, both to impose some structure on subsequent bargaining and to attempt to ensure that a party's key policies will be included in the government's agenda for action.

The Search for Credible Commitment

Reputation and Credibility

Reputation and credibility are the currency with which politicians and parties hope to procure executive power. "Credibility is a politician's main stock in trade. . . . Part of the essence of being a senior politician is the association with a set of policy positions believed by others to be either sincere or strategic positions with which the politician has become so inextricably associated that the reputational costs of deviating from them are very high" (Laver and Shepsle 1996, 248). In Laver and Shepsle's portfolio allocation approach, the forecasted policy output of any particular cabinet depends upon the distribution of portfolios. In other words, policy promises are made credible by appointing politicians with particular policy reputations to particular ministries. The portfolio distribution matters because although cabinet governments are formally collectively *responsible,* there is a departmental structure to actual cabinet *decision making.*

While Laver and Shepsle are undoubtedly correct in pointing out the "very strongly departmental character [of] government decision making" (1996, 31), this, of course, is not the whole story. Given the volume of work in each ministry and the time and information costs incurred in "interfering" in other ministries, ministers concern themselves primarily with the work of their own department.[3] However, precisely because the ministerial structure of cabinet government provides ministers (and, by implication, parties) with considerable discretion over the policy outcomes of the departments that they direct, *parties* are always in danger of losing control of government policy in the departments managed by their coalition partners. This is a potentially serious problem if the portfolios not held by a party are responsible for policy jurisdictions that are of major concern to the party. And of course, this is likely to happen in practice unless a party manages to capture all of the important ministries. Assuming that this rarely happens, a party has credibility and enforcement problems when it does not control the ministry involved. Thus, even if a key policy of party A was agreed on at coalition formation, there is a real danger that it may be sabotaged if party B controls the relevant ministry. While ministers do not have the time or resources to check on all of the details of all the policy areas, there is a party incentive to cross-check on the key policies that define the party's raison d'être. And while such intervention is an uphill task, parties simply cannot afford to allow full ministerial discretion, essentially because politicians from party B cannot be trusted to implement policies close to party A, even if these were previously accepted as part of the initial policy bargain.

Thus, parties have incentives to underwrite the credibility of their key policies—their brand identity items—by negotiating their inclusion in the coalition policy document drafted at government formation. The coalition policy document is part of the process whereby a party attempts to credibly commit its coalition partners to at least some of the party's main policies.

Coalition Policy Documents

The coalition policy document[4] is the immediate policy output of the government formation process and can be interpreted as a statement of the initial policy equilibrium of the incoming government. It also provides a rough estimate of the relative bargaining strengths of the parties concerned. This does not require the naive assumption that the content of the document should be read in a strictly literal fashion. Since the document is highly strategic (Laver and Schofield 1990; Laver and Budge 1992), some items that are included are almost entirely aspirational and have little prospect of even being attempted, while conversely other key areas of outstanding policy dispute may be omitted altogether in order to deemphasize discord. Nevertheless, the parties' own election manifestos and a whole range of policy documents and leaders' speeches set out the policy basis on which parties appeal to voters. It is against performance of these policies that credibility ultimately is assumed to be judged.

It is worth being a little more explicit about the highly strategic nature of coalition policy documents. This is best illustrated with a strategic scenario. Consider a bargaining structure—like the coalition governments that formed in Ireland in the 1970s and 1980s—of a prospective two-party coalition with one "large" party (Fine Gael) and one "small" party (the Labour Party). Given the respective size of the potential coalition partners, there was a structural imbalance in the negotiations—not so much in terms of formal bargaining power (after all, both parties were necessary to be minimum winning) as in terms of what each wanted to get out of the talks. It might be assumed that since Fine Gael's overriding motivation was to get into office, its leader (and prospective prime minister) had an interest in keeping the program for government as vague and aspirational as possible, especially given the likelihood of retrospective voting. For the Labour Party the negotiations had a different logic. Clearly, in the short term the Labour leadership had an interest in satisfying their own office-seeking motivations by negotiating what they believed their wider party would consider a "good" policy package (hence allowing the coalition to form).[5]

Such considerations are likely to be reinforced by longer-term motivations in that small parties in government are always in danger of having their policies blocked in cabinet. Given Irish governments' adherence to the doctrine of collective cabinet responsibility, and because a threat to bring down the government can be used only infrequently if it is to remain credible, a minority coalition partner has an incentive to demand that specific and detailed policy commitments be written into the coalition document as an insurance policy. Fine Gael as the far larger partner could afford to trade away a section of its preferred policies in order to get into office, since it could be confident of controlling a large proportion of the government's ongoing policy agenda by virtue of its control of over 70% of cabinet votes (and ministries). A minority partner like Labour, on the other hand, is always fearful of the progressive erosion of its policy commitments and political identity through the accumulation of lost cabinet votes.[6] It therefore had an incentive to attempt to imprint a selection of its key policies on the "tablet of stone" (the coalition policy document) in an attempt to stem the tide of policy erosion by executive decision in cabinet. In this vision, then, the coalition policy document for a minority partner in government is a kind of court of appeals, outside the logic of cabinet arithmetic and portfolio distribution, that can be periodically summoned to protect the junior partner's vital interests.

European political parties increasingly resort to lengthy and detailed coalition policy documents (e.g., Müller and Strøm 1997; Laver and Shepsle 1994). Despite this, it remains an interesting but as yet open question as to whether this development has a conflict-increasing or conflict-reducing function in the life of cabinet governments. On the one hand, such documents seem to provide a useful purpose in terms of forcing explicit or at least implicit policy trade-offs between parties with perhaps widely different priorities, hence providing a mechanism for establishing an initial minimum level of policy coherence that might otherwise be totally lacking. On the other hand, the detailed enunciation of coalition policy, as distinct from party policy, in such a joint government program, means that each party has publicly accepted a cost: the distance that it has moved away from its own preferred policy position.

Given, then, that a party is likely to have suffered substantial costs (the extent depending on how successful it was) during coalition formation, in terms of the watering down or elimination of part of its policy agenda, it becomes even more likely that the party will be prepared to fight tooth and nail for those of its policies that were included in the coalition document. The tendency of the media to evaluate each party in terms of the extent to which it is successful in implementing *its parts* of the supposedly joint policy program is likely to exacerbate these tensions further.

It may be, then, that in a government whose constituent parties have substantially diverging policy positions, the role of published coalition policy documents is

1. To identify the benefits and costs of the opening phase of policy bargaining
2. To provide a "holy grail" of bottom-line policy commitments as an insurance device
3. To map out the likely battleground of future conflicts

Part of the explanation as to why the coalition policy document often fails to exercise a conflict-reducing function is, of course, that a policy commitment in a coalition document is a long way from an enacted policy and that even in a long document the crucial details of the measure usually must still be fought over.[7] Moreover, experienced politicians are aware in advance that the inclusion of an item in a coalition agreement is only the first stage in a long battle. "The real settlement of the issue will take place later: by including many types of issues within the government agreement, they seek a tentative assurance that they will have a voice in that settlement" (Nousiainen 1993, 264). What then becomes important for any given policy is the battle to decide who is accepted as the interpreter of the spirit of intention behind the policy as it appears in the government program. Clearly, the power to decide on the detail may well amount to the power to undermine totally the original aim of the policy.[8]

Nevertheless, at least for the subsequent life of the government, the coalition policy document does impose some structure on policy bargaining, identifying some areas of "legitimate" debate and almost "ruling out" other items. It is an institutional evolution that plays some role in reducing uncertainty: "Political institutions constitute *ex ante* agreements over cooperation among politicians. They reduce uncertainty by creating a stable exchange structure" (North 1990a, 191). Thus, the negotiation and subsequent policing of the coalition treaty induce some stability by defining the areas of legitimate contestation. Of course, the amount of detail in the coalition policy document and how strictly its provisions are adhered to are empirical matters that vary from country to country. In Germany, for example, the "treaty" appears to be almost a binding contract: ministers are "bound to the coalition policy 'treaty,' which is a very precise agreement over draft bills and leaves hardly any room for deviation or interpretation. Bureaucrats in the ministries as well as in the chancellor's office constantly control and monitor the implementation of this coalition treaty" (Müller-Rommel 1994, 165). One former minister in the Netherlands is reported to have said, "The coalition agreement has gradually assumed greater significance. Eventually we have come to regard it as something like a law" (Andeweg and Bakema 1994, 64).

Thus, coalition treaties now play a substantial role in European cabinet government. Their utility for parties is that they help underwrite the credibility of their most electorally salient policies and help commit their coalition partners to their implementation. Of course, one of the reasons that political markets are inefficient is that there is "no direct enforcement mechanism to see that 'contractual agreements' are carried out" (North 1993, 18). Nevertheless, while coalition policy documents amount to more than the "cheap talk" (Strøm, Budge, and Laver 1994) of many manifesto commitments, ultimately the only reliable "enforcement mechanism" is the competitive behavior of the parties themselves.[9]

Interparty Competition: The Incentive to Defect

In anticipation of trouble, parties attempt to ensure ongoing government commitment to at least some of their key policies by trying to negotiate their inclusion in the coalition policy document as insurance. However, while this document provides some protective armor in future battles, it does not ensure victory. Interparty coalition bargaining is characterized by a pervasive incentive to defect from prior commitments. Thus, the policy output of the government is not decided at coalition formation but is the subject of continual and sometimes fierce bargaining throughout the life of the government.

Indeed, much of what makes coalition politics so intriguing is the continual battles by parties to push their favored policies to the top of the government's agenda. The policies with which the parties entered government are not simply "implemented" in some technocratic or preordained fashion. While this is also true of single-party administrations that might be thwarted in their policy efforts by the civil service or "economic realities"—to name just two possible obstacles—the key difference with coalition governments is that parties have electoral rivals *within the cabinet* who may try to undermine and subvert their policies. Even if some collegiality develops between parties in a coalition, they will rarely lose sight of the fact that they will soon be opponents once again in a forthcoming election. Parties are always concerned with their underlying level of popularity because their anticipated electoral prospects may condition their current, and certainly their future, bargaining strengths.

Attempted defections from commitments made in the coalition formation document will be vigorously resisted by parties keen to demonstrate that they can "deliver" the key party policies that they have advertised to supporters. If a precise commitment was secured at formation and included in the coalition policy document, attempted defections from this policy by a party's coalition partners will be highly destabilizing, since they will be regarded not simply as "ordinary" policy debate but as a "breach of faith" and an assault on formation conditions. Nevertheless, despite the foreknowledge that defections from commitments will be resisted, there is a constant incentive to defect. This is partly because parties are induced to make "insincere" promises at formation as the immediate attraction of getting into government clouds (or overrides) the policy costs involved. Once the parties are installed in office, the policy costs quickly come into focus, and the parties will typically find good reasons that certain costly commitments cannot be implemented, at least as specified. However, the incentive to defect is ultimately based on much more than the fact that each party at formation may have made "insincere" policy promises. More significantly, the incentive derives from the exigencies of day-to-day party competition.

While the coalition policy document is an important regulatory device in the life of coalition governments, it is not in any sense a "done deal." Coalition cabinets are an ongoing bargaining process in which much still exists to be played for. It is almost always in the interests of an incumbent party to try to drag government policy toward party policy (the limit being the extent that would cause coalition breakup). Thus, there is a constant tension as parties attempt to avoid implementing policies that have been identified as deriving from their colleagues' preferences and endeavor to substitute their own policies. Although occasionally this tension manifests itself in well publicized head-to-head coalition conflicts, it will more frequently take subtler forms, partial engagements in which ministers and parties aim to disguise their defections as "policy development." In short, a party that is less than vigilant in policing its policies will quickly find that they have been subjected to stealth attacks and erosion by detail, irrespective of what the coalition agreement says.[10]

Unitary Actor Status and Intraparty Revolts

Intraparty Dynamics

Battles between party leaders in a coalition government are only one type of destabilizing policy event that can undermine policy implementation. While ministers can make any kind of deals they like behind the secrecy of the cabinet door, these are all to no avail if they cannot secure the support or at least the acquiescence of their parliamentary parties. As the first chapter in this volume argues, "Party cohesion and discipline are very much two-way streets, and certainly much more than the emphasis on whipping—with its connotations of disciplining the unruly rank and file—might suggest." Clearly, rebellious backbenchers have the potential to torpedo even the most carefully crafted compromises between ministers.

The unitary actor assumption implicit in almost all studies of coalition formation (for exceptions, see Luebbert 1986 and chap. 2 of this volume) is reasonably serviceable, given the generally high level of party discipline in most European countries. At least for the purposes of government formation and dissolution, European political parties can be treated as if they were unitary actors, primarily on the basis that "parties do in practice tend to go into and come out of government as single actors, however painful the wounds inflicted upon them inside the black box [of intraparty decision making] might have been" (Laver and Schofield 1990, 15). The implication of unitary actor status is that "decisions will be adhered to once they have been arrived at by the whole party, whatever its method of arriving at them" (14). Obviously the monolithic actor assumption is a stylization, and in practice, parties sometimes split, backbenchers rebel, and some resign or are even expelled.

One exception to this silence on what happens inside parties is Gregory Luebbert's (1986) study, which develops an approach to coalition formation premised on assumptions about intraparty politics. Luebbert assumes that while party leaders are highly office oriented, they are "motivated above all by a desire to remain party leaders" (46). Thus, since leaders are anxious to get into government and since party activists (who derive little or no office benefit) are more likely to be militant and uncompromising, for Luebbert, lengthy periods of government formation are likely to be all about the leaders' generating intraparty consent. Thus, "Most negotiation in cases of protracted government formation takes place between leaders and their followers and among rival factions within parties" (52). Luebbert's approach is both theoretically intriguing and intuitively plausible. Many analysts (and party activists) have long suspected that most leaders would do just about anything to get into government if only they could circumvent the costs inherent in sacrificing their policy credibility with followers. This need for credibility greatly reduces their latitude for maneuvering. Of course, this does not mean that intraparty politics governs all else. Leaders (at least of European political parties) typically have immense resources with which to seduce, cajole, or discipline recalcitrant militants who get in their way (as shown in various chapters throughout this volume). Powers of promotion and patronage, especially when in government, provide a substantial array of "sweeteners" for the rank-and-file member struggling with his or her conscience.[11]

Nevertheless, credible revolts do occur. Most cases of serious revolt involve intraparty objections to the interparty concessions made in cabinet by a party's ministers. A destabilizing event occurs if the cabinet ministers have miscalculated the preferences of their supporters and a *revolt* ensues. The revolt generally becomes "serious" if it threatens the government's legislative coalition[12] or the continued leadership of the party's ministers. Once a revolt occurs, two outcomes are possible: the revolt either fails or succeeds. Failure of a revolt typically means that the threatened legislation passes (the legislative coalition holds) and/or that the defectors either are effectively disciplined or back down from the standoff with their leaders. In this sense the policy jointly announced by the cabinet continues or is implemented. A successful revolt means that the government is defeated in the legislature or, more likely, that the parties, anticipating defeat, renegotiate the policy at cabinet level.

A government with any chance of surviving and implementing its policies must be able to manage most of these standoffs with its supporting legislative coalition. Sometimes the government will play tough and face down the conflict with its supporters (the revolt fails). However, any revolts that are credible and from which the instigators do not quickly back down should be treated as serious warnings by the cabinet. The viability of the government will depend on how it responds to such revolts. Faced with a credible revolt, the party's ministers will often de-

Table 12.1

Events Destabilizing Irish Coalition Governments in the 1980s, by Arena

Arena	No. of Events		
	1981–82	*1982–87*	*Total*
Policy:			
Interparty conflicts	3	12	15
Intraparty conflicts	2	12	14
Electoral	—	4	4
Legislative (confidence motions)	1	1	2
Party organization	—	2	2
"Other"	—	2	2
Total	6	33	39

cide that the troublesome policy will have to be renegotiated by the cabinet (the revolt succeeds). Alternatively, if the party leaders feel that the policy must be upheld, the party will have to impose (expel) or accept (resignation) losses. Either way, the government's legislative coalition will atrophy. In sum, a governing party cannot simply ignore intraparty pressures; it must manage those revolts by sections of the parliamentary party that do occur. Any losses are highly significant for the party's reputation and strength as a coalition actor.

Intraparty Revolts: Some Evidence from Ireland

A recent study of coalition governments in Ireland in the 1980s examined the types of events that typically destabilize cabinets and the event management techniques with which parties respond (Mitchell 1996). One of the surprises to emerge from the identification of the events that destabilized these coalitions (the 1981–82 and 1982–87 governments) was just how many of them were primarily revolts within the coalition's parliamentary parties.

Indeed, almost half of all destabilizing policy events were intraparty revolts (table 12.1). Numerous government decisions were undermined by backbench revolts. The clear pattern that emerged was that sections of the parliamentary parties periodically punished their leaders either for conceding too much of party policy at the cabinet table or for taking decisions (especially spending cuts) that backbenchers believed would bring opprobrium on the party and thereby threaten their parliamentary seats. The evidence strongly suggests that intraparty politics may be a very significant constraint on interparty coalition policy bargaining.

Table 12.2

Intraparty Revolts in Ireland

Coalition	Policy Area	Period	Principal Instigator	Outcome
1981–82				
	Education	Nov. 81	Indep. MPs; unions	Succeeded
	Food subsidies	Jan. 82	Lab. PP and org.	Succeeded
1982–87				
	Education	Dec. 82–Feb. 83	Community; unions	Succeeded
	Social welfare	Mar. 83	Lab. PP, esp. 2 MPs	Failed
	Abortion	Apr.–Jun. 83	FG PP; community	Succeeded
	Food subsidies	Jan. 84	Lab. PP	Succeeded
	Food subsidies	Aug.–Sep. 84	Lab. PP	Succeeded
	Farm tax	Aug.–Sep. 84	FG PP	Failed
	Contraception	Nov. 84–Feb. 85	FG and Lab. PPs	Failed
	Industrial policy	Apr. 85	Lab. PP	Succeeded
	Local radio	Jun.–Jul. 85	Lab. PP	Succeeded
	Divorce	Apr.–Jun. 86	FG PP	Succeeded
	Social welfare	Nov. 86	2 Lab. MPs	Succeeded
	Social welfare	Nov. 86	1 FG MP	Failed

Notes: Total (both coalitions): 14 revolts. Succeeded: 10. Failed: 4.
PP = parliamentary party; FG = Fine Gael; Lab. = Labour.

Moreover, most of these revolts (10 of 14) "succeeded" in the sense that they destabilized the policy compromise made by the cabinet and forced a renegotiation of the policy (table 12.2). While leaders have general incentives to retain the consent of their parties, many of these revolts succeeded because their instigators threatened to defect in pending legislative votes.

Clearly, the legislative weight of these governments—the first was a minority coalition and the second had a small majority—did help to empower potentially dissident parliamentarians; certainly, the cabinet ministers in a government with a 100-seat majority would be expected to have more latitude to face down revolts. Nevertheless, since many European governments have slim majorities and around 35% have no majorities at all (Strøm 1990), credible backbench revolts are not unique to Ireland.

Unitary Actor Status Reconsidered

From time to time, credible revolts do occur that must be managed by party leaders. This need not be interpreted, however, as evidence that the unitary actor assumption of most coalition theory is entirely unwarranted and unrealistic.[13] The parties in these Irish governments, like most other European parties, generally behaved in a disciplined fashion, most obviously in legislative votes. Indeed, perhaps one of the more significant conclusions is that parties typically behave "as if" they were unitary actors *when they have to,* in situations where undisciplined behavior will impose high collective costs. Election campaigns and the government formation arena are two such occasions when fractious behavior is likely to seriously damage a party's reputation and strength. Of course, one of the reasons that most of the coalition theoretic literature has been able to retain the unitary actor assumption is that it deals primarily with the formation of coalitions. However, even if the key actors in a party have incentives to behave in a fairly unified manner at the point of government formation, this does not mandate continued unitary behavior during the actual life of the government (Daalder 1983, 21; Laver and Schofield 1990, 14–19).

The strategic incentives change once the government is installed. During the life of any particular coalition, intraparty conflicts may be unleashed and do not impose such high collective costs because they are not essentially about choosing between the current coalition and some alternative government. Whatever else they may do, backbenchers rarely endeavor to bring down their own government and facilitate its replacement by a coalition of their rivals. But what they can do without setting out to break the government is to rebel on particular policy items, punishing the party's ministers for drifting too far away from party policies and reminding their leaders that they cannot always be taken for granted. Most of this activity will not be revealed in a legislative roll call analysis, since European parties usually behave in a very disciplined fashion once a vote is called. Of the revolts listed in table 12.2, very few resulted in government MPs' actually voting against the government. For example, in March 1983 two Labour MPs planned to vote against a social welfare bill. The government decided to "hang tough," warning that anyone voting against the government would be expelled. One of the backbenchers backed down, but another, Michael Bell, did vote against the bill. Anticipating certain expulsion, he resigned the party whip in advance of the vote. This, however, was very unusual, and rebellions by individual MPs are often faced down. One of the more dramatic examples was the rebellion in November 1986 by Michael O'Leary. By this time the coalition was a minority government that needed O'Leary's vote to survive. Even though he had been clearly stating all day (on national radio and television) that he would vote against the government, O'Leary ultimately acceded to the pressure to remain loyal. One of his colleagues "told O'Leary in no uncertain terms that he was dead, gone as far as Fine Gael was concerned if he didn't support the government" (Kenny and Keane 1987, 19). Control of candidate selection meant that Fine Gael could credibly threaten to end his political career. Of course, this may be less feasible if a group of backbenchers threaten rebellion. The only other cases of backbenchers' actually voting against the government were the revolts that concerned abortion and contraception policies. In both cases a few conservative MPs felt that these were issues of moral conscience that outweighed normal loyalty to the party.

However, even if parties are highly disciplined and generally behave as unitary actors in actual legislative votes, to leave matters there would be to miss much of what is going on during a coalition's time in government. The clear pattern that emerges from these cases is that intraparty politics were a significant *constraint* on coalition bargaining between the parties' ministerial teams. Typically, these revolts consisted of hostile reactions by sections of the government's parliamentary parties to policy compromises made by the party leaders in cabinet. The structure of incentives and opportunities facing cabinet ministers and ordinary members of the parliamentary parties may diverge. In particular, the parliamentary party may see little virtue (and much danger) in effectively abandoning some party policies. Key party policies included in the coalition policy document are promises made by the leadership to the parliamentary party. In a sense they are the latter's price for agreeing to the compromises involved in forming a government. By contrast, a party's ministers, facing the constraints of governing and the incentives of ambition, are more likely to recognize and accept the necessity of compromising some of the party's policy agenda.

In discussing the impact of intraparty politics on coalition formation, Laver and Schofield (1990, 24) highlight the possible conflict of interest between the parliamentary party and the party as a whole: "The general rule is that the rank-and-file, more concerned with ideology and less in line for the other spoils of office, tend to resent the policy compromises necessary to enter coalition and hence to oppose them." The same logic applies to the life of a coalition government, although the key conflict of interest shifts to *a party's cabinet ministers versus the rest of the parliamentary party.* Since the existing set of cabinet ministers have the top jobs and therefore have strong incentives to try to keep them, they are more likely to manage interparty conflicts by recognizing the virtues of policy compromise in cabinet. By contrast, other members of the parliamentary parties (who are not in line for the top jobs) are less likely to tolerate clear departures from party policy or decisions that they believe will hurt their reelection prospects.

Table 12.2 makes it clear that almost all of the dissent that resulted in destabilizing events was instigated by members or sections of the parliamentary parties. This is because, at least for the life of any particular government, only the parliamentary party has the resources—the votes—to force a policy reversal. While other sections of the party organization or the party rank and file may make a lot of trouble—and may be able to replace leaders in the longer term—at least during the government's tenure this is mostly just "noise." Activists do not have the resources to bring ministers to heel on particular policy questions unless they can convince members of the parliamentary party to act on their behalf and rebel.

Conclusion

Political markets are inefficient because it is difficult to measure what is being exchanged and because there are no immediate enforcement mechanisms that guarantee that commitments will be honored in the future (North 1990a, 1993). Nevertheless, since politics is all about promise and performance, politicians assiduously cultivate the reputation that they are committed to their policy promises. However, since coalition formation and governing involve reputational costs in terms of concessions to coalition partners, there is a subsequent incentive to renege on these compromises. This produces further uncertainty such that parties will find that they have to spend considerable time and resources policing commitments that they thought they had secured at formation. Hence the increasing importance of coalition policy documents that perform the dual functions of underwriting the credibility of a party's brand-item policies (promises to activists and voters) while attempting to commit one's coalition partners to implementation of the measure.

Intraparty politics play a greater role during the life of a government than assumed by traditional coalition theories that concentrate on a period when unitary behavior is most imperative. In reality, coalition policy bargaining is clearly multilateral. Coalition maintenance primarily involves continuous bargaining in which a delicate trade-off has to be struck between negotiations among and within parties. In particular, interparty negotiations in cabinet occur in the context of an anticipated need to "carry" the coalition's parliamentary parties. Intraparty revolts that do materialize can be interpreted as miscalculations by the cabinet as to how much compromise their backbenchers will tolerate. And while the ministers in the Irish examples occasionally tried to face down the rebellion (with mixed results), the more typical response was to take the threat seriously and renegotiate the policy. In this sense, intraparty dynamics form an important part of an enforcement process for the coalition policy document, a counterbalance to the policy drift embraced by a party's ministerial team due to the institutional pressure to compromise entailed in cabinet bargaining.

Most rebellions (even those that are "successful") are quickly forgotten and become a part of the government's policy development phase, since the proposal is sent back to the cabinet for amendment. Thus, most revolts do not show up as legislative defections. Unless the government has a huge majority, the threatened revolt may be enough to force a policy change. Thus, despite generally high levels of party discipline in legislative votes, the cabinets of most European coalition governments will not play fast and loose with their parliamentary supporters.

NOTES

1. Opinions vary on this and are extensively reviewed in Laver and Schofield (1990, 36–61).

2. The assumption that voters are motivated by policy is common to both office-seeking and policy-seeking accounts of party behavior and is an underresearched area. The assumption is essentially residual in that since voters are assumed to receive no office benefits, "they must" therefore be motivated by policy concerns. While voters may be motivated by other incentives, such as patronage benefits or symbolic aspects of party identification, it does seem reasonable to assume that voters are to some extent motivated by public policy, notwithstanding doubts about the "purity" of voters' policy motivations.

3. Blondel (1993, 191) concludes, "Ministers are more anxious to be better departmental heads than to be part of a collective decision-making process in the cabinet, as if, for many at least, to participate truly in collective decision-making was a kind of luxury while the "real" activity with which they have to be concerned is that of their department." After all, the ministry represents the ministers' "own turf," a particularized arena in which the minister can demonstrate his or her personal contribution, in contrast to the diffusion of responsibilities (and benefits) inherent in collective decision making.

4. *Coalition policy document* here refers to the formal government policy program and not to any preballot electoral pacts signed by prospective coalition partners.

5. The Labour Party had decentralized the final decision on entering coalitions to a party Special Delegate Conference. See Gallagher (1982, 232–33).

6. This is not intended to suggest that formal voting is common practice in cabinets. This is usually unnecessary, since the outcome can be predicted in advance. The imbalance in bargaining power is manifest irrespective of whether a formal vote takes place.

7. Commenting on the first conservative-socialist coalition formed in Finland in 1987, Nousiainen (1994, 95) notes: "With respect to these general goals, the parties reached an agreement easily, but the following year was filled with heated discussion over the precise specification of these goals and the proper means to achieve them. In more general terms it is clear that a cabinet's agenda can never be fully determined in advance. New problems, goals, and solutions are introduced continually during a policy process."

8. This is not intended to imply that the respective parties necessarily shared the same interpretation of the original aims of the policy.

9. The parties may devise explicit mechanisms to monitor the coalition policy document. For example, in Austria, "All coalitions had their own forum for permanent interparty negotiations, namely the coalition committee, which consisted of a small number of high-ranking politicians from both parties" (Müller 1994, 29).

10. Of course, the transaction costs inherent in such policing are not zero (North 1990b, 1993).

11. Laver and Schofield (1990) also point out that it is usually much more difficult for the rank and file to control leaders once they are in government. When in opposition the parliamentary party is subject to party rules. In government, ministers are subject to constitutional rules such as collective cabinet responsibility. Thus, at the extreme, "The actual moment of going into government . . . may represent the point at which the rank-and-file loses control of the parliamentary party" (23).

12. Strictly speaking, then, "serious" revolts are not exclusively intraparty but rather are those that threaten the government's legislative coalition, its ability to win periodic legislative votes.

13. See Laver and Schofield (1990) for an extensive review of the utility of this assumption.

REFERENCES

Andeweg, Rudy, and Wilma Bakema. 1994. "The Netherlands: Ministers and Cabinet Policy." In Michael Laver and Kenneth Shepsle, eds., *Cabinet*

Ministers and Parliamentary Government. Cambridge: Cambridge University Press.

Blondel, Jean. 1993. "Individual Ministers and Their Role in Cabinet Decision-Making." In Jean Blondel and Ferdinand Müller-Rommel, eds., *Governing Together: The Extent and Limits of Joint Decision-Making in Western European Cabinets.* New York: Macmillan.

Daalder, Hans. 1983. "The Comparative Study of European Parties and Party Systems: An Overview." In Hans Daalder and Peter Mair, eds., *West European Party Systems.* Beverly Hills, CA: Sage.

Fiorina, Morris. 1981. *Retrospective Voting in American National Elections.* New Haven, CT: Yale University Press.

Gallagher, Michael. 1982. *The Irish Labour Party in Transition, 1957–82.* Manchester, UK: Manchester University Press.

Kenny, Shane, and Fergal Keane. 1987. *Irish Politics Now: "This Week" Guide to the 25th Dáil.* Dublin: Brandon and RTÉ.

Laver, Michael, and Ian Budge. 1992. *Party Policy and Government Coalitions.* New York: Macmillan.

Laver, Michael, and Norman Schofield. 1990. *Multiparty Government: The Politics of Coalition in Europe.* London: Oxford University Press.

Laver, Michael, and Kenneth Shepsle, eds. 1994. *Cabinet Ministers and Parliamentary Government.* Cambridge: Cambridge University Press.

———. 1996. *Making and Breaking Governments: Cabinets and Legislatures in Parliamentary Democracies.* Cambridge: Cambridge University Press.

Lewis-Beck, Michael. 1986. "Comparative Economic Voting: Britain, France, Germany, Italy." *American Journal of Political Science* 30: 315–46.

———. 1988. *Economics and Elections: The Major Western Democracies.* Ann Arbor: University of Michigan Press.

Luebbert, Gregory. 1986. *Comparative Democracy: Policy Making and Coalitions in Europe and Israel.* New York: Columbia University Press.

Mitchell, Paul. 1996. "The Life and Times of Coalition Governments: Coalition Maintenance by Event Management." Ph.D. diss., European University Institute, Florence.

Müller, Wolfgang. 1994. "Models of Government and the Austrian Cabinet." In Michael Laver and Kenneth Shepsle, eds., *Cabinet Ministers and Parliamentary Government.* Cambridge: Cambridge University Press.

Müller, Wolfgang, and Kaare Strøm, eds. 1997. *Regierungskoalitionen in Westeuropa.* Vienna: Signum.

Müller-Rommel, Ferdinand. 1994. "The Role of German Ministers in Cabinet Decision Making." In Michael Laver and Kenneth Shepsle, eds., *Cabinet Ministers and Parliamentary Government.* Cambridge: Cambridge University Press.

North, Douglas. 1990a. "Institutions and a Transaction-Cost Theory of Exchange." In James Alt and Kenneth Shepsle, eds., *Perspectives on Positive Political Economy.* Cambridge: Cambridge University Press.

————. 1990b. "A Transaction Cost Theory of Politics." *Journal of Theoretical Politics* 2: 355–67.

————. 1993. "Institutions and Credible Commitment." *Journal of Institutional and Theoretical Economics* 149: 11–23.

Nousiainen, Jaakko. 1993. "Decision-Making, Policy Content and Conflict Resolution in Western European Cabinets." In Jean Blondel and Ferdinand Müller-Rommel, eds., *Governing Together: The Extent and Limits of Joint Decision-Making in Western European Cabinets.* New York: Macmillan.

————. 1994. "Finland: Ministerial Autonomy, Constitutional Collectivism, and Party Oligarchy." In Michael Laver and Kenneth Shepsle, eds., *Cabinet Ministers and Parliamentary Government.* Cambridge: Cambridge University Press.

Powell, Bingham, and Guy Whitten. 1993. "A Cross National Analysis of Economic Voting: Taking Account of the Political Context." *American Journal of Political Science* 37: 391–414.

Strøm, Kaare. 1990. *Minority Government and Majority Rule.* Cambridge: Cambridge University Press.

Strøm, Kaare, Ian Budge, and Michael Laver. 1994. "Constraints on Cabinet Formation in Parliamentary Democracies." *American Journal of Political Science* 38: 303–35.

Timmermans, Arco. 1996. "High Politics in the Low Countries: Functions and Effects of Coalition Policy Agreements in Belgium and the Netherlands." Ph.D. diss., European University Institute, Florence.

Contributors

Attila Ágh is professor and head of the Department of Political Science, Budapest University of Economic Sciences.

David Baker is a reader in political science at Nottingham Trent University.

Shaun Bowler is an associate professor of political science at the University of California, Riverside.

David M. Farrell is a senior Jean Monnet lecturer in political science at the University of Manchester.

Andrew Gamble is a professor of political science at the University of Sheffield.

Richard S. Katz is a professor of political science at the Johns Hopkins University, Baltimore.

Prisca Lanfranchi works as a scientific collaborator at the Service of the Federal Assembly of Switzerland (Parliamentary Administration Control).

Michael Laver is professor and head of the Department of Political Science at Trinity College Dublin.

Steve Ludlam is a lecturer in political science at the University of Sheffield.

Ruth Lüthi works at the Service of the Federal Assembly of Switzerland.

Carol Mershon is a professor of political science at the Department of Government and Foreign Affairs, University of Virginia.

Paul Mitchell is a lecturer in political science at the Queens University of Belfast.

Bjørn Erik Rasch is a professor of political science at the University of Oslo.

Tapio Raunio works as a researcher at the Department of Political Science and International Relations at the University of Tampere.

Manuel Sánchez de Dios is a professor of political science at the Universidad Complutense of Madrid.

David Seawright lectures at Lincoln University.

Patrick Seyd is professor and head of the Department of Politics, University of Sheffield.

Kenneth A. Shepsle is a professor of political science at the Department of Government, Harvard University.

Paul F. Whiteley is a professor of political science at the University of Sheffield.

Index

abortion, as voting issue, 282

absenteeism: disciplinary procedures in Spain's parliamentary system, 157; in the EP, 208; as means to avoid voting on an issue, 132, 138n. 12

abstentions: in Spain's parliamentary system, 158; in Swiss parliamentary roll calls, 106, 118n. 5

accountability, executive, and identifiable legislative blocs, 3–4

activists, local party: and coalition government policy compromises, 282; political agendas and party as unitary actor, 25; and role of their members in British Parliament, 53–70; survey of attitudes toward role of an MP, 63–64

actors, political: as attempting to set prices in coalition bargaining, 233–34; in autocratic party leader coalition models, 36–41; in winning coalition systems, 12–13

actors, unitary: and Irish intraparty revolts, 280–83; in Norwegian parliamentary politics, 121, 133; parties as, in models of intraparty competition, 23–25, 28, 186n. 2; status and intraparty revolts, 277–83

AFD (Alliance of Free Democrats), Hungary, 172, 182, 185

agendas: electoral and party ideology, 15; EP as setter of, 209; government control in Italy and the Netherlands, 236–37; reelection, and party as unitary actor, 24–25

Ágh, Attila, 19, 141, 152, 165

Agrarian/Center Party (KP), Finland, 244, 246–47, 253–54, 263n. 12

agrupaciones (small groups), in Spain's parliamentary system, 150

airport, Oslo, location of as party issue, 135–36, 138n. 15

Alianza Popular (AP), Spain, 148–49

Alliance of Free Democrats (AFD), Hungary, 172, 182, 185

Alliance of Young Democrats (Fidesz), Hungary, 174, 185

alliances, in Swiss system, 110–11, 117

Allison, Rupert (Britain), 79

alternative proposals: in preferential voting behavior patterns, 125–26; voting on, and Norwegian party unity, 131–32, 135–36

amendment(s): attempt to defeat Maastricht Treaty bill in Britain, 75, 77, 79–80, 91n. 8; process in Spain's parliamentary system, 151

Andalusian Socialist Party (PSA), Spain, 150

Andreotti, Giulio (Italy), 260

anti-Mafia Network (Rete), Italy, 259

AP (Alianza Popular), Spain, 148–49

Arndt, Rudi, 194

Asher, H., 213

Ashford, D., 75

attendance, parliamentary: creation of Whip's office to enforce in Britain, 10; at EP sessions, 195; use of roll calls to encourage, 9; and voting behavior in Hungary's First Parliament, 171–78

Austria, use of committees to monitor coalition policy documents, 285n. 9

Axelrod, Robert, 233

backbenchers: discipline of, 3, 14–15, 67; information given to, 56, 156; opinions of, 16; revolts to thwart party's coalition commitments, 277, 279, 281; role in British Conservative Party's vote on European integration, 72–88; role in multiparty systems, 19

Baker, David, 52

balloting, secret: in Dutch parliamentary system, 244; in Italian parliamentary system, 11, 236–37, 259; use in the EP, 195

rules
legislative, as norms of behavior in the
EP, 194–95, 211, 218–20
party: affecting roles for members, 7–8,
9; decision-making regimes based
on, 28–29; governing Spain's parliamentary parties, 154–57, 159
Rules of Procedure (EP, 1994), 194–95

salaries, of MPs in Spain, 154, 157
Sánchez de Dios, Manuel, 19, 97
Sani, Giacomo, 239, 262n. 9
Sartori, G., 125, 169
Schofield, Norman, 121, 282, 285n. 11
Scotland, devolution issue, effect on
Labour MPs, 56
Searing, D., 212
seats, parliamentary: Dutch and Norwegian ministers not allowed to hold, 244,
250; splits and consequent loss, 127,
128
secret balloting: in Dutch parliamentary
system, 244; in EP, 195; in Italian parliamentary system, 11, 236–37, 259
secularization, effect on religious-based
parties, 239
separation-of-powers, "in" parties and
"out" parties in parliamentary systems,
108
Seyd, Patrick, 8, 51–52
Shaffer, William R., 131
Sharon, Ariel (Israel), 35–36
Shaw, Malcolm, 114
Shepsle, Kenneth A., 33–34, 141, 186n. 2;
portfolio allocation models, 19, 225,
231–32, 271
single-member simple-plurality systems,
7, 9, 97, 127
single-party governments, factions within
and portfolio allocations, 43
single preference vote, in Italy, 259
single transferable vote (STV) system, as
Ireland's version of PR, 236
Social Chapter Amendment (Maastricht
Treaty), debates on in British Parliament, 75, 77, 79–80, 91n. 8
Social Democratic Party (SPD), Germany, influence on EP party cohesion,
190
Social Democrats (SSDP), Finland, 247,
255

Social Democrats (PSDI), Italy, 251, 254,
257, 259
Social Democrats, Switzerland: MAD
score, 116; power sharing in the executive, 101–2; representation in bicameral
legislature, 100; roll call voting record,
107, 108, 116
Socialist Group, role in the EP, 192, 194
Socialist Left Party, Norway, 128, 133
Socialist Party (PSI), Italy, 238, 240–41,
250, 252–53, 257
social movements, as origins of initial
Hungarian parliamentary parties, 178
Spain: absenteeism and disciplinary procedures, 157; abstentions, in parliamentary system, 158; *agrupaciones,* in
parliamentary system, 150; Congreso,
constitutional formula for, 144, 149,
161n. 7; information given to backbenchers, 156; party discipline, 157–59;
party statutes, 154–57, 159; role of the
portavoz, 97–98, 150–51; speakers in
parliamentary debates, 151
Spicer, Michael (Britain), 75
splits: in British Conservative Party, 72–
73, 90n. 1; and consequent loss of parliamentary seats, 127, 128; in
Hungarian parties, 176; strategic party
voting on regional or moral issues,
134–36
SSDP (Social Democrats), Finland, 247,
255
stability, government, and disciplined
parties, 143
standing orders: in Hungary's parliamentary system, 184–85; regulating Spain's
parliamentary system, 150–51, 152
state socialism, plebiscites against in ECE
countries, 171–72
statutes, party: governing Spain's parliamentary parties, 154–57, 159. *See also*
rules, party
Steffani, Winfried, 99, 108
Storting, Norway, party discipline and
cohesion, 121–37
strategic party splits, in Norwegian parliamentary system, 134–36
Strøm, Kaare, 232, 261n. 2
strong party: in cabinet portfolio allocation models, 33–34, 37, 41–46; as government or unified opposition, 143
Suarez, A. (Spain), 148

Parliaments and Legislatures Series

General Advisory Editor
SAMUEL C. PATTERSON, OHIO STATE UNIVERSITY, USA

The aims of this series are to enhance knowledge about the well-established legislative assemblies of North America and western Europe and to publish studies of parliamentary assemblies worldwide—from Russia and the former Soviet bloc nations to Asia, Africa, and Latin America. The series is open to a wide variety of theoretical applications, historical dimensions, data collections, and methodologies.

Other books in the series

Citizens as Legislators: Direct Democracy in the American States
Shaun Bowler, Todd Donovan, and Caroline J. Tolbert

Cheap Seats: The Democratic Party's Advantage in U.S. House Elections
James E. Campbell

Coalition Government, Subnational Style:
Multiparty Politics in Europe's Regional Parliaments
William M. Downs

Creating Parliamentary Government:
The Transition to Democracy in Bulgaria
Albert P. Melone

Politics, Parties, and Parliaments:
Political Change in Norway
William Shaffer